TYPESETTING
and COMPOSITION

Also from Blueprint

The Print and Production Manual
The Print and Production Manual Practical Kit
Magazine and Journal Production
Wordprocessor to Printed Page
The Publisher's Guide to Desktop Publishing
The Publisher's Guide to Copy Prep
The Publisher's Guide to Litho Printing
Web Offset Directory

TYPESETTING
and COMPOSITION

Geoff Barlow
Simon Eccles

Second Edition

BLUEPRINT
An Imprint of Chapman & Hall
London · New York · Tokyo · Melbourne · Madras

Published by Blueprint, an imprint of Chapman & Hall,
2–6 Boundary Row, London SE1 8HN

Chapman & Hall, 2–6 Boundary Row, London SE1 8HN, UK

Van Nostrand Reinhold Inc, 115 5th Avenue, New York NY 10003, USA

Chapman & Hall Japan, Thomson Publishing Japan, Hirakawacho Nemoto Building, 7F, 1-7-11 Hirakawa-cho, Chiyoda-ku, Tokyo 102, Japan

Chapman & Hall Australia, Thomas Nelson Australia, 102 Dodds Street, South Melbourne, Victoria 3205, Australia

Chapman & Hall India, R. Seshadri, 32 Second Main Road, CIT East, Madras, 600 035, India

---

First edition 1987

Second edition 1992

Typeset in Great Britain by the Heronwood Press
Printed in Great Britain

ISBN 0 948905 72 7

A catalogue record of this book is available from the British Library

Library of Congress Cataloging-in-Publication data available

Contents

Acknowledgements

I would like to thank my many colleagues and contacts in the trade who fielded (at times unwittingly) queries relating to this book, and the following organisations who answered my requests for information: AM Varityper; Apple Computer (UK) Ltd; Atex Inc; Pica Systems; GB Techniques; SII Ltd; L & M Ltd; Linotype Ltd (with special thanks to Tim Cordell for the demonstration of that company's equipment; Miles 33 plc; Monotype International (UK) Ltd; Pagitek Ltd; Scangraphic Visutek Ltd; Xyvision Ltd.

In particular I am grateful to the following individuals for therir help with the preparation of the book: Kathy Munro, who helped to adapt files from *The Print and Production Manual* to create the glossary and bibliography; Blueprint Publishing for permission to use parts of those files; Charlotte Berrill, who remained patient as deadline after deadline came and went; Juliet Brightmore, who tracked down the picture of a print shop in the 17th century; Derek Turpin of Universe Typesetters, for his virtuoso performance at the Scantext keyboard which produced the illustration 1.22; Michael Card for sorting out my confusion of floppy disks and answering (at all hours of the day!) my cries for technical assistance; Brenda Stephenson, who somehow produced a coherent text from my incoherent galleys; Robert Updegraff, who inspirationally converted my grey ideas for illustrations into black and white; and Priscilla, who advised, encouraged and remained cheerful even while discovering new meanings in the term 'typesetting widow'. Lastly, my thanks to Mark Hammer, who introduced me to type and without whom this book would not therefore have been possible.

Illustrations

I am grateful to the following individuals and organisations for permission to reproduce the illustrations on these pages: Agfa UK Ltd: 199; Michael Card: 73, 86, 87, 111, 132, 159; DPS-Typecraft Ltd: 147; Interset Computer Systems (UK) Ltd: 191; Linotype Ltd: 28, 59, 60, 76, 120, 182, 184; Monotype International (UK) Ltd: 59; Scangraphic Visutek Ltd: 12, 134, 170, 172, 177; Derek Turpin: 5, 27, 178; Xyvision Ltd: 84.

Introduction to the first edition

The last thirty years have seen typesetting in the throes of a revolution. In this short space of time a technology and a tradition evolved over a period of five hundred years have been swept away, and the introduction of digital computing and electronic imaging systems have made possible new techniques of data processing and image manipulation unimaginable in the days of hot metal composition. The assembly and typesetting of text and graphics is now an integral part of a complete new world of information technology.

The development of this new technology has brought huge benefits in terms of the speed, cost and efficiency with which text can be processed and manipulated. At the same time the pace of these changes continues to pose fresh challenges for those who must control and understand the new procedures. Confronted with a technology that refuses to stand still, anyone involved with contemporary typesetting can no longer approach the job with the familiarity that comes of working within a fixed and established set of conventions. A new sense of professional awareness is required so that both the potential and the problems presented by the new composition processes can be fully explored.

The current trend in publishing is for ownership to be increasingly concentrated in the hands of a few large companies, and for the various editorial, design and production functions to be performed by large and specialised departments. The economies of scale involved in this approach are attractive, yet the risk of isolating the different yet interrelated roles of publishing staff is very real, and I would argue that it is difficult for any member of a publishing house to operate effectively if their knowledge of their own specialist field is not reinforced and balanced by an appreciation of the needs and responsibilities of the people working alongside them. Nobody except a very few individual printer- publishers can be in a position to control all the aspects of the publishing process, but I would contend that all those involved in the preparation or presentation of words in typeset form can only benefit from a grasp of the principles, capabilities and, most importantly, the practical implications of contemporary typesetting technology. What this book therefore attempts to do is to explain how this technology has evolved from traditional typesetting processes, how it may affect the conventional role of author, editor, designer and production executive, and how it can provide fresh opportunities and new solutions to publishing problems.

It is in this context also that I have included the very brief discussion of the basic principles of typographic layout and a short history of the evolution of typeface design. These subjects have been treated in far greater depth elsewhere and specialists in these areas will find little new. I firmly believe however that a knowledge of typesetting methods and systems must be balanced by at least an acquaintance with typography if type is to be effectively handled, and this book would have seemed incomplete without a brief outline of the conventions of sound typographic practice.

Because the book concentrates on the practical implications of typesetting for the publisher, I have wherever possible avoided explanations of the complex computer operations that underpin much of contemporary typesetting. This technology is no doubt fascinating to those who are prepared to learn to be experts in computer science, but the fact remains that for most people working in publishing, it is the practical implications and results that will be of more importance. The well-worn analogy of being able to drive a car without understanding the detailed workings of the internal combustion engine is once again valid.

The more salient points are illustrated with diagrams or photographs, but it is an inescapable fact that many of the most exciting typesetting processes take place in the microcosmic world of the silicon chip, and are to all intents and purposes invisible. The hardware of contemporary typesetting is frequently mundane in appearance, and rather than produce a photographic essay on the theme of 'the grey box' the illustrations are confined to those of real significance.

Typesetting and computing professionals seem to take a perverse delight in creating a specialist vocabulary of 'buzzwords' with which to shroud the technicalities of their craft. Such technical terms as may require explanation will be found in the glossary. The first occurrence of any word which is described there is set in italics in the text.

The earliest known manual of printing was published in 1683-4. In the *Mechanick Exercises on the Whole Art of Printing* Joseph Moxon gave a complete account of everything to do with printing at the end of the seventeenth century, including the construction of the equipment, the techniques used in printing and the day-to-day activities of the printer's workshop. He prefaced the book with the following definition

> *By a Typographer I do not mean a Printer... but by a Typographer, I mean such a one, who by his own Judgement, from solid reasoning with himself, can either perform, or direct others to perform from the beginning to the end, all the Handy-works and Physical Operations relating to Typographie.*

The processes and equipment which Moxon describes have of course long since lost their relevance to commercial typesetting, but over three hundred years after it was written, his definition of the 'typographer' still rings true.

GB

Introduction to the second edition

If proof of the rapid technological change within the composition industry were needed, it could be taken from the fact that this book required a major revision only four years after it first appeared. When Geoff Barlow first wrote this book, the computerisation of typesetting was well-established. But since then, the concepts that first saw light in desktop publishing systems have made mighty strides to affect all aspects of the modern industry. Low costs and ease of use have 'democratised' both type and page assembly, to the point where it can be directly handled by the information creators – authors, journalists, copywriters, designers – and not just skilled and trained compositors. The use of standard microcomputers and software interchanges has put a vast range of facilities at users' fingertips – pages can be assembled from not just type, but high quality graphics, colour photographs, tints and vignettes, with special effects and distortions readily accessible. At the same time, the falling costs and increasing power of computers have forged links between composition and colour reproduction systems, to the point where two once separate industries are starting to overlap and merge due to common equipment and operator requirements.

It is notable how little of the equipment referred to as current in the first edition was still in manufacture as the second edition was written. It's a far cry from the time when it took an expert to tell a Linotype caster of the 1920s from one made forty years later! For this reason, little emphasis has been placed on the capabilities of specific items of equipment available in the early 1990s, so where equipment is named, it is generally as a typical example of its class. Readers wishing to keep up with specific equipment trends are referred to the regular trade press, not just of the printing industry, but also the graphic design and computing sectors.

The first four chapters of this book deal mainly with the 'timeless' subjects of typography and the history of mechanical composition, so little has been changed here, except to emphasise which equipment is now obsolete, and which is still to be found in frequent use. From the second half of chapter four, however, things started to change radically for the second edition. The requirements for graphics and colour to be incorporated alongside text have necessitated major advances in the design of data input terminals and graphics scanners, control computers and software, storage systems and output devices.

The way typesetting companies work is also changing. The bottom end of the 'typesetting' market is coming under threat as office word processors and laser printers gain the sophistication to allow unskilled secretarial staff to do significant amounts of this work in-house. In the professional publishing markets, typesetters are more and more often being presented with disks containing elaborate completed pages, and expected merely to record these to film rather than controlling all aspects of composition as before. That so many are prepared to do this is the consequence of shifting trade union attitudes as much as technical feasibility. To keep their businesses operating as more than an automated film recording service, some typesetters are looking to develop 'value-added' services, and the inevitable direction is upmarket, into repro and other pre-press facilities. These trends are reflected in this second edition.

When the first edition was published, it seemed that much of the demand for 'direct input' by clients would be in the form of word processed files, with formatting codes inserted which would be interpreted by the typesetting computers to make up pages in the correct font, column widths etc. For newspaper, magazine and brochure work, much of this has now been rendered unnecessary by 'codeless' desktop and professional publishing systems, which can make-up and proof pages directly. However, coded mark-up looks likely to survive in book and technical documentation work for some time, so the details are retained in this book. It will be interesting to see if they are still relevant when the third edition is due!

SE

1 Typography

For five centuries, text composition for printing was accurately described as a 'black art'. This referred both to the arcane practises of the trade, which took years to learn and used a sometimes deliberately obscure terminology, coupled with the observation that the heavy reliance on black ink made for a pretty messy industry. Today the blackness and some of the art have largely vanished. Type composition takes place in a clean environment where computer technology is stretched to the limit and advanced laser devices are commonplace. Composition is rapidly becoming an aspect of a larger electronic prepress process which combines type with computer graphics and colour photographic manipulation. Access to composition has become much more widespread, thanks to low cost and easily learnt desktop publishing. Even the printroom is less 'black' than it used to be, partly because of the increased use of colour, but also thanks to stricter health and safety laws and presses that virtually clean themselves.

As recently as thirty years ago any description of typesetting methods would have concentrated on the arrangement into lines and blocks of individual letter shapes cast in lead and designed for printing by impression onto paper. At that time hot metal composition for letterpress printing, even by the most advanced mechanical methods available, was a dirty, slow and laborious business, involving the painstaking assembly of large quantities of heavy and expensive type metal for each job.

In those thirty years, progress has been rapid, and shows no sign of slowing. Growing pressure to reduce the costs of letterpress printing led to the increasing acceptance of photolithography, to the point where today it is the dominant printing process. Lithography in turn demanded a faster and more flexible means of composing type. Phototypesetting proved the answer, being able to produce the photographic original needed for photolithography, and being more inherently suited to computerisation.

Phototypesetting produces type by exposing a light sensitive material in a controlled manner. The exposure source can be a spot of light drawn across the surface of a cathode ray tube, the horizontal scans of a laser beam, or the passage of light through an array of transparent or opaque cells.

In many modern typesetting systems, type is electronically created and processed as a pattern of minute dots which can be modified by a controlling computer to produce a wide range of alternatives to the basic character design. These dots can equally be used to produce graphic elements such as halftoned photographs, line art or tint blocks. For this reason most modern phototypesetters are termed imagesetters, to stress that they can produce any visual component, not just type.

The traditional appearance of any letter, cast solidly in lead for over five hundred years, is now only one of an infinite number of possible variations on the theme.

The operator of a modern typesetting system generally communicates with the imagesetter through special software running on a standard microcomputer, hence the term 'computer typesetting'. The software codes are turned into on-off instructions for the light source through a device called a 'raster image processor', or RIP.

Metal typesetting is increasingly viewed as an historical curiosity in rich Western economies, although it is still in widespread use in Third World countries. Yet even the most modern typesetting systems derive much of their terminology from metal composition, so a grasp of the traditional elements of type is a useful aid to understanding contemporary typesetting technology.

TERMINOLOGY

Any single letter, figure, mark or symbol is known as a *character*, or *sort*, and consists of two distinct elements: the *face* of the type carries the image that will print, and governs the shape and design of the character, while the *body* of the type dictates the size of this image. Body size is conventionally measured in terms of *point size*.

The width of the character is described as its *set*. Within any alphabet of type, the set widths of individual characters vary: the letter i is narrower in set than n or m, for example. The degree of sophistication with which differing set widths are assigned to characters in a type-

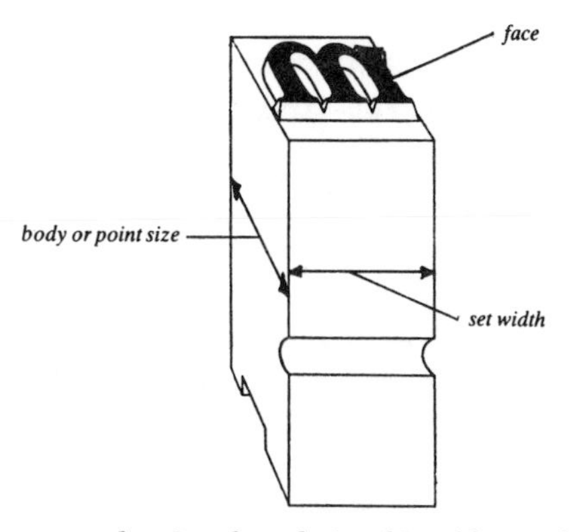

A metal type character showing the relationship of face to body size and set width.

setting system has a great influence on the legibility and visual quality of the typeset image. A conventional typewriter may use the same set width for all characters and so is termed a *monospaced* device; in Monotype hot metal composition 12 different width sets are used within the alphabet.

The set width of a character is usually expressed in terms of the number of units of space that the letter takes up relative to the widest character of the alphabet; this is conventionally assumed to be capital M. Each character is assigned a particular number of units which determines the relative width of the letter. Because this method is based on proportional values, the relative widths of different characters remain the same regardless of the point size used. The Monotype hot metal system, for example, divides the M (generally pronounced and spelt *em*) into 18 units: the letters i and n have values in this system of five and nine units respectively. The number of units into which the em is divided varies with different manufacturers' systems: 18-, 36-, 54- and 96-unit systems are all in operation.

The term *set* is also used to describe the width of a typeface design relative to its size; a design which is wide in set will use more space than a narrow-set design when used in the same *appearing size*. A piece of copy typeset in Aster, for example, will take up more space than if set in a size which is visually equivalent (the same appearing size) in Ehrhardt. The relationship between appearing size and set is therefore very important when setting copy to fit a predetermined space or preferred extent. The relative set of a type design can be measured as its *alphabet length*, the space taken up by the letters a-z set together; comparative alphabet lengths show which typefaces are more or less economic for text composition.

abcdefghijklmnopqrstuvwxyz
abcdefghijklmnopqrstuvwxyz

Linotype Ehrhardt (top) and Linotype Aster (bottom) set to approximately the same appearing size to show the difference in alphabet length and relative set width between the two faces.

The *fit* of a character describes the degree of space apparent between the outer edges of the strokes of characters when set together and is important for the way in which letters combine into words; loosely fitted setting will tend to 'fall apart' and appear as a collection of individual characters rather than words, while setting that is too tightly fitted may be equally difficult to recognise as groups of words, phrases and sentences. In metal typesetting, each letter contains a small amount of space, integral to the design of the specific character, between the face of the character and the edge of the metal body on which it is cast; letters cannot be fitted more closely than this allows. In computer typesetting there are no such restrictions: the fit of any typeface design can be progressively tightened in minute increments by adjustment to the width tables stored in the memory of the typesetting system's computer. Extremely tight setting is possible, and certain characters may even touch or overlap each other. The tendency in contemporary phototypesetting is to take advantage of this ability and to set type much more tightly than was possible with metal composition. This is most evident in advertising work, where words are often set so tightly that the individual characters run into one another to form a continuous block. The results may have impact in large-character setting such as headlines, where only a few words need to be recognised, but excessively close letter-fitting in continuous text tends to diminish readability by hiding the shapes of letters and destroying the unique patterns recognisable to the eye as words and phrases.

The more sophisticated modern typesetting systems also allow adjustments to be made to the spacing between certain specified combinations of characters whenever they appear; preferred spacing values are stored in the computer's memory for each of the various combinations which are considered to need amendment. The excessive space which otherwise appears between character pairs such as 'To' or 'Wa'

Sample of −4 per cent. Character Compensation
Sample of −3 per cent. Character Compensation
Sample of −2 per cent. Character Compensation
Sample of −1 per cent. Character Compensation
Sample of +1 per cent. Character Compensation
Sample of +2 per cent. Character Compensation
Sample of +3 per cent. Character Compensation
Sample of +4 per cent. Character Compensation

Adjustments in overall letter-fitting, or character compensation.

can thus be automatically reduced to appear visually even with the spacing of the surrounding setting. This process is known as *automatic kerning*. Many typesetting software programs allow users to set up their own kerning values, which are stored as *kerning tables*.

The *base-line* of type is an imaginary line through the base of the letters upon which most characters in the alphabet appear to sit; this line therefore determines the alignment of the different letters at a common level, and is dependent on the design, not the size, of the typeface. In metal typesetting different designs of typeface rarely aligned evenly on the base-line, and for this reason typefaces could seldom be mixed in the same line of setting. All modern computer typesetting systems have the ability automatically to align types of different design on a common base-line, enabling complete flexibility in the mixing of typefaces within any line.

The *mean-line* is a similar imaginary line drawn along the top of the small letters – a c e g, etc. – which have no *ascenders*. The *x-height* of an alphabet is the distance between the base-line and mean-line, and is equivalent to the height of the character x; this particular letter is chosen because it has *serifs* on both the base-line and the mean-line.

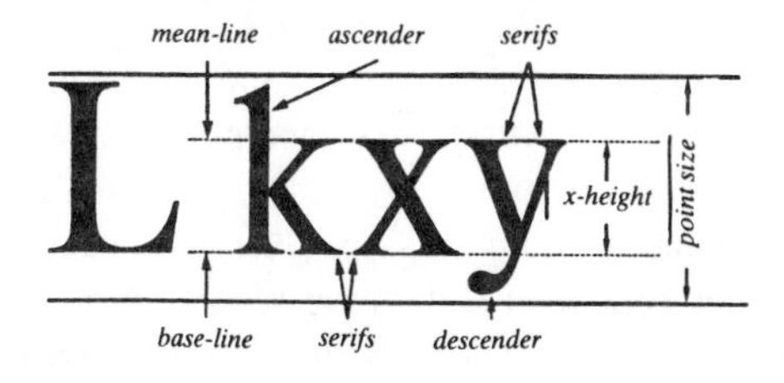

The printed image of type. Note that the measurement of point size does not relate directly to the size of any part of the type.

The x-height governs the appearing size of an alphabet; types with a large x-height will have a greater appearing size than those with a comparatively small x-height. The relative x-height of a type will determine the apparent blackness or colour of a page of setting, as well as the amount of space which is required between lines to ensure that the text is easily readable. Different typefaces may have the same body size yet widely varying x-heights and it is the appearing size of the type, rather than its specified point size, which determines the final look of a piece of setting.

Ascenders are those strokes of a character which rise above the x-height, as in b d f h k l and t. *Descenders* are the strokes falling below the x-height, as in g j p q y. The relationship between x-height and the length of ascenders or descenders is also important for the appearing size of a type; ascenders or descenders which are short in relation to the x-height produce a type that appears large in proportion to its body, in whatever point size it is used.

Serifs are the small terminal strokes at the end of the main strokes of letters. Visually, they help to combine individual characters into words by linking the predominantly vertical strokes together, and are also needed in certain cases to distinguish between different characters, such as 1 (one), l (el) and I (cap i). In weight, serifs can vary from hairline to slab, and in direction from horizontal to oblique; they may also be bracketed - that is, joined to the main stroke of the letter by a curve or angled wedge.

The *kern* of a letter is any part of the face which overhangs a neighbouring character. Roman f, and several italic letters, need kerns to avoid a distortion of their traditional shapes. Hot metal characters required a small extension to be cast which extended beyond the type body and rested on the shoulder of the next character; photosetting does not have this problem.

Preferentially

Vertical rules drawn to show the kerns on the characters f and y.

The term *kerning* has been adopted by manufacturers of typesetting systems to mean the automatic tightening of fit between any pair of characters, as described above. Where groups of characters, such as whole words or sentences, are uniformly tightened up, this is called *tracking*.

The *counter* of a letter is the space either completely or partially enclosed by a stroke of the character, such as the hollow of C or the spaces between the strokes of E.

MEASUREMENTS

Early printers cast their own type and no attempt was made to standardise the various sizes used. Even when typefounding became a specialist craft typesizes were still approximate, and were described by traditional names rather than by any exact terms of measurement. One commonly used size, *pica*, has survived as a basic unit of typographic measurement; the other traditional names are unlikely to crop up in use in contemporary typesetting.

The earliest attempts to assign exact measurement to specific sizes were made in France in the eighteenth century and developed into a system with a basic unit of the point (now known as the 'didot' point to distinguish it from the Anglo-American point) equivalent to 0.0148 in. However, this system met with little success in the English-speaking world, where sizes standardised only in the 1870s with a point measurement of 0.01383 in, or roughly one seventy-second of an inch. There are 12 points to the pica em (0.166 in), and six pica ems to the inch. The term *em* is often used in place of *pica* in modern typesetting parlance.

The relationship between the point system and the metric system are shown below; the point system is still generally used for typographic specifications and layouts, while the dimensions of pages and books are measured by the metric system. To further complicate the issue, American printers and publishers often use inches rather than the metric system to describe formats.

Point size	*Inches*	*Millimetres*
1pt	0.014" ($\frac{1}{72}$")	0.35mm
12pt (1 pica)	0.166" ($\frac{1}{6}$")	4.20mm
72pt (6 picas)	1 inch	25.4mm

The body size of type is expressed in points; this book is set in Times type, in 10$\frac{1}{2}$pt size, with two points of extra space between lines, otherwise expressed as 'Times 10$\frac{1}{2}$/12$\frac{1}{2}$pt'. This system derives, as shown, from metal typesetting, where the point size actually defines the depth of the metal body on which the type is cast, and not therefore the dimensions of the face itself, which is always slightly smaller than the body: in a printed sample of 11pt type, no part of the typographic image will measure 11 points! The appearing size of faces can vary considerably yet still be classified as the same point size, and the only sure way to ascertain the point size of a typeset sample is to match it against comparative settings in a specimen book.

abcdefghijklmnopqrstuvwxyz

abcdefghijklmnopqrstuvwxyz

Linotype Perpetua (top) and Linotype Ehrhardt (bottom) both set in 12pt size. Note the difference in x-height and appearing size.

Modern typesetting is not subject in this way to the restrictions of a physical body of fixed dimensions, and the existing point system of measurement seems therefore no longer completely relevant; some new system relating to the dimensions of the printed image itself is required. Recommendations for metric typographic measurement have in fact been drafted by the International Standards Organisation, but have not been widely adopted. Some typesetting companies which recognise the problems involved in the unambiguous specification of phototypesetting have introduced their own methods; one such alternative proposes that type be specified by reference to two separate dimensions – the height of the capital letters as printed (*cap height*), and the distance between base-lines of successive lines of setting (*line feed or film advance*) – with both these measurements to be taken in millimetres.

Clients of typesetting companies, such as design or advertising agencies, often take this process into their own hands. They will often just specify the desired character height, and leave the typesetter to find out which point size this corresponds to.

ALPHABETS, FONTS, SERIES AND FAMILIES

The letter-forms used for continuous text composition in English and many other languages are called *roman*, after their place of origin; *italic* letters, used to emphasise or contrast words in the text, developed originally as a separate style for texts where economies of space were needed, but soon came to be considered as a companion face to roman.

Certain of the more cursive italic typefaces contain extremely beautiful letter-forms, including decorative *swash* letters.

Modern typesetting systems are capable of electronically distorting roman letter-forms to produce a type which retains the stress and serif construction of roman type but is slanted like italic; these type styles are known as *sloped roman*. Since the stress is the same as for roman letters and the angle of inclination is the same for all characters (which it is not in true italic), sloped romans fail to provide sufficient contrast with their original face and are generally used only where true italic is for some reason unavailable.

Both roman and italic letters are available in CAPITALS (*upper case*) and small letters (*lower case*); the terminology derives from the way in which cases of metal type were arranged for hand setting.

SMALL CAPITALS are similar in size to the x-height of their related roman lower case and are used for emphasis in places where full-size caps would be intrusive and over-emphatic. As contemporary type-setting systems can change the sizes of type set in the same line, smaller-sized capitals are often substituted for a small-cap design; true small caps are, however, proportionally heavier and wider than capitals reduced to the same size.

Bold type is used for emphasis, and was a relatively late development in typeface design; many roman faces were originally created without any considerations of a bold version, and the later addition of a bold face has often resulted in a distortion of the shape of the original letters. The best bold faces are those which have been designed as an integral part of a coherent family; even so, bold type can appear very heavy when used within continuous text and is best reserved for headings and display work.

An *alphabet* comprises all 26 letters in any specified design and size; it usually also includes a few additional letters such as *diphthongs*, and the tied letters known popularly as *ligatures*.

A *font* is a set of alphabets in any specified design and size. A font usually comprises five alphabets – roman and italic upper and lower case plus roman small capitals – but may also include bold upper and lower case roman, and possibly italic. A font also contains figures, punctuation marks, reference marks, miscellaneous signs, accents, and a selection of mathematical symbols, fractions and commercial signs.

The exact constitution of a font varies between typesetting systems, and can be defined only by reference to a comprehensive specimen from the relevant manufacturer's system. A basic roman (three-alphabet) font normally contains at least the following:

Upper case	ABCDEFGHIJKLMNOPQRSTUVWXYZ
Lower case	abcdefghijklmnopqrstuvwxyz
Small caps	ABCDEFGHIJKLMNOPQRSTUVWXYZ
Diphthongs	Æ Œ Æ Œ æ œ
Ligatures	ff fi ffi ffl
Figures	1 2 3 4 5 6 7 8 9 0

Figures are described as *arabic* to distinguish them from the roman numerals I V X L C D M. Arabic figures can be

lining: 1 2 3 4 5 6 7 8 9 0

or *non-lining* 1 2 3 4 5 6 7 8 9 0

Lining figures are also known as aligning, or modern, figures; non-aligning figures as non-aligning or old-style figures.

Lining figures are approximately the same height as capital letters, and therefore suitable for setting with them in the same line; non-lining figures look awkward when set with capitals, but are less obtrusive when set with lower case letters or small caps. Alternative designs may not, however, always be available in every typeface.

Arabic figures are specified as either 'italic' or 'upright', to prevent confusion with 'roman' figures.

Punctuation marks

. full stop	? question mark	- hyphen
, comma	' opening quote	– en rule
: colon	' close quote/apostrophe	— em rule
; semicolon	" " double quotes	

Reference marks

* asterisk	† dagger	‡ double dagger
§ section mark	‖ parallel	¶ paragraph

Miscellaneous signs

( ) parentheses	[ ] square brackets	& ampersand
/ oblique		

Accents

´ acute	` grave	^ circumflex	¨ diaresis
¸ cedilla	~ tilde	ß eszett	

In professional typesetting systems, accents are usually floating and can be positioned over any upper or lower case letter as appropriate.

An accent is understood to be visually separate from the letter to which it is applied; marks which form part of the letter itself are properly called diacritical.

The PostScript fonts which are increasingly used in desktop and professional typesetting generally have pre-determined accent positions. For English language versions these generally correspond to the most common French or German accent positions. The fonts do contain accents for other languages and positions, but special type manipulation software is required to access them.

Mathematical signs + − × ÷ = ° ′ ″

Fractions ⅛ ¾ ⅔ ⅝ ½ ¾ ¼ ⅛

The more common mathematical signs are included in fonts designed for text composition, but any other symbols required for a particular job may need to be included in the font as *pi* characters, or accessed from a special mathematics font; complex fractions may have to be built up using a mathematics typesetting program.

Commercial signs % @ © # £ $ ¢

Special fonts may be needed for particular purposes, such as the setting of phonetics, mathematics, or non-roman alphabets (of which the most commonly required are Arabic, Cyrillic, Greek and Hebrew).

A wide range of pi characters is available on most contemporary typesetting systems, allowing a great variety of signs, symbols and typographic ornaments to be included in any piece of setting. Specialised symbol fonts are also available – Zapf Dingbats is in widespread use due to it being supplied with many PostScript laser printers.

A *series* describes a complete set of fonts of the same typeface design but in a range of different sizes (Times 7pt, Times 8pt, Times 9pt, etc.).

A *family* comprises a group of series which are related in basic design but differ in either the weight of the design, from ultra-light to 'black' or ultra-bold, or width, from ultra-condensed to ultra-expanded. The normal weight of design, from which other variants are derived, is usually described as medium. Popular typeface families may contain a considerable number of variant series; the family of the Helvetica type design, as issued by Linotype, includes 45 different faces.

Modern digital typesetting can be programmed to distort the design of characters in very fine progressive increments, producing electronically condensed, expanded, lightened or emboldened variations from the one master design. As a result, it is becoming increasingly difficult to identify and specify typeface design by reference to standard alphabets.

Excellence in typography is the result

Excellence in typography is the result

Excellence in typography is the result

Excellence in typography is the result

Above *Type electronically slanted to various angles from the normal roman face of the top line.*

Below *Type electronically condensed and expanded; line three shows the standard setting*

Excellence in typography is the result
Excellence in typography is the result
Excellence in typography is the result
Excellence in typography is the result
Excellence in typography is the result

A new development by Adobe Systems for its PostScript font format will take this a step further. Multiple Masters gives the font user the option of creating customised variations in a typeface's characteristics. The typeface is encoded with pairs of characteristics, say ultra light and ultra bold, and the user can specify any desired weight between these points. Additional masters, such as 'true' light, medium and bold, can be encoded by the typeface manufacturer if desired. Apart from weight, other characteristics that could be encoded for variation include width, visual scaling (cuts for small and large point sizes), the degree of italicisation, and kerning. Exactly which variations are permitted are decided by the font manufacturer.

This development is compounded by the wide availability of type manipulation programs such as LetraStudio or TypeStyler. These can take the outline information for letters from standard typefaces and distort them into completely new forms. Several PostScript line drawing programs, such as Adobe Illustrator and Aldus Freehand 3.0, can also be used to create lesser distortions, and very sophisticated graphical effects in groups of PostScript Type 1 characters. Programs of this type produce one-off modifications to the letterforms, and are largely intended for graphical effect. Font creation programs such as URW Ikarus, Altsys Fontographer or Letraset FontStudio, can modify typefaces permanently so that they can be accessed from a keyboard, and they are available at prices low enough to make them widely accessible. Completely new typefaces can be created in any form the designer chooses. They can also be used to modify existing typefaces, and save the result as new designs.

With such potential for customisation, letterforms are rapidly becoming a matter of individual preference, and conventional methods of classification are likely to lose their precise meanings.

SPACING

To communicate effectively, type must be not only legible but also readable: that is, it must not only be identifiable as isolated letter-forms of a particular shape, but must also be easily recognisable as patterns of letters grouped together to form words and phrases. The way in which characters and words combine with each other or are spaced apart has an important effect on how fluently this readability is achieved.

Spaces may be either fixed or variable. Fixed spaces are defined by reference to the set width of the typeface, so that they remain proportional to the size of type. The terminology used to describe fixed spaces derives from hand composition of metal type and still survives in contemporary professional typesetting. The various spaces are known as *hair, thin, mid, thick, en (or nut)* and *em (or mutton)*, which have values of 6, 5, 4, 3, 2 and 1 to the em respectively. Desktop publishing programs rarely distinguish spacing from tracking and kerning, and so use the same controls and numerical values.

Em spaces provide a kind of invisible full point, which can be used to separate items in tables, display matter, or to demarcate side-headings from text set in the same line.

En spaces fulfill a similar role, but less emphatically, and can be confused with the variable spaces between words if the latter become too wide.

A mid space is equivalent to the normal word space; setting which is not justified is often set with mids as word spaces.

Hair spaces are sometimes needed to avoid collisions between characters in such combinations as f'.

The width of a line of setting is referred to as the *measure*, usually measured in picas and points.

Typesetting which has an even edge only at the left of the measure is described as *ranged left, unjustified.*

Alice was beginning to get very tired of sitting by her sister
on the bank, and of having nothing to do: once or twice she
had peeped into the book her sister was reading, but it had no
pictures or conversations in it, 'and what is the use of a
book,' thought Alice, 'without pictures or conversations?'

Typesetting with an even right-hand edge and ragged left edge is *ranged right, unjustified.*

Alice was beginning to get very tired of sitting by her sister
on the bank, and of having nothing to do: once or twice she
had peeped into the book her sister was reading, but it had no
pictures or conversations in it, 'and what is the use of a
book,' thought Alice, 'without pictures or conversations?'

Typesetting where every line is positioned on the same central point is *centred line for line.*

Alice was beginning to get very tired of sitting by her sister
on the bank, and of having nothing to do: once or twice she
had peeped into the book her sister was reading, but it had no
pictures or conversations in it, 'and what is the use of a
book,' thought Alice, 'without pictures or conversations?'

Typesetting with even edges at both left and right is *justified.*

Alice was beginning to get very tired of sitting by her sister on
the bank, and of having nothing to do: once or twice she had
peeped into the book her sister was reading, but it had no pictures or conversations in it, 'and what is the use of a book,'
thought Alice, 'without pictures or conversations?'

In unjustified setting, consistently even spacing, usually equivalent to a mid space, can be used between words. In justified setting, the word spaces, although consistent within the line, must be allowed to vary from line to line to fill the measure without creating an excessive number of broken words at the line endings; the value of the different spaces required in each line is calculated by the typesetting system's computer. This can be programmed by the operator to define the ideal, minimum and maximum word space values allowable in a line. The specification of these word-spacing parameters greatly affects the appearance of the finished typesetting; if the spaces are too wide, rivers of white space appear to disrupt the overall texture of the finished setting, and the type breaks up into random blocks of words. Excessively tight word-spacing has the opposite effect of closing words together into unintelligible strings.

The visual effect of word-spacing is also dependent on the apparent space between successive lines of text. Type set without any extra space between lines is *set solid*, but most setting is improved by the addition of some space between lines. In metal composition this is achieved by adding thin strips of lead, in varying thicknesses, between the lines of type, and the term *leading* is still commonly used to describe interlinear space in computer typesetting. This book is set in Adobe PostScript Times 10½pt with two points of extra interlinear space or leading, or 10½/12½pt Times.

Even when set solid, typesetting in metal retains a minimum degree of legibility due to the space inherent in the relationship between the face of the type and the rectangular body on which it is cast. With phototypesetting it is possible to set type on a body that is smaller than the point size of the type itself in order to create extremely closely spaced lines of text. This treatment does not usually improve the readability of continuous text but is often used for effect in advertising and display work, especially in larger type sizes; careful attention is needed to prevent the possible collision of ascenders and descenders!

> With phototypesetting it is possible to set type on a body that is smaller than the stated point size of the type itself in order to create extremely closely-spaced lines of text. This treatment does not usually improve the readability of continuous text, but is often used for effect in advertising work; careful attention is needed to prevent the collision of ascenders and descenders! This copy is set in 10/9pt Avant Garde Book.

Letter-spacing is not normally required for words set in lower case, where the individual characters combine best when closely fitted.

Words and lines set in capitals or small capitals are, however, more difficult to read due to the inconsistent visual space between the letters, and increased space is often considered desirable between characters to allow each letter-shape to be easily recognisable to the human eye.

When large sizes of type are used for display work, any extra space should ideally be visually, rather than mechanically, consistent, and should therefore vary according to the individual letter-shapes involved; adjustments to the spacing produced by the typesetting machine can be easily made by cutting and pasting a bromide of the setting, which is then stripped into the text as artwork. Alternatively, if a high quality preview of the text is shown on the computer screen, the characters can be adjusted visually before output.

TYPEFACE DESIGN

The history of typeface design is complex and intriguing, and it is not possible to do it justice in this book. The following brief outline is intended to enable the reader to identify in the broadest terms the typefaces and type families in frequent use today; the bibliography lists several books which treat this fascinating subject in greater detail.

The main features of type design which identify the varying families and faces are:

Proportions Important features are the relationships of x-height to set, including the appearing size of the type on the body, the relative length of ascenders and descenders, the weight and 'colour' of the face, and the degree of tightness or looseness in the character fit.

Stress The forms of types used in printing derive ultimately from the letter-shapes of writing. The square-ended pen used by scribes in the fifteenth century when typography was invented in Europe gave a diagonal stress to letters; the angle at which the pen was held produced thick or thin strokes according to the direction in which the pen was moved. This angle of stress still survives in most printing types, varying between oblique (diagonal stress from left down to right) and vertical.

Serif structure The weight, direction, and bracketting of serifs may all be distinctive.

The classifications used below are those prepared by British Standard 2961 in 1967, although the names of the traditional groupings, shown

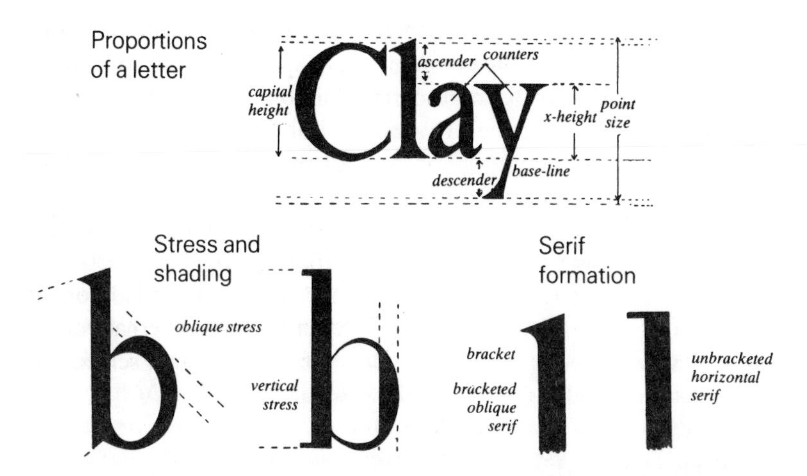

in brackets, are probably more likely to be met with in day-to-day practice. The German typesetter and font manufacturer Scangraphic has created a new classification method for its font catalogue, reasoning that the availability of computer modified forms makes the original descriptions too restrictive. So far no other manufacturer has adopted its proposals.

Any distinctions of the sort detailed below must in any case be to some extent arbitrary, as the history of typeface design is one of constant and gradual evolution. It should also be understood that when talking of any particular typeface, what is meant is usually a modern reissue by a contemporary type-founder, or manufacturer of typesetting equipment, of a face based on an historical model, and not the original face itself. Each generation of printers used the styles of type developed under the cultural and historical influences of their own age, and only in recent times has it become usual for designs of earlier periods to be reissued. Many of the typefaces in use today were re-cut for metal composition by the Monotype Corporation in a period of intense typographic activity between the two world wars. Manufacturers of early phototypesetters used adaptations of these designs for filmset output. This policy did not always prove successful; type designed for printing by physical impression into paper, with a consequent thickening and blackening of strokes, can often lose its character completely when exactly reproduced as a two-dimensional photographic image. Later developments in type design for phototypesetting produced fresh versions of the classic metal faces remodelled for film output and lithographic printing, as well as some highly successful new designs. The need for type which retains its character on low resolution devices such as CRT screens, televisions and laser printers prompted another wave of new versions in the 1980s.

Humanist (Venetian)

The first successful roman type is attributed to Nicholas Jenson, the great Venetian printer. Early roman typefaces were developed from the calligraphic hands used for formal volumes in late fifteenth-century Venice; these scripts had themselves been influenced by a revival of interest in classical Roman lettering. The designs are characterised by a lightness and freedom of form, with irregular thickness to the main strokes of the letters. The shading is oblique, and the serifs are strongly 'cupped'. The angled bar of the lower case e is diagnostic. Examples of this style of typeface include Kennerley, Veronese and (shown below) Centaur.

abcdeghijklmnopqrstuvwxyz
ABCDEFGHIJKLMNOPQRSTUVWXYZ

Garalde (Old Face)

The manner in which metal types were created very soon came to be reflected in their appearance, and the influence of the typecutter's engraving tool began to oust that of the scribe's pen. The first major evidence of this development appeared in a type cut in 1495 for the Venetian printer Aldus Manutius, and first used for a work by a scholar named Pietro Bembo. Like other Garalde designs, it is of much greater regularity and consistency than earlier Venetian forms. Although the stress is still oblique, the main strokes are more even in weight, the serifs are no longer cupped, and the inclined bar to lower case e has disappeared. Garalde type appears in many forms, bearing witness to the varying national and cultural traditions of the sixteenth and seventeenth centuries, during which it was the predominant style of typeface.

Reissues of these designs are among the most popular 'classical' faces for book typography: Bembo, Garamond, Plantin, Ehrhardt and Caslon Old Face, while possessing great individuality, are all examples of the Garalde tradition. The face shown opposite is Bembo.

abcdefghijklmnopqrstuvwxyz
ABCDEFGHIJKLMNOPQRSTUVWXYZ

Transitional

The regularity of metal engraving continued to exert an influence on typeface design. This trend was accelerated by the gradual displacement of wood-engraving as a method of book illustration by copperplate engraving. This intaglio process allowed for much finer detail to be reproduced in illustrations, but also introduced letter-shapes of greatly increased contrast and regularity in its engraved captions. This influence can be seen in the typefaces of the mid-eighteenth century known as transitional types, although the pre-cursor to these designs appeared as early as 1702 in the 'Roman du Roi', a type designed and cut by Grandjean for the exclusive use of Louis XIV of France. The serifs of this type were horizontal and virtually unbracketed, and the overall stress was almost vertical. The face exerted a great influence over contemporary typefounders, including the French designer Pierre Simon Fournier and John Baskerville in England, and types from the mid-eighteenth century display a mix of features drawn from both the old-face tradition and the new designs.

The trend towards increased contrast and vertical shading was made possible only by improvements in the mechanics of printing presses and the invention of smoother 'wove' paper, which enabled the thinner and more delicate cross-strokes of the new type to be satisfactorily printed.

Fournier, Baskerville (below), Bell and Caledonia are examples.

abcdefghijklmnopqrstuvwxyz
ABCDEFGHIJKLMNOPQRSTUVWXYZ

Didone (Modern)

The move towards precision and regularity of stress reached its limit in this style of typeface, which is known as 'modern' although the influences which ultimately produced it had been at work since the end of the seventeenth century. The stress is absolutely vertical, with extreme contrast between thick and thin strokes, and abruptly horizontal, often unbracketed, serifs. Although types such as Bodoni and Didot were designed and used for text setting, it is in the stark and simple layouts of title pages and other display work that they look most at ease. Modern faces require extreme care with regard to size, spacing and paper to produce an effective and legible result when used for continuous text. The modern face illustrated here is Bodoni.

abcdefghijklmnopqrstuvwxyz
ABCDEFGHIJKLMNOPQRSTUVWXYZ

□ □ □

The Industrial Revolution gave rise to an entirely new development in type design – the display type. Although ornamental type appears on title pages and elsewhere as early as the middle of the seventeenth century, increased commercial activity and changes in relationship between producer and consumer in the early nineteenth century introduced a new and aggressive style of advertising, and the need for a new fashion of typography to serve it. Above all the advertising poster, in its scale and emphasis, generated the intense experimentation in modification and distortion of letter-form that dominated Victorian typography. Display types defy rigid classification, and it is not possible to do more than loosely group such designs under convenient headings, which cover both display types and the text faces which share their characteristics.

Slab Serif (Egyptian)

The earliest display types proper were over-developed and grossly enlarged versions of the modern face, known as 'fat faces'. The tendency for the hairline cross-strokes to become damaged during printing led to the introduction, in 1815, of the slab-seriffed type called Egyptian. The many variations on the basic form include expanded, condensed, shaded and ornamented designs.

Playbill is a typical display face, while Rockwell (shown here) is an Egyptian for text composition.

abcdefghijklmnopqrstuvwxyz
ABCDEFGHIJKLMNOPQRSTUVWXYZ

Lineale (Sans-serif)

Sans-serif types first appeared in 1816, and were very popular by the middle of the nineteenth century because of their adaptability of form in all sizes and weights. There are four main styles of sans-serif type:

Grotesques: nineteenth-century in origin, sometimes also called 'Gothic' due to the influence of the Gothic revival. Examples include Grot 215.

abcdefghijklmnopqrstuvwxyz
ABCDEFGHIJKLMNOPQRSTUVWXYZ

Neo-Grotesque: more modern in origin, mechanical and monoline in weight, with all strokes of even thickness. Univers (illustrated below) and Helvetica are types of this style.

abcdefghijklmnopqrstuvwxyz
ABCDEFGHIJKLMNOPQRSTUVWXYZ

Geometric: types constructed on circular or rectangular models, such as Futura.

abcdefghijklmnopqrstuvwxyz
ABCDEFGHIJKLMNOPQRSTUVWXYZ

Humanist: although without serifs, these types reflect the influence on old-face designs in their shading and the proportions of their main strokes – Gill Sans and Optima (below) are good examples.

abcdefghijklmnopqrstuvwxyz
ABCDEFGHIJKLMNOPQRSTUVWXYZ

Glyphic

Glyphic types reflect the stonemason's chisel in their overall feel and the treatment of serifs. Faces of this design, such as Albertus (shown below), Chisel or Latin, are intended for display work and are best identified by reference to typeface catalogues.

abcdeffiflffghijklmnopqrstuvwxyz
ABCDEFGHIJJKLMNOPQQRSTUVWXYZ

Script

There seems an inherent paradox in attempting to imitate the essential freedom of cursive writing in the regularity of typeforms, yet script types are conventionally used for such kinds of jobbing work as formal announcements and invitations. Styles range from formal copperplate to more loosely designed forms.

abcdefghijklmnopqrstuvwxyz
ABCDEFGHIJKLMNOPQRSTU

Graphic

These faces are distinguished from scripts by the appearance of having been drawn, not written. As with script faces, the wide variety of available designs makes it difficult to illustrate universal identifying features, but Cartoon, Klang and Brush (below) are examples of graphic faces.

abcdefghijklmnopqrstuvwxyz
ABCDEFGHIJKLMNOPQRSTUVWXYZ

Hybrids

Contemporary type designs are strictly categorised by reference to their hybrid origins – e.g. Humanist-Garalde – but are most conveniently treated as separate group.

The design and production of new typefaces for phototypesetting is both easier and cheaper than for metal composition systems, and new faces are continually being released by all the manufacturers of contemporary typesetting systems. Display typography, subject to the volatile trends of the advertising world, is at the centre of this explosion in typographic activity, and many of the new faces issued defy even the very loose classification outlined above.

The most interesting of the new types for continuous text composition are those which have been specifically created to suit contemporary production methods, and are designed for reproduction by phototypesetting and printing by offset lithography on smooth, white, coated papers; such types have strong, even strokes with no abrupt contrast or pointed serifs and thus avoid the risk of appearing 'thin' when reproduced. Apollo, Photina and Melior (below) are examples.

abcdefghijklmnopqrstuvwxyz
ABCDEFGHIJKLMNOPQRSTUVWXYZ

TYPOGRAPHIC DESIGN

Typographic design is a skilled discipline, which relies not only on creative flair and imagination but also on a sound understanding of the way in which typefaces behave when used in different circumstances. The choice of type design, and the way in which type and space are arranged in the presentation of the text, are influenced by many factors, including the nature of the editorial copy, the age group of the intended reader, the required design impact, the paper and print process, economic considerations, and, above all, the purpose of the printed work and the circumstances in which it is to be used. All these questions are inter-related, and a sensible compromise is often necessary before the 'right' typeface can finally be selected.

Type must suit its purpose: both the design of the face and the size and manner in which it is employed must be sympathetic to the overall editorial concept, whether this is the newspaper that will be read in the swaying crowd of a commuter train, the huge advertising hoarding glimpsed for a few seconds at the side of the motorway, the functional presentation of an educational textbook, or the gracious and elegant display of lines of poetry. If it seems obvious that a delicate old-face design is inappropriate for a motor-repair manual, there are also dangers in allowing the subject material to dictate too forcefully: many computer manuals strive for a hi-tech style by using sans-serif typography, even if the running text becomes as a result much less easy to read and assimilate. To convey its message effectively, typography must be unobtrusive and lucid: the reader must be conscious of the message, not the medium.

In its fullest sense, 'design' encompasses not only the specification of typeface, size, measure and spacing, but also control over choice of format, paper, print process and relevant suppliers. Today this is rarely so in practice, as the increasing pressure towards specialisation leads to the many various, but connected, aspects of the design process being divided up among several people. Designers who consider a particular face 'right' for a job on the evidence of their finished visuals may still be betrayed by the quality of the paper or the standard of printing imposed on them 'further down the line'. These situations can lead to a good deal of what can only be described (on good days!) as 'creative tension' between those specifying typography and those responsible for producing the final job. As long as commercial pressures continue to work towards the mutual isolation of the design and production functions there can be no magic solution to this problem; the only answer is increased communication and mutual consideration by the involved parties of both the ideals of the planned design and the practical constraints of reality.

Foremost among the practical considerations of any project are the format, materials and process to be used.

Format is determined not only by the proposed extent of the work, but also by the size and capabilities of the printer's equipment. The sheet size which can economically be printed influences the choice of page size, which in turn affects the measure used for the typesetting. Economic factors determining the required length of the work as a result govern the choice of type of a set width suitable for either driving out copy to fill the extent, or pulling it back to save space. It is here that the relationship between the x-height and alphabet length of a typeface becomes a critical factor.

The inclusion of type as an integral part of illustrations, as in advertisements, also affects the choice of typeface. If type is to print over part of a picture, it should be in a strongly contrasting colour, and in a size which shows up clearly against the illustration; the 'busier' the background against which it must appear, the larger the type must be to remain legible. Type designs with thin strokes or sharp serifs should in any case be avoided, as these tend to disappear, making the text hard to decipher against the illustration.

Type which is intended to reverse to white out of either pictures or flat areas of colour should be at least 10pt in size, and of a robust design; even at this size, the finer strokes of letters reversed out of heavy solids can fill in during printing, while any slight misregistration of the different colours on press may cause fringes of colour to appear round the edges of type which is too small or delicate for this treatment. Wherever possible, the number of colours combined to produce the shade in which small sizes of type will print, or from which it will be reversed, should be limited to a maximum of two.

The characteristics of paper which exert the greatest influence on the choice of typeface are shade and smoothness of surface. As a general principle, the whiter and smoother the paper used for the final job, the more closely the type, when printed, should resemble the original image produced by the typesetting machine. Conversely, printing on rough or absorbent stock, such as newsprint, distorts details of the typographic characters, thickening the strokes and filling in the counters of letters. Elegant faces, with delicate strokes or small counters, should therefore be avoided for any work in which economy has been the overriding factor behind the selection of paper.

The effects of paper surface on the reproducibility of type were possibly more important when letterpress was the dominant print process; all images were created by the impression of relief metal type into paper, and typefaces cast in metal were designed with allowances for the thickening effect, or 'squash', inherent in this process. Certain types of Venetian or old-face design are considered to be at their best only when printed by letterpress, with considerable weight of impression, on a rough-surfaced paper; even versions of the same face subtly redrawn for phototypesetting can appear very anaemic when faithfully reproduced by the planographic process of offset lithography. For printing by lithography, types without excessive contrast between strokes, but with even colour and strongly drawn serifs, are preferable, especially if there is any danger of grey or inconsistent inking in the final printing. This is even more relevant for jobs printed on white, coated papers, where strong contrast between the thick and thin strokes of type, and between type and paper, can create a dazzling effect detrimental to continuous reading. The types most suitable for the integrated illustrated work for which coated stocks are often used are the darker, more robust designs such as Plantin, Ehrhardt or Palatino, and some of the newer faces specifically created for phototypesetting.

The principles of photogravure influence the choice of typeface and type size that can be satisfactorily used in the long-run colour catalogues and magazines produced by this process. In photogravure the image is transferred photographically to the surface of the printing cylinder through a screen which breaks the image into a regular pattern of tiny recessed cells; these are flooded with ink, and the surface of the cylinder is wiped clean by a blade before contact with the paper, which lifts the remaining ink from the cells. The screen pattern covers the entire printing surface, including type, and its effect is to break the edges of the characters and cause a loss of sharpness and definition in the typographic image; under a glass, the serrated edges of the characters can be clearly seen. Types with strong colour, low contrast, and blunt serifs are ideal for reproduction by this process, but it is advisable to avoid the use of types of delicate design, or those with hairline or pointed serifs. In larger sizes, the problems are not so acute, since the screen is proportionally smaller and less obtrusive, and a wider variety of faces can be used. The limitations of flexographic and screen printing processes also demand the use of typefaces of robust design.

TYPEFACE VARIETY

Before the invention of mechanical typesetting systems which cast and set type in one operation as it was required, the printer wishing to offer variety to his customers had to hold in stock cases of metal type for hand composition in all the sizes and designs necessary for his kind of work; this could involve a huge investment in expensive and space-consuming type-metal. Even after the introduction of mechanical type-casters such as the Linotype and Monotype machines, it was still necessary to stock cases of type for hand-correction of the machine-set matter. To a large extent, this limited the variety of typefaces that all but the largest organisations could afford to hold. The labour-intensive and expensive processes involved in the design and production of a new typeface in metal also tended to restrict the range of faces available. Each size of every alphabet in all the variant faces of the typeface family required the creation of separate drawings, punches and matrices. As a result, the typical bookwork house of the 1960s might offer 20 or so faces available for composition in text sizes, with a few extra faces held in a limited range for display or jobbing purposes.

With the advent of computerised typesetting, these restrictions have been swept away. Instead of physical masters, the type is stored as electronic instructions which are interpreted by the exposure device to build up the characters. Not only is the manufacturing process for a new type design quicker and, in relative terms, cheaper than before, but in many systems only one master of the design is necessary. The effect is that many trade typesetters can now afford type libraries of 1,000 fonts or more.

The new ability to manipulate typeforms for every purpose, from the stunningly original typographic effect to the more mundane but

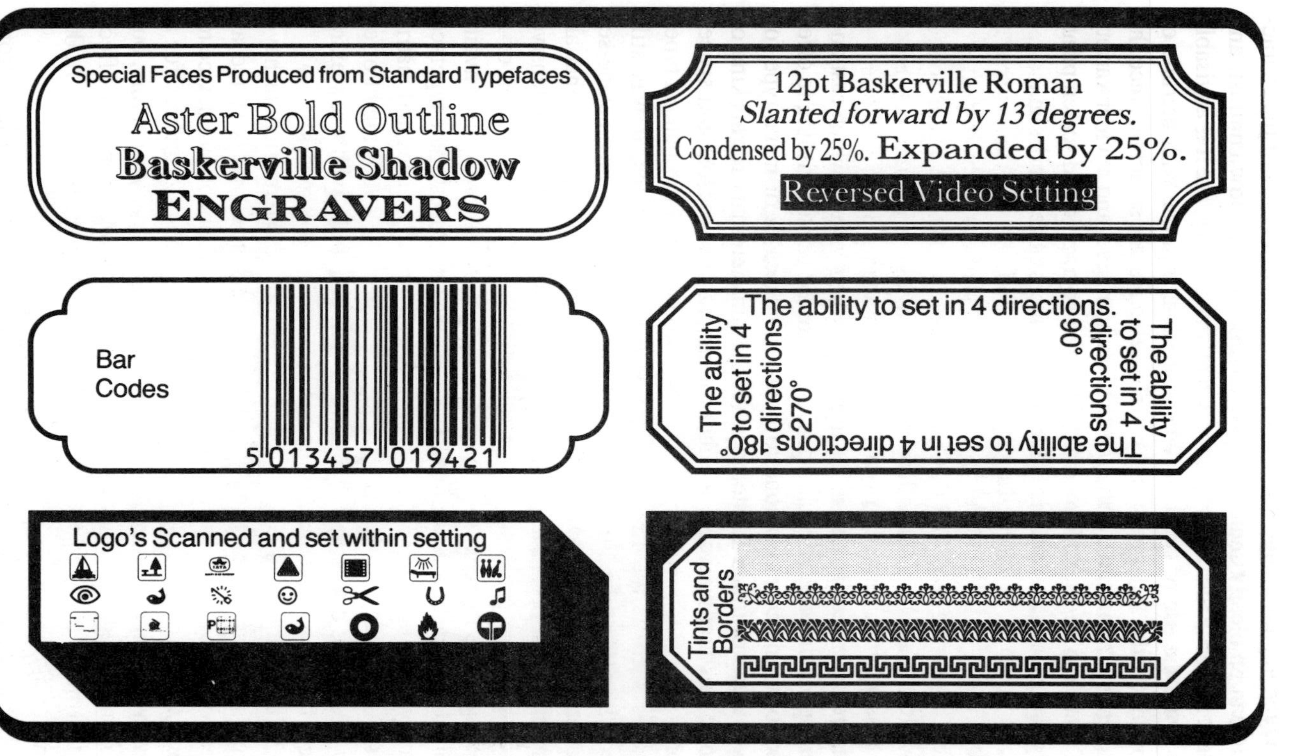

Typographic flexibility: this illustration was composed, arranged and output as one piece of bromide.

equally valuable copy-fitting solution is exciting, but carries some dangers. In metal composition, each image was the product of an individually designed and typecast design. This had two major implications: it made possible subtle variations in character design to cope with the different proportions of letter-forms necessary for varying type sizes, and it gave a sharpness to each image because each impression was, in effect, produced directly from its own master. If a typeface is enlarged or reduced across the whole range of sizes from one master, as in some phototypesetting systems, it follows that the character shapes will all be identical in proportion, regardless of the demands of their appearing size, and this is not always satisfactory. More noticeable, the image may in its larger sizes show ragged outlines caused by excessive enlargements from the single image master; this effect is known as *indexing*, and is most evident when large sizes of type are printed on smooth or coated papers. There are two possible solutions, both of which are now adopted by type suppliers. The first is to provide more than one image master to cover the complete size range, with one master used for text sizes, another for intermediate sizes, and perhaps a

Hamburgefons 8 pt Design

Hamburgefons 12 pt Design

Hamburgefons 18 pt Design

Hamburgefons
8 pt Design

Hamburgefons
12 pt Design

Hamburgefons
18 pt Design

Comparisons, enlarged and reduced to the same size, of the three different image masters used to cover the full range of point sizes for Linotyope Bodoni roman, showing how the proportions of characters are adjusted in the different design sizes. In the smaller size the characters are drawn slightly wider, with thicker serifs and looser letter-fit, to preserve the characteristic features of the face. In larger sizes the characters are proportionally taller, narrower and more closely fitted to retain the elegance of the design.

third for display titling. Some fonts are also available with special cuts to ensure optimum image quality at large sizes. The other solution is to build typesetting machines capable of higher-resolution output, so that the outline of the image is more finely and smoothly constructed. (There are also other reasons behind the current move towards higher-resolution output and these will be discussed later.)

A further important consequence of the increased typographic activity of recent years is that there are now many more sources of typefaces than in the days of metal type; the computer technology of modern typesetting has enabled manufacturers with no tradition of metal composition to join the established names like Linotype and Monotype. Perhaps the largest of these is Bitstream, a company set up in 1980 specifically to supply digital type. Adobe, a company set up in 1983 specifically to develop the PostScript computer language, is also now a major font manufacturer.

The introduction of page description languages, such as PostScript, means that any typeface design issued in that page description language can be output by any imagesetter or other output device capable of interpreting that language. Thus it is common for Monotype founts to be output from Linotype imagesetters, Berthold faces from Agfa devices, while designs issued by independent type manufacturers such as Bitstream or ITC are equally device-independent. The wide availability of type design programs has prompted the development of many small type creation companies, which can supply custom fonts and logotypes.

The competitive impetus which this has provided has been beneficial to typography as a whole, but the increased number of suppliers can itself cause confusion. Each supplier has, for copyright reasons, adapted and patented its own interpretation of the traditional classic typefaces, each of which differs in more or less subtle details from the designs of its competitors. To further complicate the situation, manufacturers of typesetting systems now also offer many alternative design interpretations, with slight differences of emphasis, of the same historical typographic models. The terms 'Baskerville' or 'Garamond' are thus becoming increasingly ambiguous without detailed clarification or reference to a particular typesetting system and classification number. This is particularly vital if the input and output of type is performed by separate operations. Such a case would arise where a small publishing operation was composing pages in-house, and sending the work for output by a bureau. If the two operations used different manufacturers' versions of Garamond, then the text might not fit the pages precisely on output.

abcdefghijklmnopqrstuvwxyz
ABCDEFGHIJKLMNOPQRSTUVWXYZ

abcdefghijklmnopqrstuvwxyz
ABCDEFGHIJKLMNOPQRSTUVWXYZ

abcdefghijklmnopqrstuvwxyz
ABCDEFGHIJKLMNOPQRSTUVWXYZ

abcdefghijklmnopqrstuvwxyz
ABCDEFGHIJKLMNOPQRSTUVWXYZ

*A range of different 'Garamond' typefaces available from one typesetting system manufacturer. Note the differences in weight, fit and design detail between the Linotype faces (*from top*) Garamond Original, Garamond No 3, Garamond ITC Light and Garamond Simoncini.*

In typeface nomenclature as in all other areas of typography, the invention of computer typesetting has brought new freedoms and possibilities, but with this potential comes a corresponding need for awareness and for precision. Today, more than ever before, type specification demands that the designer or publisher arrive at a full understanding of the possibilities and problems of current technology before attempting to manipulate the 26 basic letter-shapes for the purpose of his own communication.

2 Hot-metal composition

Hot-metal composition can today be considered obselete. It is commercially viable only in certain extremely specialised areas, and in countries where letterpress printing still predominates. As recently as 30 years ago a composing room would have been clearly recognisable, at least in principle, to printers from any age since Gutenberg's invention of moveable type, but during this brief period the technology of metal composition has been abandoned. The processes have been discarded, the machinery sold for scrap, and the knowledge and vocabulary of hot metal live on only as nostalgic memories in generations of 'ex-comps'. Even the few remaining applications for metal composition seem, with one exception, to be without a future, and certain to disappear before long.

This chapter can be considered of largely historical interest, as it explains the principles out of which current computerised typesetting grew.

APPLICATIONS

Jobbing printing

The production of small ephemeral items – invitations, business cards, letterheads, menus or programmes – was until recently the province of the small jobbing printer which existed in every town. The most economic printing process for this kind of work was letterpress, and most general printers kept a few cases of the most popular types specifically for these jobs which would be set by hand and printed on a small platen machine. The advent of inexpensive strike-on or phototypesetting composition systems and the use of small offset-lithography printing, combined with aggressive marketing techniques, have established the instant print shop on every high street in the country, often replacing the more traditionally equipped local jobbing printer; instant print is cheaper, faster and more easily accessible to the customer.

The introduction of desktop publishing systems and the growth of bureau typesetting services to output disks produced on clients' own personal computers seem certain to hasten the decline of the general jobbing printer, and, unless they are quick to adapt to these changes, may in time also threaten the instant print shops themselves.

Reproduction proofs

Not all the typefaces originally cast for metal composition have been reissued for phototypesetting. It is still reasonably common, when setting correction lines for books printed from metal type, to need access to the original metal typeface; this is becoming increasingly difficult as the number of hot-metal typesetters continues to decline.

Newspapers

Until the mid-1980s hot-metal composition still played a considerable role in the reproduction of some London newspapers, with linecasting machines sometimes driven by more modern computerised control systems. The introduction of photocomposition systems was a central part of the revolution in the national newspaper-publishing scene, and even those papers which are continuing with letterpress printing use photocomposition to originate the relief printing plates.

Fine printing and the private press

It is in the current renaissance of fine book production that metal composition has retained a significant role. As a relief surface, metal type is a natural companion to wood-engraving, and there are now a growing number of private presses producing limited editions of books that combine elegant typography with the best of contemporary illustration. Some of these presses have profited greatly from the wholesale disposal of obsolete typesetting plant by commercial printers, insuring themselves against the future by acquiring a complete range of composing room equipment. The private presses may well prove the final surviving stronghold of metal composition and letterpress printing.

TYPEFOUNDING

From the invention of moveable metal type until the end of the nineteenth century, types were produced by a process completely separate from composition itself. Each alphabet of type was cast from hand-held moulds by the printer – or, from the end of the sixteenth century, by specialist typefounders – and supplied in cases for hand composition.

The first step in typefounding is the cutting of the *punch*: the shape of the letter, reversed left to right, is engraved in relief on the surface of the end of a steel rod. This punch is then struck into a small slab of softer bronze alloy to create a right-reading image of the character in recess – the *matrix*. The matrix is fitted to the mould, and molten type-metal is poured into it. When cooled, the metal casting combines a reverse-reading relief image of the letter, produced from the matrix, on a *shank*, or body, of metal formed by the mould. Very few typefounders are still in operation today.

HAND COMPOSITION

Type for hand composition is stored loose in cases – wooden trays divided into many different-sized compartments; these compartments are arranged so that the letters most frequently required lie closest at hand to the compositor. Before the invention of the mechanical composing machine, when all composition was by hand, two cases for any size of each typeface were required: a top one for the capital letters and a bottom one for the small letters – hence the terms upper and lower case still in use today. Nowadays a single 'jobbing' case which contains both upper and lower case letters is more usual.

The compositor places the case on a sloping stand or frame in front of him and 'sets the line measure' by means of an adjustable screw on a composing stick held in his left hand. Taking letters and spaces in order from the case, he arranges them upside down and left to right in the stick, so that the first line of type set lies at the bottom of the stick and subsequent lines on top of it. The compositor's eye is on his copy and the typecase, and he arranges the letters the correct way up by feeling for the nick on the back of each piece of type. With practice and good co-ordination, speeds of over 1000 characters an hour are possible, depending of course on the copy and the size of type being set. Lines are justified by using a combination of fixed metal spaces – em, en, thick, mid, thin and hair – until the line is a snug fit. This is a skilled and important task, as both loose and forced setting cause problems during the process of make-up and printing.

MAKE-UP

When the stick is full, the type is transferred to a metal galley and setting continues until the entire job has been composed. The type is then carefully lifted onto a flat surface – the *imposition stone* – and locked tightly up inside a metal frame, or *chase*, using strips of wood known as *furniture* and expandable metal wedges called *quoins*. Proofs are

A print shop in the early seventeenth century. On the left a compositor sets type from a case while a bespectacled reader checks a proof; in the background a pressman is inking a forme as the proprietor exhorts his companion at the nearer press to greater efforts! The main features of this scene remained unchanged for over four hundred years until the invention of mechanical composition.

taken from this locked chase or *forme*, and corrections are made – either 'on the stone' if they are minor, or back 'in the stick' if they involve the rejustification of lines.

Once the galleys of type are passed as clean, all the various elements of the job, set in the different faces and sizes required, are imposed together in the correct sequence and layout, and a further proof is taken. This manual make-up can be very time consuming and expensive for complex work which involves many changes of typeface or size, or disparate elements such as extracts, tables or footnotes. When these proofs have been corrected, the forme is ready for press.

The type may alternatively be used to create moulds for the production of rubber or plastic plates for printing by rotary letterpress, as with some newspapers and paperback books, or may be proofed to supply high-quality pulls for reproduction by photolithography.

After use, the type is *dissed* or distributed; if the type was founder's type, which must be kept for future use, dissing involves putting the lines back into the stick and reversing the procedure of hand composition, taking extreme care to put all the letters back into their correct compartments in the case. A 'foul case' was historically an offence punishable by instant dismissal! Type cast by machine is melted down in a furnace and recycled through the casting and typesetting process.

The advantage of hand composition is the ease with which small jobs destined for letterpress printing can be set: the variety of typefaces and sizes required in the average piece of jobbing work can be accommodated readily and quickly. Setting by hand also allows for great finesse in the hands of a skilled compositor.

Against these benefits, it must be accepted that typesetting by hand is slow, even by metal composition standards, and 'wrong fonts' can creep in, however careful the dissing of the previous job; consistent spacing is also difficult to control when setting by hand from a case. If continually re-used, even founder's type will eventually begin to wear: the image will thicken, and letters will become damaged or battered.

Today, hand setting is a dying art, and much jobbing printing has passed to high street instant printers, with lithographic 'small offset' printing presses and no requirement for metal typesetting. They find that rub-down letttering, high quality typewriters and simple desktop publishing systems provide the quality and productivity needed, and have lower skill requirements.

MECHANICAL COMPOSITION

Many attempts at inventing mechanical typesetting devices to overcome the slow speeds of hand composition were made during the nineteenth century. The earliest machines concentrated on the idea of composing pre-cast founder's type into lines, but the problems of maintaining the flow of types, justifying the composed lines and redistributing the used type proved difficult to overcome. Those machines which succeeded did so only by labour-intensive means, which necessitated the employment of juvenile labour and invoked the consequent opposition of the London Society of Compositors. The solution lay in the concept of a machine which, rather than assembling pre-cast types, combined typecasting and composition in one operation, and this was made possible only by the invention in 1885 of a mechanical punch-cutting device which allowed mass-production of the punches necessary for mechanical composing. Two machines came to dominate the scene – the Linotype, which cast type in lines or slugs, and the Monotype, which produced setting composed of individual characters.

It is a tribute to the original design of these machines that only relatively minor changes were made from the 1880s until production was wound down in the 1980s. They were even able partially to accommodate the computer revolution: adaptations were latterly produced to allow them to be driven by paper tape punched by typesetting terminals.

Line Composition – Linotype and Intertype

The principle of the Linotype, and the closely related Intertype machine, is that type is cast in complete lines rather than as single characters. Brass matrices stored in channels in a flat magazine at the top of the machine are released by the operator tapping the relevant key on the keyboard. The matrices are assembled in order in a line, and wedge-shaped expandable spacebands are driven up between the words to justify the line. The matrices are then transferred against the mouth of the mould, and molten type-metal is forced into them; the width of the mouth is the measure of the line and the depth is the body size of the type. As the operator is keying the next line, the slug of cast type is ejected from the matrices, which are automatically transported to the top of the machine; they run along a distributor bar which consists of a series of serrations partly cut away in pre-determined positions. The matrices have teeth to support them as they travel along the bar; as they reach the appropriate position, they are allowed to fall back into the correct channel of the magazine. The composed slugs are meanwhile collected on a galley tray, from where they are taken to the stone for make-up and imposition.

The capability of the linecasting machine depends on the particular model used; there are many variants. Most machines can carry a maximum of four main magazines and four side-magazines, which hold 90 and 34 matrices respectively, but whereas the simpler 'non-mixer' variants cannot use matrices from more than one magazine in any one line, the 'mixer' models can access matrices from any two adjacent main and side magazines in the same line: this gives these machines a potential choice from 248 matrices in a single line, and 496 in the entire piece of setting. As some matrices can carry two characters, the number of characters available is still further increased. Type can be set in sizes between 4¾pt and 18pt, or, with some models, 24pt.

The huge capacity of the magazines and the speed of casting ensured the linecasting machine's popularity in magazine and newspaper setting; simpler variants of the design tended to be used for bookwork, but even these had a far greater flexibility than Monotype machines, and Linotype and Intertype casters proved particularly popular for this work in the USA.

The typographic standards of linecasting machines have, however, never been comparable with those of Monotype casters. Because the matrices are assembled before casting takes place, kerned characters are impossible in line composition. Obviously cramped and irregular designs of characters such as italic 'f' are an obvious feature of line-cast setting. Strange, loosely fitted italics are another giveaway: if these characters are carried on the same matrix as their roman counterparts – *duplexed* – the set width of the letters must of necessity be the same.

In the composition process itself, problems arise from wear of the matrices. If they do not fit snugly together, excess metal can be forced up between them to print as fine hairlines between letters. Tiny pieces of grit between the matrices can cause the same problem. Minute variations in the type-height of different lines are another frequent fault in slug setting and show in darker or lighter lines in the final printed job, while worn matrices can also lead to uneven base-alignment of characters in the slug, so that characters appear to drift up and down along a line.

As a greater area is cast in one operation on a linecasting machine than in single-type composition, slightly softer type-metal must be used, and for this reason Linotype and Intertype setting was never very suitable for extremely long runs or for repeated impressions: in newspaper work, moulds were usually produced from the slug setting and the final job printed from harder plates cast from these.

Corrections are more difficult to perform than with single-type setting, as the entire line must be reset, ruling out late corrections on the bed of the press. On the other hand, slugs are far easier to handle than lines of individual types, and it is not so easy to drop and *pie* setting.

Display matter is cast, using the same principles of the line composition, on machines such as Ludlow or Nebitype casters. The matrices for display sizes of type are assembled by hand in a special composition stick and cast in a complete line.

Today, one hundred years after its introduction in the composing room of the *New York Tribune*, the linecasting machine might seem to be on the verge of extinction but production continues, although the handful of new machines are destined for foreign markets.

Single-character composition – Monotype

The Monotype machine was first produced a few years after the Linotype, in 1889, and had become established by the turn of the century. The main innovations of its creator, Tolbert Lanston, were a solution to the problem of justification, and the use of paper tape to drive a casting and composing machine.

The Monotype system comprises two machines: a keyboard, which is used to perforate a spool of paper tape, and a casting machine which casts single types according to the perforation codes on the tape. The splitting of the input (keying) and output (casting) functions, and the use of a storage medium (paper tape) to transfer the data, anticipates modern computer typesetting practice. Because the caster could operate faster than a keyboard operator could type, the practice was generally for there to be several keyboards for every caster. The extremely noisy casters were often located in a separate room.

Monotype keyboard

The keyboard has a seven-alphabet layout, and the operator can thus cause any character from these alphabets, in one type family and size only, to be set. Any matter to be set in different faces or sizes must be keyed and cast separately and made up manually on the imposition stone. The operator first sets up the keyboard for the type size and the measure required, and by keying the copy causes codes, in a combination of two holes according to the different characters keyed, to be punched in a 31 channel paper tape. At the same time as the codes are punched, a toothed wheel registers the width of the characters which have been keyed, and a mechanism known as a justifying drum indicates to the operator the space which remains in the line. As the end of the line approaches, the mechanism calculates the correct amount of space necessary to justify the line, and the pointer on the drum indicates which two justification keys need to be tapped. These keys punch holes in the paper tape which direct the caster to produce consistent and even spaces throughout the line.

On completion of the line, a key is depressed to return the justifying drum to its original position for the start of the next line.

Monotype caster

When keyboarding is complete, the spool of paper tape is transferred to the caster, which produces single metal types corresponding to the letters keyed by the operator.

The caster comprises three main elements: the *die-case*, the *mould* and the pump. In the die-case, either 225, 255 or 272 matrices are arranged in rows. These matrices correspond to the seven alphabet font of type represented by the keyboard, and are of one typeface and size only. All the characters in any one row have the same set width. The die-case is positioned on moveable rods over the mould; the mould's body, regulating the point size of the type, remains unchanged for the casting of any job, but the set width of the characters being cast is controlled by the operation of a steel wedge which alters the set of the mould.

When the paper tape is presented to the caster, a compressed-air mechanism reads the perforations, causing pins to move the draw rods which control the movement of the mould. Of the two-hole perforations produced for each character at the keyboard, one controls lateral movement and the other movement at right-angles to this. As the holes punched last are the first to be read by the caster, the perforations of the justification keys operate wedges which produce word spaces of correct width in the line. The die-case is moved over the mould as controlled by the tape, and molten type-metal is pumped into the matrix presented to the mouth of the mould. The mould is water-cooled, and as the metal solidifies the excess is cut off at the foot, and the piece of newly cast type is ejected into a channel. Meanwhile the die-case is moved to a new position to cast the next character. The types accumulate in the channel until the line is complete, when they are removed automatically to a galley tray. Make-up and imposition is then the same as for type composed by hand.

The Monotype Composition Caster can produce type in sizes from 4½pt to 14pt. Display matter to accompany Monotype setting is normally set by hand from types cast on a Supercaster, a machine working on similar principles but which can cast up to 72pt; alternatively, founder's type may be used. Since the type is cast singly, the type-metal can be made hard enough to withstand proofing, moulding, and relatively long print runs, as well as subsequent reprints; it is not, however, as durable as founder's type.

'Monotype' was for a long time considered a synonym for the highest possible standards in mechanical composition, and is still often used as a benchmark against which phototypesetting systems are measured. This stems from the range and quality of the Monotype typeface library that resulted from the design programme initiated in the years between the wars, and also from the standards set by the letter-fitting and spacing parameters of the system. As a result Monotype composition was long regarded as the obvious choice for those jobs where quality of typesetting was of critical importance.

One great advantage of Monotype composition is the ease with which corrections can be made. Simple corrections involving single characters can even be made on the bed of the letterpress printing machine itself, if necessary. Corrections to matter held in standing type are similarly cheap and easy to effect. But this facility is countered by the enormous cost of the metal and associated paraphernalia necessary for a letterpress printer, and the slow and expensive make-up required for matter set in different typefaces and sizes.

Today there are few typesetters who can offer metal composition, and even fewer printers retaining letterpress facilities. As metal type looks at its best when printed by letterpress on a sympathetic paper, there seems little purpose in pursuing a typographic ideal with Monotype composition only to reproduce it by the completely alien process of repro pulls and photolithography. This is not to imply any criticism of the latter process, but rather to underline the unsuitability of this kind of hybrid production.

3 Strike-on composition

One of the great advantages of lithography as a printing process is that any drawn or written image can be treated as an original and used as a master to produce multiple copies of the same design; any method of getting words onto paper, from handwriting to the most complex electronic composition process, is therefore a potential way of creating an image master, subject only to considerations of cost and typographic quality. The term *strike-on composition* is used to define those devices which produce camera-ready copy by the impact on paper of an image-carrying surface. In the past this has been synonymous with the various kinds of manual and electronic typewriter, but now the scope of the definition must be extended to include also the different types of printers used as output devices with personal computers. Non-impact printers, such as laser printers, have more affinity, both in imaging system and typographic capability, with typesetting systems proper, and are discussed under the heading of *Proofing methods* in Chapter Seven.

TYPEWRITERS

Both manual and electric typewriters create text by striking a relief image of individual characters onto paper through a pigmented ribbon. The main advantage of typewriter composition is economy, against which must be set considerable limitations in both typographic flexibility and output quality.

In fixed-space typewriters all characters share the same set width, and are as a result very unevenly and loosely fitted. There are three categories of character width:

Pica	10 characters to the inch
Elite	12 characters to the inch
Microelite	15 characters to the inch

The body depth of each face is equivalent to 12pt and is the same for all three categories, even though they have very different set widths and appearing sizes. The set width of the word space is fixed at the same size as the character width, and as a result all lines look loosely spaced in comparison to conventional typesetting with variable word-spacing. Justification of lines is not possible, and interlinear space can be adjusted only in crude increments. The individual letter designs are monoline, and lack any stress or shading; a typical font is limited to 88 characters, consisting of upper and lower case alphabets, figures and a small selection of punctuation marks, and each machine is restricted to one font. In manual typewriters the weight of impression can often vary between individual characters, and the overall clarity of the image is also affected by the condition of the pigmented ribbon.

Electric typewriters with proportionally spaced fonts overcome some of the above restrictions: set widths vary from character to character, allowing improvements in letter design and closer fitting of individual letters into words. Justification of lines is possible on most models: the line of copy is keyed and shown on a marching display or CRT screen, which also allows for corrections. It is not printed until the typist, alerted by a bell that the line-ending 'hot-zone' has been reached, makes a decision about the line end. The justified line is then printed out automatically. A range of different type-styles is often available, carried on *golfballs* or daisy wheels which can be removed and replaced as required to change alphabet style or typeface. The impression from an electrically-powered typewriter is likely to be more even than that from a manual machine.

Lack of typographic versatility, however, still precludes typewriter composition from all work except where economy is a priority above all other considerations. When a typescript is to be used as camera-ready copy, the machine should be fitted with a new, preferably wax-coated, ribbon and the same smooth, hard, white paper should be used throughout the entire job to ensure a crisp and even impression. A slight photographic reduction of the text will also improve image quality. Once the copy has been printed out, any corrections must be set as correction patches and stripped into the original by cut-and-paste methods.

IBM COMPOSITION

The IBM Selectric Composer is no longer made, but remains in common use, though gradually being replaced by desktop publishing and low cost phototypesetting systems. It is a sophisticated typewriter which combines economy and ease of operation with an improved quality of typographic output. A range of typefaces is carried on golf-ball heads, each containing 88 characters; the typeface designs are derivatives of those used in conventional typesetting, and most are available in series which include bold and italic alphabets, although not small capitals. Type sizes range from 7 to 12pt. The IBM proportional spacing system is based on nine units that permit seven different widths for characters of the alphabet.

While a considerable improvement over most typewriters, this system is much less flexible than conventional phototypesetting and as a result, characters can often appear loosely fitted. The set of each bold or italic character is exactly the same as its roman counterpart, meaning that bold characters appear rather more narrowly, and italic more widely, fitted than in the roman alphabet. There are only three escapements, or alphabet widths, to cover the seven different point sizes in each typeface: as a general rule, 6, 7 and 8pt sizes share the narrow (colour-coded blue) escapements; 9 and 10pt the medium (yellow); and 11 and 12pt the wide (red). Each size in each face is colour-coded on the golfball to ensure that the operator adjusts the escapement control on the machine to the correct setting before keyboarding commences. It follows from this that where two point sizes share the same escapement, the larger of the two will tend to be closer fitted and more successful.

These restrictions, together with the details of the actual type designs, demand extreme care when type is being specified for IBM setting; certain combinations of face and size are much more successful in appearance than others. The more acceptable include the following:

10pt and 12pt Aldine (Bembo)
11pt Baskerville
12pt Bodoni Book
11pt Century
11pt Journal (Sabon)
10pt and 11pt Press Roman (Times)
11pt Theme (Optima)
11pt Univers Condensed

Different sizes of type or face are achieved by manual changes of golfball; different sizes align on the base-line, allowing smaller-sized capitals to be used as a substitute for true small caps.

Interlinear space is adjustable in increments of one point; solid setting should be avoided, as it will make the cutting and pasting of corrections necessary with IBM setting extremely slow and laborious. The sharpest image quality is achieved when special proprietary forms of baryta paper or polyester film are used for the camera-ready copy; the weight of impression can be adjusted on the machine for optimum results.

Justification of lines on manual models of the Composer is achieved by a process of double keying. The line is keyed once, without being printed, until a bell requests the operator to make a line-end decision; the line is then re-keyed to this point to produce justified output.

With the IBM Electronic Composer the first keying of the text produces a proof output of the setting, ranged left, while the keystrokes are stored in a memory capable of holding up to 8000 characters. After proofreading, corrections are keyed into the text in the memory by overtyping the relevant original copy, and the setting is then played out automatically at high speed in a clean and justified form. Other models offer the facility for storing keystrokes on magnetic tape for correction and automatic justification.

IBM Composer setting is most suited to straightforward text with few changes in typeface or size, and with simple layout. One advantage of the system is that final camera-ready copy can be made available as keying is in progress, and no subsequent processing is required; in this respect the machine is ideal for short takes of copy such as stationery, publicity copy, illustration labels and general jobbing work. Any work containing a significant number of changes in typeface or size should be avoided, as the manual changing of the golfball causes disruption to the speed of keyboarding. Corrections after proofreading are often more economically handled by separate keying and cut-and-paste techniques than by attempting to correct and replay the original tape; this can, however, prove very time consuming if correction levels are high, and may also lead to variations in density of image in the final camera-ready copy.

Most IBM setting, even if designed in a carefully selected combination of face and size, can usually be identified by slight irregularities of base-line alignment between characters. The overall quality of IBM composition, although superior to that produced by conventional typewriters, is not comparable with that of modern phototypesetting.

Alice was beginning to get very tired of sitting by her sister on the bank, and of having nothing to do: once or twice she had peeped into the book her sister was reading, but it had no pictures or conversations in it, 'and what is the use of a book' thought Alice, 'without pictures or convers-ations?'

Alice was beginning to get very tired of sitting by her sister on the bank, and of having nothing to do: once or twice she had peeped into the book her sister was reading, but it had no pictures or conversations in it, 'and what is the use of a book' thought Alice, 'without pictures or conversations?'

Alice was beginning to get very tired of sitting by her sister on the bank, and of having nothing to do: once or twice she had peeped into the book her sister was reading, but it had no pictures or conversations in it, 'and what is the use of a book' thought Alice, 'without pictures or conversations?'

Alice was beginning to get very tired of sitting by her sister on the bank, and of having nothing to do: once or twice she had peeped into the book her sister was reading, but it had no pictures or conversations in it, 'and what is the use of a book' thought Alice, 'without pictures or conversations?'

Output from (reading from top) a Hermes S.40 electronic typewriter, a Microline dot matrix printer, a Brother daisy wheel printer and an IBM Electronic Composer. Note the differences in character design, letterfitting and word-spacing between these four samples of strike-on composition.

WORD-PROCESSOR PRINTERS

The earliest printers supplied with personal computers provided only monospaced fonts, of a quality that differed greatly according to the speed at which the printer was required to run. Manufacturers are now becoming increasingly aware of the value of offering higher-quality output, and some attractive proportionally spaced fonts can be obtained. Various different types of printer are available.

Matrix printers

In this type of printer, each character is represented by a pattern of dots, and a set of fine needles is activated by data from the computer to construct the shape of the relevant character by striking through a ribbon held against the paper. The font information is determined by a chip within the printer which holds the matrix patterns for each character code.

The quality of image produced varies according to the size and cost of the machine, but also depends on the size of matrix, and the speed at which the printer is driven: in *draft mode* speeds of up to 200 characters per second are possible, but to achieve *near letter quality* (NLQ), speeds will be much slower. Letter quality is used in this context by suppliers of word processor printers to define the standards of the average office typewriter. Output from a printer in draft mode does not usually have sufficient density to be used as camera-ready copy, and any text produced in NLQ mode will require careful checking; as the definition implies, typographic quality cannot be expected to exceed that of a conventional typewriter.

Daisy wheel printers

These printers can offer much higher image quality than dot matrix printers. The characters are held as relief images on the end of plastic stalks radiating from a central hub; it is the resemblance of this wheel to the flower that gives the daisy wheel printer its name. The wheels each contain 90 to 100 characters, and are interchangeable. In operation, the wheel is mounted vertically in front of a pigmented ribbon and rotates until the required character is brought to a vertical position, when it is struck by a hammer against the ribbon to create an image on the paper behind it. The wheel moves one character space across the paper at each impression, at speeds of up to 60 characters per second. A variety of proportionally spaced fonts is available, and with sufficient care a crisp image suitable for photographic reproduction can be obtained. The output is normally defined by manufacturers as letter quality. Best results are achieved by using a carbon film ribbon, and a metallised, rather than a plastic, daisy wheel.

Output from a word-processor printer is most suited to work where control over the initial keyboarding and correction stages is to be retained by the originating source, and where economic pressures do not permit resetting of the text. Output from printers using even the best proportionally spaced fonts does not stand comparison with conventional phototypesetting, and progress toward higher quality seems to have been halted by the greater commercial acceptibility of laser printers and ink jets (which are virtually silent compared to noisy strike-on printers). Many word processing programs can now incorporate elements of page composition, including a selection of electronically stored outline fonts, and some can even import graphics for output on a page. This requires a printer that is not confined to the rows-and-columns approach of many strike-on printers; again laser printers and ink-jets are more suitable. This leads towards the discussion of desktop publishing systems explored in Chapter Eight.

SETTING DISPLAY SIZES

No strike-on composition system offers the ability to set type in display sizes. Various options are possible to incorporate the larger type sizes or different faces that may be needed for headings and other titling.

It is always possible simply to have any display matter photo-typeset and pasted into the camera-ready copy of the text, but the use of strike-on composition for the text implies a need for maximum economy, and this is therefore unlikely to be an ideal option. One alternative is to set all display matter in the same size as the text, and enlarge it photographically to the required size; the irregular letter-fitting which is characteristic of most strike-on setting, and visible even in composition sizes, does however tend to be accentuated as the image is enlarged, and considerable cutting and pasting of individual letters may be necessary to close up the characters into an acceptable final form.

Dry transfer lettering is the setting method for display titling most often used as a companion to strike-on composition; various types are marketed under such proprietary names as Letraset, Normaset or Mecanorma. A huge variety of different type styles in a complete range of sizes is available, together with ornamental flourishes, symbols and other decorative material; most manufacturers print spacing guides on the sheets as an aid to correct visual positioning and no great expertise is therefore required to produce an acceptable result. Care should, however, be taken to ensure that the sheet of transfer lettering has been stored flat and is in good condition, with no cracked or chipped letters although small blemishes can sometimes be retouched with black ink. The lettering should be rubbed down onto a smooth-surfaced sheet, and never onto the original camera-ready copy; any errors in spelling, spacing or alignment of characters can be more readily corrected on a separate sheet, after which the titling can be cut up for pasting into position in the text.

4 Electronic output machines

The first attempts to create lines of text on paper without the use of metal type date from the late nineteenth century but, although it was proved that photographic methods of typesetting could work in theory, none of the early prototype machines were effective enough in practice to warrant development. Although the growth of photolithography as a printing process during the twentieth century demanded a fast and economical means of producing an image master, for a long time the usual way of creating this was by a process of metal composition and reproduction pulls. To a large extent it was the development of computer technology in the late 1940s that paved the way for the first commercially successful phototypesetting devices. From that time to the present, the history of typesetting has been one of increasingly rapid change.

Typesetting systems that set 'hot' metal type using typecasting equipment, like the Monotype and Linotype, are known as mechanical composition systems. Composing machines setting 'cold' type onto film or bromide paper without the use of metal type are often loosely described as phototypesetters. Four generations of machine are identified. Of these, only the first- and second-generation devices are truly phototypesetters, equipped with photographic masters, lenses and light sources for exposing images onto light-sensitive paper or film. Later composing machines abandoned these photo-mechanical principles, adopting digital techniques for the storage of type masters, and cathode ray tube or laser devices for output under computer control. These designs of machine are more properly described as *electronic typesetters*, and those machines which can output digitised graphics and illustrations as well as type are further distinguished as *imagesetters*. The last generation of machines that could only produce type was the AM Varityper Comp/Edit 6700/6800 series, introduced in 1986. Since then all new output devices, whether laser or CRT based, have been in effect imagesetters, although graphics handling ability varies from design to design.

Although it is convenient to classify machines in this way, it is wrong to consider developments as falling into neat and discrete periods. Research took place simultaneously into many different output technologies, and categorisation is best used as a clarification of operating principles rather than of exact chronology.

FIRST GENERATION: PHOTO-MECHANICAL MACHINES

First-generation phototypesetters were developments of existing mechanical composing machines, utilising the same principles but replacing the metal typecasting equipment with photographic devices. The Monophoto Filmsetter substituted a die-case of negative film matrices, a camera unit and a photographic film carriage system for the recessed metal matrices, mould and pump of its hot-metal predecessor. The keyboard, the paper tape and, most importantly, the drive system that aligned the correct matrix in the die-case in front of the camera lens were still almost exactly those of the Monotype caster.

Linecasting machines underwent similar conversion to emerge as phototypesetters. In the Intertype Fotosetter the individual brass matrices contained negative image masters of characters; the linecasting principle was changed slightly to allow individual exposure of the matrices, although these were still first assembled in lines. But the basic principle of image-carrying matrices circulating through the machine from a central magazine remained.

These early phototypesetters inherited not only the mechanical principles but also the limitations of hot-metal composing machines. Each die-case, or set of matrices, held film masters for one design of typeface only; the Monophoto die-case held 272 matrices, exactly the same number as its metal equivalent. Any copy in a different face had to be composed separately using another die-case and stripped in manually at make-up stage; corrections were handled in the same way. Both make-up and corrections were laborious and time consuming operations; most work was output in film, and this proved difficult to control accurately. Inconsistent processing of the exposed film often caused problems in matching the density of correction patches to the original setting. Crooked correction lines, and dark or light areas in the final printed type were common faults of early photo-mechanical typesetting.

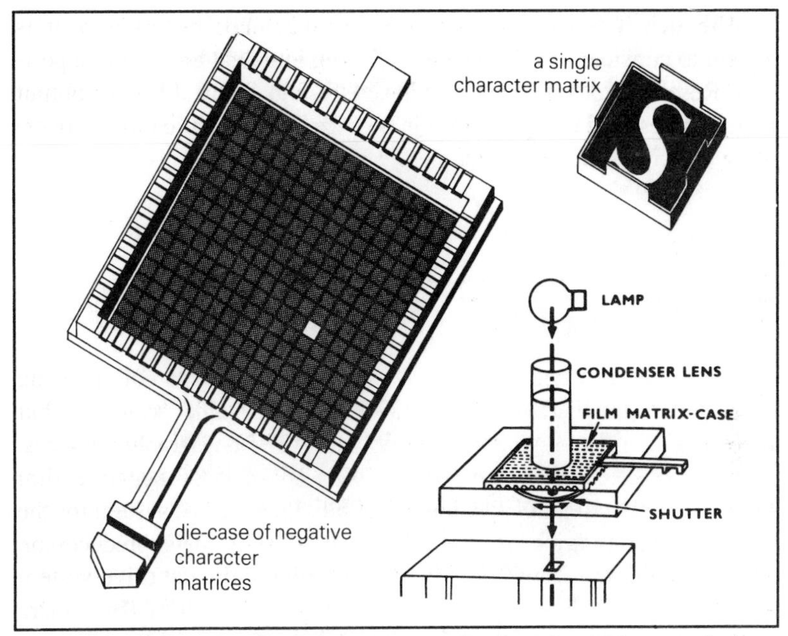

The imaging system of a first generation photo-mechanical typesetting machine.

The Monotype machines at least retained the high-quality typography that distinguished Monotype composition in metal, and the die-case was held stationary at the instant of exposure, resulting in a photographic image of extreme sharpness and clarity; a system of zoom lenses was used to produce a range of different sizes from the one negative master of each character. But the mechanical operations which made possible this image quality seriously limited the speed of the machine. In the next generation of phototypesetters, typographic quality was subordinated to the demands of higher output speed.

The most common of the first-generation phototypesetting machines were the Intertype Fotosetter and Fotomatic, and the Monotype range, Marks I-V. The only machine based on these principles that is still likely to be found in operation today is the Monophoto 400/8, later developed further and rechristened the 1000 system. This embodied several modifications to the original design: the die-case was enlarged to carry 400 matrices, each of which could be replaced to allow the introduction of special sorts. Corrections were made simpler by the development of a paper-tape reader which could merge tapes of correction setting with those of the original keyboarding to produce a new, correct master tape for re-running through the output machine.

But although these developments went some way to overcoming the restrictions of early phototypesetters, new solutions to the mechanical problems were already being sought through the introduction of electronic control.

SECOND GENERATION: ELECTRO-MECHANICAL MACHINES

The earliest phototypesetter recognised as belonging to the second generation – the Photon 540 machine – was introduced commercially in 1962. The main design features which distinguished second generation machines from earlier phototypesetters were the use of valves, electro-mechanical relays and circuits to reduce mechanical movements within the machine, and the stroboscopic flash exposure of characters from a continuously spinning photo-matrix disk. Both these developments were to allow a considerable increase in the speed of access to characters and the exposure of the images on film. Information required for the characters and spaces tapped at the keyboard was coded and stored in the memory units, which also held information about character widths, thus enabling automatic justification of lines to be performed; the keyboard unit produced justified paper tape to drive the output device in slave mode. The image masters of the individual characters were still photographic negatives as on first-generation machines, but in the Photon these negatives were arranged in concentric circles around the circumference of a disk. During output, the disk rotated continuously at high speed in front of a light source, which was synchronised to flash and expose the relevant character as it spun past. A lens system was used to control the sizing of the image.

Other machines were developed, working on similar principles, but with progressive modifications. Later designs held the logic which controlled hyphenation and justification in the output machine itself, thus allowing the use of unjustified tape from the keyboard. In 1970 the Merganthaler Linotype VIP became the first phototypesetter to incorporate a minicomputer with programmable software which could be used to process raw text within the output machine.

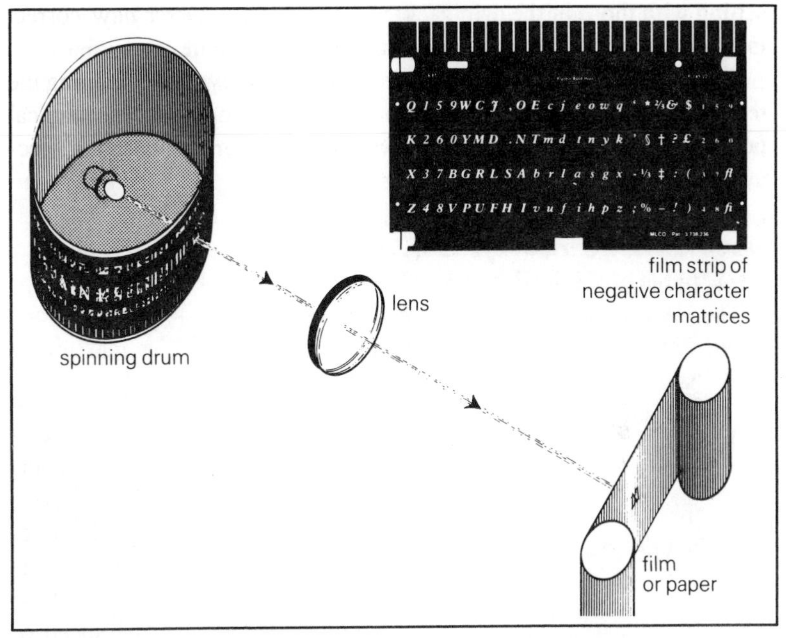

The imaging system of a second generation electro-mechanical typesetting machine

The matrices used as image masters in these machines were usually negative (transparent) images on a black (opaque) ground, and could be stored in a variety of ways: rectangular grids, disks, segments for attachment to parts of disks, and film strips for mounting on drums were all used. The common feature of all the variants was the increased capacity and flexibility of the character store, with many more sorts, in a number of different typefaces, available at any one time for exposure. In the later Photon machines, 224 characters were carried in each of four circles on a rotating disk, giving a total of 896 characters *on-line* at any time. Systems in which characters were fixed in position on grids or disks and could not be individually replaced compensated by allowing a number of different matrix carriers to be held in the machine; these could be switched by electronic control from the keyboard. Segmented disks allowed even greater flexibility, as each segment or quadrant, of which there could be from two to eight per disk, could be removed and replaced, enabling special sorts or alternative typefaces to be included; the same principle was used to mount different film strips on a main carrying drum.

Sizing of the image could be achieved in a number of ways. Some machines used a different font matrix, carrying separate image masters, for each size; this method produced the highest image quality, but limited the capacity of the character store and the overall productivity of the machine. To reduce the number of image masters required by these 'same-size' systems, turrets of lenses were developed, with each lens used for one specific type size; switching between the different lenses was controlled from the keyboard. Zoom lens arrangements also allowed a wide range of sizes to be exposed from a single negative master.

The clear advantages of the second-generation phototypesetter were the increased speed of output due to the reduction in mechanical movements, and the wide range of characters available on-line. These benefits were not achieved without some compromise in typographic quality. Type produced in a range of sizes from a single image master cannot retain all the subtleties of weight and proportion that are inherent in the *same-size* designs of either metal or photoset type, where individual masters are designed specifically for each size. Image quality from some second-generation typesetting machines also suffered from the technique of stroboscopic exposure of characters from a continuously spinning disk or drum adopted by most manufacturers: this could often produce an image that was slightly blurred and unsharp. Character positioning was another source of problems: irregular letter-fitting and faulty base-alignment of characters could result from mistimings of the flash exposure.

Corrections were still handled by tape-merging, or by cutting and pasting into the original setting lines or patches output separately at a later stage; most output was now on bromide paper, which was cheaper and easier to handle than film, but uneven density of correction patches was still a potential danger.

Production of electro-mechanical typesetters continued until the early 1980s, long after the introduction of all-digital laser and CRT phototypesetters. Many electro-mechanical typesetters are still in operation today, usually in smaller print shops where volume of throughput is relatively low. They include the Compugraphic Universal and EditWriter series, a range of economical machines which played an important role in popularising phototypesetting in the 1970s. Second generation machines, with their design of character store, include:

A-M Comp/Edit – early models (disk)
Berthold TPU 3608 (grid)
Compugraphic EditWriter series (film strips on drum)

Compugraphic Universal series (film strips on drum)
Itek Quadritek (quadrant)
Merganthaler Linotype VIP (film strips on drum)
Monophoto 2000 system (disk)

THIRD GENERATION: CATHODE RAY TUBE MACHINES

The photographic principle of flashing a light source through a negative image of the required character is abandoned in this design of machine. Instead images are generated on the face of a cathode ray tube (CRT) and exposed from there onto photographic material.

A cathode ray tube crudely resembles a flat-bottomed glass bottle, in which the bottom serves as a screen. This is coated with a phosphor salt which glows (fluoresces) under the impact of high-speed electrons. The electrons are fired as a concentrated beam from a cathode in the neck of the tube, and the light beam appears as a microscopic spot on the screen. The beam can be diverted to move across the screen under the control of electronic data fed to deflector plates between which the beam passes, enabling the beam to 'draw' images on the screen; the phosphor continues to fluoresce for a very short time after the beam has moved past (persistence), and so the image can be redrawn at very high speed to give the appearance of a continuous image. This is then transferred to the photographic material via a lens system or a fibre-optic faceplate. Early designs of CRT machines use the light spot as a pencil of light to draw the shape of the required image in a technique known as vector scanning. Another technique is for the CRT to create the image by drawing a series of vertical and parallel lines of light, with the beam switched on or off under electronic control to create image or non-image areas as required. Modern CRT typesetters utilise this latter method of imaging, with the light beam exposing type as a series of very fine vertical lines, from left to right, character by character.

The first CRT typesetters held type in photographic character stores, with negative matrices carried on grids, drums or disks. One cathode ray tube scanned this master, generating scan lines which were converted by a photomultiplier into electronic pulses; these signals were then amplified according to the size of type required and reconstructed into optical form by a second cathode ray tube for exposure to film or paper. Font changes were achieved by mechanical switching of the grid or drum containing the image masters. This photo-mechanical character store limited the output speed and productivity of the typesetter, and also tended to reduce typographic quality. With the cathode ray tube came the ability for the first time to manipulate type electronically: all sizes could be produced from one image master, more quickly and flexibly than with lens systems, and type could be expanded, condensed or slanted at will. This new-found flexibility encouraged some manufacturers to abandon such so-called inessential characters as small capitals (which could be replaced by capitals of a smaller type size) and ligatures (ff, fi, fl, ffi, ffl), while in some systems sloped roman, electronically generated from a roman master, was offered as a substitute for true italic. These typographic distortions were genuine attempts to overcome the 'matrix poverty' imposed on typesetting by the limitations of mechanical character storage. The true advantages of electronic composition lie in speed of output coupled with total typographic flexibility, but these could not be fully realised until the introduction of digital character storage.

The average CRT typesetter is so fast that output is normally quoted not in terms of characters per second but in newspaper lines per minute (nlpm), with a newspaper line defined as an 11 pica measure of 8pt type. An average quoted performance would be 700 nlpm at a resolution of approximately 1000 lpi, but many machines can achieve faster speeds than this; the Autologic APS-5 is rated at 3000 nlpm.

With cathode ray tube devices, both type sizes and interlinear space can be adjusted in fractional amounts, as small as one tenth of a point with some machines, and a wide range of electronic effects can be applied to type. By decreasing the set width of characters while keeping body height constant, a condensed version of the original typeface can be produced; increasing set width with constant body height creates an expanded face. Type can be sloped forwards or backwards in increments of as little as one degree to offer the facility of sloped roman faces in varying inclinations. These surrogate forms may not always be as aesthetically satisfying as their 'true' counterparts, but the ease with which they can be created is impressive. Because of this power and speed, coupled with extreme reliability, CRT typesetters have proved very popular in a wide range of applications and are found in all environments from small general printers to national newspapers and directory typesetters, where the volume and speed of throughput is all-important.

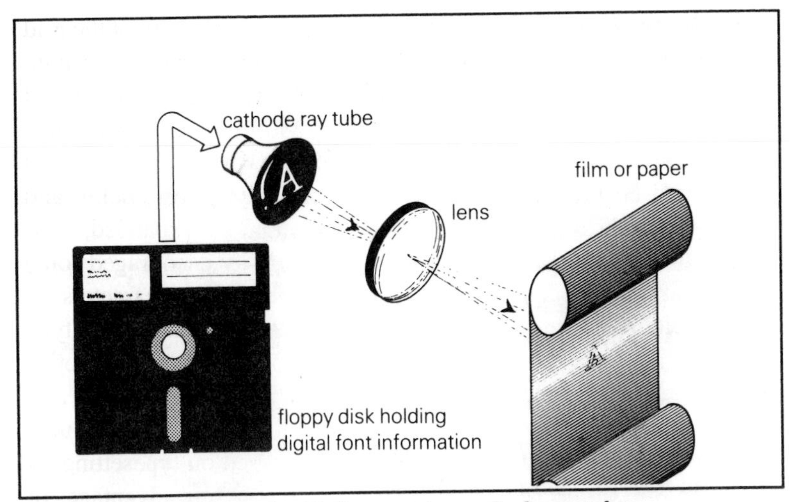

The imaging system of a third generation cathode ray tube typesetting machine.

Launched in 1978 and still in limited production in 1991, Linotype's Linotron 202 was one of the most successful CRT typesetting machines ever made, and is still in widespread use. The details from its manufacturing specification which will be of most interest to those responsible for buying type are listed below:

Input Paper tape (6 or 8 level), floppy disk, magnetic tape. Can be driven as 'slave' typesetter by justified input, or by unjustified input using the hyphenation and justification program of the 202 itself.

Point size range 4½–72pt in ½ increments.

Speed 700 nlpm for 8/9 pt type at 11-pica line length.

Line length 48 picas maximum.

Film advance ¼ pt increments.

Font master and capacity Fonts stored as outline shapes on 8-inch floppy disks. Digitised fonts each having up to 150 characters with approximately 32 per side. Two disk drives are standard. Standard font capacity is 64 fonts. Double-sided option offers twice that number. Each 40Mb of fixed disk can store approximately 2000 standard fonts.

Number of required digitisations One master digitisation produces all point sizes and also, expanded, condensed and slanted effects.

Expanding/condensing Expanded and condensed versions of all fonts are produced by changing set width independently of point size. Type can be expanded to 400%, and condensed to 25%, of original.

Character widths Based on 18- or 54-unit system.

Mixing Mixing and base-alignment of all typefaces, point sizes and set widths within the same line is possible.

Resolution 975 scan lines per inch, or 1950 scan lines per inch in high-resolution mode.

Output Paper or film, right or wrong reading, as galleys or pages.

Other common CRT machines include the following:

AM Comp/Edit 6700 and 6800 series
Autologic APS-5 range
Compugraphic MCS 8000 series
Information International Grafix (triple-I) VideoComp 570
Linotype CRTronic 320/340/360
Scangraphic Scantext 1000

Manufacturers have now turned their attention to laser based imagesetters, and these third generation machines are now either out of production or only available to special order. However, CRT technology is by no means abandoned, and is used in some modern imagesetters, such as the Berthold Recorder CI and the Chelgraph IBX series.

FOURTH GENERATION: IMAGESETTERS

Machines of this generation, like CRT typesetters, use digital storage to carry typeface font information. Most of them, however, use a completely different method of imaging, which has important implications for graphics and full-page output.

Unlike most CRT typesetters, which expose type in a series of vertical strokes, character by character, imagesetters operate by sweeping horizontally across the full width of the area being exposed, building up lines of type scan line by scan line from the top of the image area; this process is known as raster scanning. The significance of this is that a device scanning horizontally has the potential to output not only

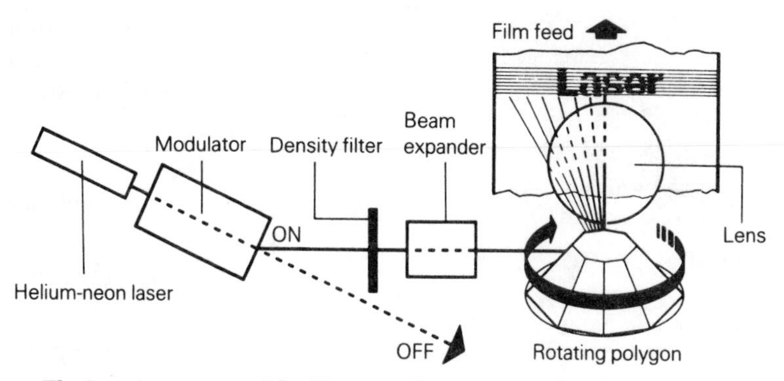

The imaging system of the Monotype Lasercomp, a fourth generation laser imagesetter.

typographic characters, but any image presented from the controlling computer in digital form: the image/non-image pattern produced by laser can be used to build up the strokes of type characters, line graphics, or the screened dots of halftone illustrations. Raster scan setters can therefore in theory output complete pages of text and illustrations, with all elements in the correct position. Manual page make-up becomes unnecessary, and the film delivered from the imagesetter is ready for platemaking. There are great attractions in this concept for work which has regularly to be produced to critical deadlines.

To produce full pages of integrated text and tone, the imagesetter's computer must have a complete picture of the page in digital form in its memory before starting to output. This task is performed by a *raster image processor* (RIP). The first commercial use of a RIP was in the Monotype Lasercomp in the late 1970s; the man responsible for its development, David Hedgeland, has defined the RIP as 'a device which creates a symbolic description of a page, with type, point size, shapes and pictures, and processes that description into an organisation of scan lines for output by a raster device.' This 'description of a page', composed of individual *pixels*, is known as a *bitmap*. In practical terms, the raster image processor is fed from the composition front-end system with a series of computer codes that define the characters and elements required; the RIP then creates the page by accessing the digital type fonts from memory and regenerating the stored outlines into correctly sized bitmap form, by creating any tints, patterns, rules or boxes required, and by using logic to convert the continuous-tone

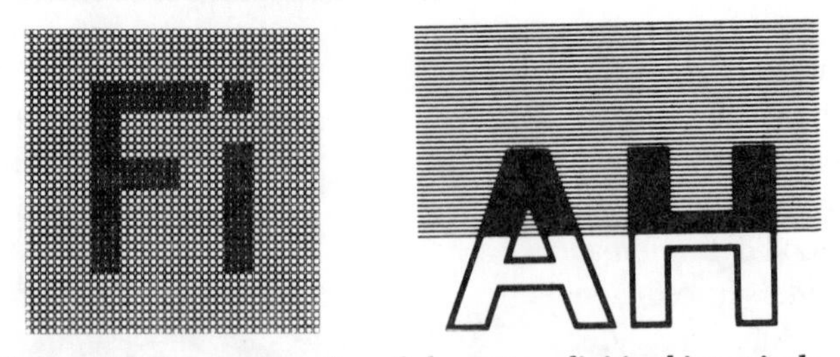

Left *Simplified representation of characters digitised into pixels.*

Right *Raster scanning: showing how images are built up by horizontal scan lines. In reality, both pixels and scan lines touch or overlap slightly, and are at much higher densities.*

data of illustrations into screened halftone output. The bitmap of the page is then processed for output, with the raster image processor controlling the switching of the modulator to reproduce the predefined images.

The raster image processor itself is ideally an independent device and can drive different output recorders at different resolutions; these may be imagesetters accessing high-quality type fonts for output on film at 2500 lpi or laser-proofing devices using fonts specially designed for output at 300 dpi on plain paper. The resolution of the image produced depends on the output device driven by the RIP. Until recently, however, the front-end systems on which pages were created were linked to output devices by proprietary software and hardware interfaces; to achieve complete independence of output device, the text and graphic elements of a page must be described by the computer which creates the page in a consistent software language, allowing output to be generated by any equipment which can accept data in this language.

Page description languages enable computers to encode information about type fonts, sizes and positioning, the screen rotations and positioning required for graphic elements, into a description of the contents of the page which can then be computed by the raster image processor into the bitmap required for the output recorder. Several page description languages have been developed, of which PostScript, introduced in 1984 by a US software company called Adobe Systems, rapidly became the industry standard; all imagesetter manufacturers now include PostScript-compatible models in their ranges, and a wide range of publishing and graphics software is available which can output in this language.

The output of integrated text and graphics requires the use of a raster scan device exposing the image in horizontal sweeps across the image area, and most manufacturers have adopted lasers as a suitable imaging system: the virtually parallel beam of light produced by a laser can give good definition and sharpness.

Imagesetters, together with their controlling electronics and software programs, extend the electronic manipulation techniques that were introduced by CRT machines. Type can be expanded, condensed and slanted, and point size and interlinear space are adjustable by infinitesimal amounts. In addition, a wide variety of geometric shapes can be produced, in any weight of line, with square or rounded corners, and filled with varying screen tints or patterns. Elements on the page, or the entire page itself, can often be rotated through 360 degrees: this facility makes possible the exposure of fully composed display advertisements, or of pages correctly imposed for printing on a one-piece foil, and even the imaging by the laser of the printing plate itself.

Direct-to-plate systems have had a long and difficult birth, hampered by the difficulty of producing light sensitive coatings that were 'fast' enough to be exposed by laser devices, and the technical problems of producing laser exposure units big enough to handle common plate sizes. Both problems seem to have been overcome, so direct platemaking should start to be increasingly common. In the meantime, the main emphasis is on the production of imposed foils.

The potential ability of the imagesetter to output screened halftones of a high quality is another exciting development, and is the subject of major research work by many manufacturers; quality halftone setting makes exacting demands on digital storage techniques, data processing speeds, and the accuracy of lasers. These problems are discussed in Chapter Seven under the heading of *Graphic Systems*.

One new phenomenon in imagesetter sales is that of OEM licenses. This stands for Original Equipment Manufacture, and basically means that one manufacturer will sell another manufacturer's machinery with its own label on it, and sometimes changes to the specification of the control systems. Thus exposure units made by Ultre, Agfa and ECRM appear under many other manufacturers' names. The Canon LPB-8 laser printer 'engine' is at the heart of the best selling Apple LaserWriter and Hewlett-Packard LaserJet series. Hyphen and Harlequin make high speed PostScript interpreters which confer PostScript compatibility on a wide range of third parties' exposure systems.

LIGHT SOURCES

Imagesetters can use a variety of light sources. The most common is the laser and the related laser diode, but several other technologies are seen in commercial use.

Lasers

A laser (Light Amplification by Stimulated Emission of Radiation) is a light beam of a special kind, which can apply vast energy with extreme accuracy. The laser comprises three main elements: an amplifying medium, a resonator and a power supply. In most typesetting applications, the amplifying medium is helium-neon (HeNe) gas, contained in a tube with highly reflective mirrors at each end acting as resonators; one of these mirrors is, however, semi-transparent to very intense light. Running down the centre of the tube is a cathode and, when an electrical current is applied, this releases electrons into the helium gas. As the helium atoms become excited, they collide with the neon atoms, causing the neon electrons each to release a photon, or light particle. The photons are reflected by the mirrors at each end of the tube, and pass back and forth through the neon atoms, causing more photons to be released until the resultant energy is sufficient to escape through the semi-transparent mirror as a highly concentrated beam of red light. A small burst of energy applied to the cathode thus causes a disproportionately high level of light to be released by the surrounding gas.

Other types of laser are available for different requirements. An argon ion gas, for instance, produces an intense blue-green light, and was used in early colour scanners and lithographic direct plate exposure systems. Carbon dioxide can give an infra-red beam of immense power, and is commonly used to vapourise soft materials such as wood, rubber and plastics. This is used to etch gravure cylinders, to engrave rollers for flexographic printing, and to cut channels in cutting and creasing formes.

Lasers are also an integral part of the optical disk technologies which are beginning to be used for high capacity digital storage of information. As the name suggests, lasers are also the exposure source for laser printers, which use a light sensitive toner drum similar to a photocopier, as opposed to the photographic material used on imagesetters.

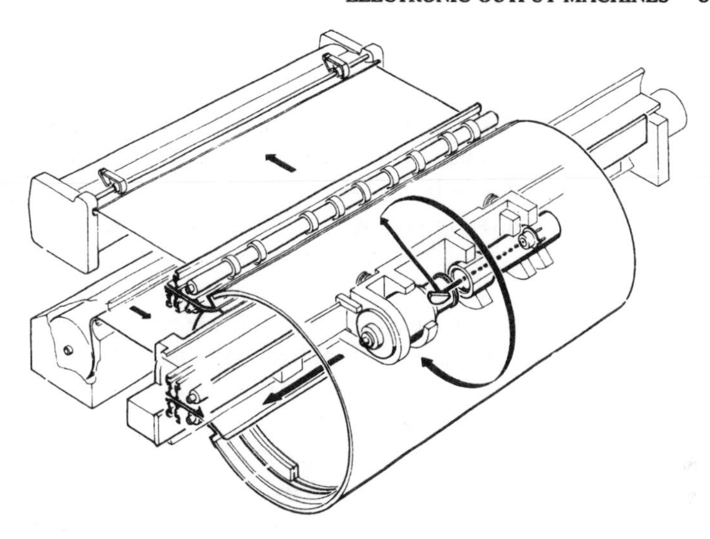

Basic principle of an internal drum imagesetter, in this case supplied by Scangraphic. The film material is wrapped around the inner surface of the drum, the laser carriage moves from right to left, and the beam exposes a series of arcs.

The helium-neon laser found in many typesetting applications produces a continuous beam of light, which cannot easily be turned on and off; the beam is therefore directed at a modulator, which, by either deflecting the beam or allowing it to pass straight through, differentiates between the image and non-image impulses presented as digital information from the computer. When imaging, the laser beam passes via prisms to a density filter which improves the intensity of the light, and a beam expander which controls balance, intensity and definition. In many systems the light is focused onto a cone-shaped polygonal mirror, which rotates at a constant speed and reflects the consecutive strokes (or *scans*) of light side by side horizontally across the photographic film or paper. In between scans, the film material is advanced slightly in the vertical direction, thus building up an image from a column of vertical strokes.

For high accuracy requirements, such as business forms or colour halftone work, an alternative arrangement called the internal drum imagesetter is coming into favour. Instead of being advanced during exposure, the film is held stationary throughout, and the laser beam is advanced in two dimensions. To achieve this, the film material is wrapped around the inner surface of a hollow drum, generally occupying about half or three quarters of the circumference. A laser beam is directed down the exact centre of the drum, and strikes a travelling, spinning mirror which is angled to redirect the beam outward at right angles to strike the inner surface of the drum. As the mirror spins, it describes a scan line across one dimension of the film. After each scan, the mirror unit is advanced slightly down the centre of the drum, and the next exposure pass is made. By keeping the film stationary, great accuracy and repeatability is possible, which is important for multiple sets of colour separations.

In all laser machines the imaging spots of light are positioned so that they just touch, and the diameter of the light beam therefore determines the resolution of the output; this varies according to machine, but values of 1000 lpi and upwards are usual.

Imagesetters intended for the production of photographic halftones as well as type generally have resolutions in the 2000–3500 lpi range. Resolution is inversely related to speed, and many machines have adjustable resolution to suit the demands of particular work: the Linotronic 300 can set in ‘high quality’ (2540 lpi), ‘normal’ (1270 lpi), or ‘proofing’ (635 lpi) modes. To guarantee accuracy and definition, all parts of a laser setter, but in particular the rotating mirror, must be engineered to extremely critical tolerances.

Laser imagesetters available include:

Agfa (formerly Compugraphic) 9550, 9600, 9700, 9880, 5000
Autologic APS-laser-6
Berthold Laser Recorder
Birmy Graphics Birmysetter
Linotype-Hell BridgIt (formerly made by Hell-Xenotron)
Linotype-Hell Linotronic 230, 230SQ, 300, 330, 500, 530
Monotype Prism, ExpressMaster, ImageMaster
Purup ImageMaker
Scantext 2030 and 2051
Scitex Dolev-PS
Varityper 4300, 5000 series

Laser diodes

Helium-neon lasers require a high voltage supply, an external modulator and, because they incorporate complex optical systems with finely tuned moving parts, can be prone to mechanical faults. Laser diodes are claimed to offer significant advantages in all these areas. As the technology is related to that used in compact disk players, volume production of the diodes has reduced initial costs, while power consumption is low and life expectancy long. Unlike gas lasers, the diode can be switched on and off rapidly, and there is therefore no need for a modulator to control the beam.

In the late 1980s, laser diodes came to be favoured in some imagesetters (generally the smaller, lower cost models) and most laser printers. They are much cheaper than HeNe lasers and have a much longer life, but initially they could only produce a relatively weak infra-red beam, requiring a special, more expensive film. Until 1985 there was no film suitable for exposure by laser diode commercially available, but several manufacturers now make film sensitive to the infra-red wavelengths in which the diode emits light.

Red light laser diodes have now been developed and are used in the high accuracy Linotronic 630 imagesetter, while blue light models have been demonstrated in laboratory conditions.

Light emitting diodes

This system is based on a screen of LEDs, each of which can be individually turned on or off by a computer controlling the voltage in order to expose images. The attraction is that banks of LEDs could theoretically be assembled in densities of up to 1000 per inch across the entire image area, giving very high-speed imaging with extreme accuracy, as there would be no problematical moving parts except the film or paper transport mechanism. The small Itek Digitek setter used an array of 128 LEDs which traversed the image area horizontally, exposing photosensitive material in a series of steps. This is no longer produced; however LEDs are used in some Dainippon Screen and Itek Colour Graphics scanner recorders, which can also be used as imagesetters.

Light gate array

The Monotype 512, introduced in 1986, exposes images by focusing a conventional light source through an array of 512 cells on a semi-conductor light gate. Each of these cells can be addressed by computer to render them transparent or opaque, and thus allow or prevent light from reaching the photographic material. Image exposure takes place in areas where the elements of the array have been turned transparent to allow light to pass through. The array is mounted on a carriage which is stepped horizontally across the film or paper, exposing as it travels. The 512 is a low-cost, medium-speed machine, aimed at smaller typesetting installations. The 512 is no longer sold, but light gates are used insead of lasers in a handful of plain paper printers.

DIGITAL FONTS

From the third generation of typesetter onward, there was a requirement to store type fonts electronically, rather than as physical masters. Today effectively all type design is for digital applications and many designers have never known any other way of working. Digital type can be stored compactly on computer disks. As every character generated from a digital source is in effect an original, there is nothing to wear or become distorted with age or constant use. With digital type fonts, characters are stored in computer memory as digital information and accessed by codes fed to the typesetting output machine in an established typesetting language, such as ASCII (American Standard Code for Information Interchange); this allows characters to be called up from store at speeds impossible with mechanical storage systems.

To produce a digitised type font, the typesetting manufacturer or supplier must first scan the original drawings of all the characters one by one against a grid pattern of extremely fine horizontal and vertical lines, to produce an image of each character as a mosaic of fine dots. These individual dots are known as picture elements or pixels. The character is displayed on a monitor at a vastly enlarged size, and individual pixels are added to or removed from the outline in order to cater for the effects of reproduction and printing processes on the appearance of the type; a curve may need attention to ensure a smooth outline, or the angles where strokes join may need 'notching' to prevent build-up of ink during printing. Once these aesthetic adjustments have been entered via a keyboard, the digital image of the character is ready for storing as a sequence of signals denoting the image or non-image values of each individual pixel. This sequence is called a bit-map. Digital font information is supplied by the manufacturer on rigid or floppy disk, ready for downloading to the typesetting machine's memory.

The highest quality of image is obtained with those systems which follow the *same-size* principle, and hold a separate digitised font master for each point size of type required. Even in digital form, this approach is very expensive in terms of storage needed: in a font which has been digitised at 1200 lines per inch, a 12pt character requires 200 x 200 pixels to carry the information about its shape, a total of 40,000 bits of information. Every pixel needs to be recorded, and a same-size system requires bit-mapped font masters for each character in each size of each typeface held.

Enlarging/reducing systems make use of a limited number of bit-mapped font masters and manipulate these electronically to produce a complete range of sizes. A typical machine might hold four masters to cover the complete point-size range, designed to produce type in sizes of 9–16, 18–32, 36–64 and 72–96 points. Type set with an enlarging/reducing system of character sizing automatically suffers a loss in typographic finesse as all sizes produced from the same master will have identical proportions. In addition on large sizes of type set on CRT or some laser machines the stepped edges of the scan lines may be visible – a fault technically known as *indexing* or, more colloquially, *jaggies*. One solution to this problem which has been adopted by most manufacturers is to store master fonts as a series of outlines or vectors built up from a combination of straight lines and arcs; these outlines are sized up or down electronically and then filled in by the imagesetter with the maximum number of vertical scan lines available. Thus every character in every size is created with the best quality available from the resolution of the typesetter, rather than being dependent on the pre-determined image points of a bit-mapped face. This approach combines the ability to manipulate type with the advantages of economic font storage and, depending on the output resolution of the imagesetter, produces a high quality of typographic output.

Most digital typesetter manufacturers now use outline fonts, including Linotype, Monotype and Varityper. The PostScript page description language also uses outline fonts. In its Type 1 variant it has a limited ability, called hinting, to modify the outlines for small point sizes or low resolution printers and monitors. The later Multiple Masters variant allows several outline masters to be incorporated in a single font, and users can choose and interpolate between them. TrueType, a type format introduced in 1991 for Apple Macintosh and PC computers running MS-Windows, can also use multiple outlines.

The apparent quality of the final printed type does not, however, depend solely on the resolution of the output machine as measured in lines per inch (lpi). Most typesetters can output at resolutions well above 1,000 lpi but this in itself is significant only when balanced by consideration of the size of type being set, the paper the job will be printed on, and the quality of the final presswork. Type output at 600 lpi may appear quite satisfactory if set in 9pt and printed by rotary letterpress on rough newsprint. There may well be readability problems, but indexing on the curves of the type is hardly likely to be the major concern! If, however, the same resolution is used to set type in 72pt for printing by sheet-fed litho on glossy coated paper, the jagged edges of the digitised type may be clearly visible. The number of lines resolution per character of the type size set is more relevant for the sharpness and legibility of the image than the number of lines resolution per inch.

SETTING DISPLAY SIZES

Any of the typesetters of the second, third or fourth generation can output type in sizes large enough for display use. With some early systems, large sizes of type may suffer from indexing, and in addition the letter-fitting from a machine set up for continuous text composition may be unacceptably loose for display work. Some outline faces, particularly the earlier PostScript fonts, were created to look best at smaller point sizes, and ink traps and similar optical devices are enlarged unacceptably at display sizes. Some systems overcome these problems by offering letter-fitting which is automatically tightened as sizes increase, and by using special display fonts: these display fonts contain extra digital information about the character shapes to guarantee smooth contours in large sizes. Typesetters offering these facilities may often be targetting their services at agency and advertising work, and single lines of display type for use in books or magazines are often more economically produced by suppliers specialising in headline setting; the film or paper output is then stripped into the text at the make-up stage. This process increases both the setting and make-up costs of the job, and therefore the decision on when to resort to specialist display setting should also take into account the frequency with which it will be required; it may be preferable to specify frequently recurring headings in typefaces held on-line by the text setting system.

Specialised headline machines are available for display setting. The simpler machines resemble small second-generation phototypesetters, and are operated by keyboard. The image masters are negative, usually held on disk, drum or film strip. These machines are very economical for the production of large amounts of display work.

Photolettering machines are much slower in operator and are reserved for top-quality work; they are operated on the principle of the photographic enlarger. Negative image masters on film strips are exposed consecutively, with letter-fitting and alignment manually controlled, thus giving the operator total freedom over the positioning of the characters. Special effects, distortions and screens or patterns can also be the subject of experimentation before the type is exposed. It follows that this type of composition is extremely expensive: rates are quoted in pounds per word, rather than per thousand keystrokes. Nevertheless, it is in high demand by advertising agencies, and it is not unusual for the bromide paper output from these machines to be subjected to further manual repositioning by a studio paste-up artist to give a perfect final result; the adjustment of spacing after capital letters, or between punctuation marks, is a typical speciality.

An advantage of the headliner machine is the huge repertoire of typefaces available. New designs, or endless variations on existing faces, are continually released as typefaces come into vogue in the advertising world. Storage of the film masters presents few problems.

Nevertheless, headliners look like ultimately being replaced by increasingly sophisticated page make-up and design software for personal computers. Programs such as QuarkXPress, Adobe Illustrator and Letraset LetraStudio can now show realistic previews of text in high magnification on the computer screen, and allow adjustment of letterspacing and baselines by fine increments. More and more PostScript and TrueType typefaces are being released that can be used with such software, although display faces are still comparatively rare.

In addition to phototypeset display work, any image which can be reproduced by offset lithography can serve as decorative or display material to be made up for camera with phototypesetting; this can include repro pulls from the few metal faces not available on phototypesetting systems, dry transfer lettering, or hand-lettering. Low cost scanning and digitising software also allows such images to be incorporated within the type matter at the electronic page make-up stage, or even turned into logotypes which can be accessed from the keyboard.

5 Control and storage media

One of the great advantages of contemporary typesetting is the ability, through the power of computers, to store, access and modify data at very high speed. Encoded typeface information, control programs and massive amounts of raw text and graphics can be addressed and manipulated with a convenience unimaginable before the advent of current computing systems and their associated volume storage facilities.

An essential distinction in computing systems is that between *hardware* and *software*. Hardware refers to the physical elements of a computer, including the computing unit itself, the disk drives, keyboard and monitor. Software describes the programs and the data which they process. Software held on small elements of hardware such as microchips is often known as *firmware*.

All computers handle data by converting it into measurable numeric form and then manipulating these values. They can do this by working with a quantity that is an analogue of the information, or by converting the quantity into a string of digital impulses. Digital information is easier to manipulate and has much lower error rates than analogue information, and is now the predominant method. Digital signals carry information through the use of the binary code, which reduces all information to a system of paired opposites, conventionally represented in written form as 0 and 1. The binary system counts only to 1 before the value is carried over to the next place: thus the numeric value 2 is represented in binary from as 10, 4 as 100, 6 as 110, 7 as 111, and so on. Binary digits are known as *bits*, and a group of bits which together carry information as a *byte*; a byte is usually composed of eight bits, although there may be 16 or 32 bits according to the computer language being used. A byte is the smallest addressable unit of computer storage or memory. Computer power and capacity is measured in kilobytes (Kb or K = 1000 bytes) or megabytes (MB = 1,000,000 bytes).

In typesetting applications, binary values can be defined in several ways: opposed polarity – north or south – of a magnetic field, presence or absence of light or current, a hole punched or not punched in a paper tape. All information describing text or graphics can be reduced to combinations of these two opposites. ASCII (American Standard Code for Information Interchange) is the binary language most often used in typesetting; it consists of seven information bits plus one bit used for error checking, and thus has 128 possible code combinations, although in certain applications the addition of an eighth bit creates 256 combinations. All the letters of the alphabet, figures, spaces and punctuation are represented by unique strings: capital K, for example, is allocated the value 75 and is defined digitally as 1001011. A character is therefore equal to one byte.

In a typesetting installation driven by punched paper tape, this information would have been recorded as a string of holes punched in specific channels across the width of the tape, to be decoded by a paper-tape reader on the typesetting machine. In a magnetic medium, such as tape or disk, the information is recorded in minute areas of the surface coating, each one of which can be magnetised in either a north or south direction. A read/write head applies a magnetic field as directed by the binary information from the computer processor; the same head is used in a read mode to detect the direction of magnetism and recover the information for storing in the computer's memory.

The most powerful and quickly accessible memory is housed inside the computer itself on silicon chips. This provides immediate access to data but, as it is relatively expensive to produce, it is usually limited in size. A chip consists of a number of transistor elements made up of different semi-conducting materials; when a current is fed to one of the transistor's three terminals, it controls the flow of current between the other two terminals, causing a switching action. A digital computer contains many thousands of such switches, which in combination with other components direct the flow of current so that certain actions are performed only as controlled by the correct combinations of current or signals.

There are many different types of microchip. ROM (Read Only Memory) chips are used to hold system programs; these chips are programmed during manufacture and cannot be erased or modified. Although the chips are cheap when produced in large quantities, specialised programs may not justify sufficient volume to guarantee this. A PROM (Programmable Read Only Memory) chip can be used for writing and storing programs permanently: once programmed, this chip cannot be erased. EPROM (Erasable Programmable Memory) chips can be programmed and then overwritten with the aid of special equipment to allow subsequent amendment or re-use.

Random Access Memory (RAM) chips are used for the temporary storage of information required by the computer whilst processing. Any stored values are lost when the computer's power is switched off. One solution is to maintain the power supply to the RAM chips by a battery or similar non-mains source. More commonly, the data which is needed for longer term storage is transferred to a more permanent medium such as a magnetic disk or tape.

The microprocessor chip or Central Processing Unit (CPU) holds the circuits which control and perform the operations of the computer itself.

Because of the limitations on the size of internal memory, computers use secondary or backing storage to hold data which is not permanently required. There are two main categories of storage medium: random access and sequential access. Cost and speed of performance vary with the different types of device, which therefore have specific applications in the typesetting industry.

RANDOM ACCESS DEVICES

With random access devices data can be retrieved by direct access to any specified address on the storage medium. Such devices can be either totally electronic, such as a silicon RAM chip, in which case access to information is virtually instantaneous, or electro-mechanical, such as a disk drive; although slower, retrieval of information is still measured in fractions of a second. The capacity of these devices – the density of packing of the magnetised areas – is governed by the quality of the magnetic coating and the closeness of the recording head to the surface of the disk. The most common media used are floppy disks or rigid disk drives.

Floppy disks

The floppy disk has a base of thin mylar coated with a fine film of ferric oxide capable of carrying a magnetic field. This surface is easily damaged and so the disk is permanently housed in a protective paper

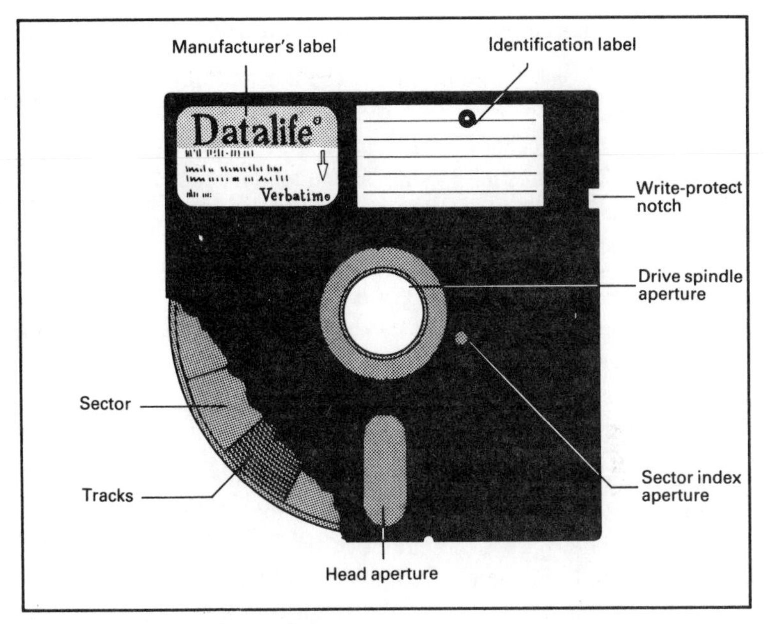

The structure of a floppy disk

envelope or plastic case, with slots cut into it for the drive spindle, read/write head and index hole. The envelope or case also has a notch which can be covered by a tab to 'write protect' the disk, allowing it to be read from, but not written to.

In use, the disk spins at high speed in an anti-clockwise direction, and the read/write head moves in and out from the centre to the rim of the disk under computer control, contacting the disk surface through the cutout.

Beyond this basic description, things become more complicated. There are few industry standards relating to the structure, formatting, or even the size of floppy disks. Disks from one manufacturer's system cannot normally be read directly by another system; the data must be unloaded and passed through a conversion process for it to be acceptable. This incompatability is a major problem with data supplied on disk from 'outside' a typesetting system and has slowed down the acceptance of direct keying by authors as a method of data capture. The most successful single-keying operations to date have involved the planned use of directly compatible equipment within a coherent environment.

The ways in which floppy disks can vary are as follows:

Size 5¼" or 8" disks were originally the most common sizes used in typesetting, but these have been overtaken by 3½" sizes, which are used as standard in recent IBM PC and PS/2 computers, and all Apple Macintoshes. The unusual 3" size is frequently encountered in typesetting from disk, as this is used by the popular low-cost Amstrad PCW word processors.

Density The number of bytes per inch (bpi) that can be stored on a disk determines its density; disks can be single, double or quad density. Error rates increase with high density.

Sectoring The surface of a disk is divided into tracks, concentric circles of different radii, each of which contains a number of sectors; a 5¼" disk has between 8 and 15 sectors. When the read/write head is positioned over the selected track, it has to locate the required sector. As the index hole passes the cutout in the disk, a circuit between a beam of light and a photocell is completed, signalling the start of a sector. Hard-sectored disks have a hole punched in them for each sector; soft-sectored disks have a single hole for synchronisation purposes, with the start of each sector being determined by software. Hard- and soft-sectored disks cannot be interchanged.

Single- or double-sided Double-sided disks require a dual-head disk drive so that data can be accessed without turning the disk over.

The exact specification of floppy disks should always be detailed when transfer of information on disk is being considered. The usual formula for this is 'diameter/sector/side/density'; thus '5¼"/soft-sectored/single-sided/double density'.

The capacity of floppy disks can vary widely according to the above factors, and also tends to increase as the technology of disks and disk drives improves. Some 8" disks can hold up to 1Mb or 1 million characters, while later, smaller 5¼" disks hold 1.2 Mb, and the even more compact 3½" size can commonly hold up to 1.4 Mb, and some have been demonstrated at 2 Mb.

Floppy disks are extremely delicate and should always be handled with great care; this cannot be over-emphasised, since damage to a disk can result in corruption of data which may not always be immediately evident. Disks must never be removed from their protective envelopes, and should not be bent, stapled, paper-clipped, left in the sun, nor, despite their tempting size, used as mats for coffee cups! The 3" and $3^1/2$" disks have rigid plastic cases and sliding flaps to protect the magnetic surface, so are less vulnerable than older designs, but should still be treated with respect.

Extremes of temperature and magnetic fields are also dangerous; keep disks away from TV sets, hi-fi cabinets, telephones and other electrical appliances. Disks that are not being used should be stored upright in rigid protective boxes. Label disks carefully, but with a felt-tip marker, not a ballpoint pen. Take care never to touch the exposed surface of a disk. As a general rule, the higher the price of a disk, the more reliable it will prove, but steps should always be taken to guard vital data against sudden disk failure. Make back-up copies regularly, keeping them in a separate place from the masters (preferably a separate building, to guard against fire, water and theft), and clearly marking any accompanying hard-copy print-out.

Even with good care, floppy disks have a limited life before the surface starts to deteriorate, and any data which needs to be permanently stored should be copied across to new disks or to tape. Floppy disks are very cheap and convenient, and are now established as a means of recording small to medium amounts of data. In typesetting, typical uses are the storing of digitised font information and the transfer of raw text data from keyboards to the front-end of the typesetting system.

Rigid disk packs

To improve capacity, the magnetised, information-carrying areas of the disks must be reduced in size and packed more closely on the surface. This can be achieved only by developing a smoother surface coating and by reducing the distance between the read/write head and the disk surface. Rigid disks use a firm aluminium base with a magnetic coating. As the disk revolves it creates a cushion of air on which the head flies, only millionths of an inch above the surface. The disks are normally housed in packs on a single spindle within a plastic housing, with a comb arrangement of recording heads for each surface of each disk. A typical disk pack will have a capacity of 300Mb, making it suitable for storing large amounts of information with immediate and random access.

The slightest defect in manufacture, or fingerprints or hairs on the surface, or the presence in the air of dust or smoke particles, can all cause disks to crash. They can only therefore be used in carefully

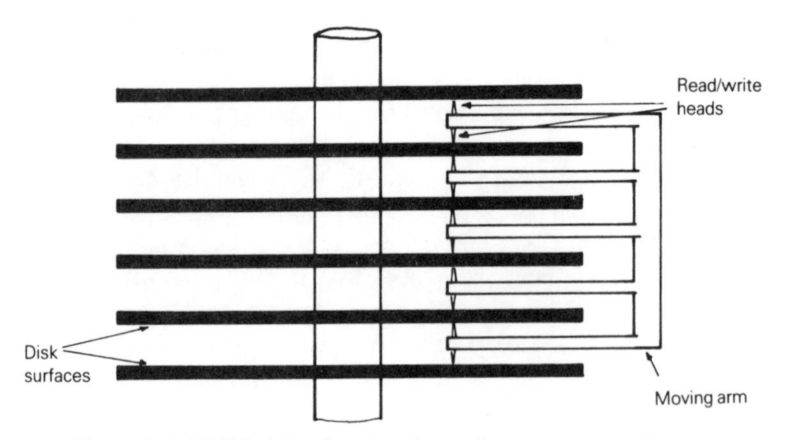

Above *A rigid disk drive showing the comb arrangement of read/write heads.*

Below *A representation of particle size in comparison with the distance of the read-write head from the disk surface.*

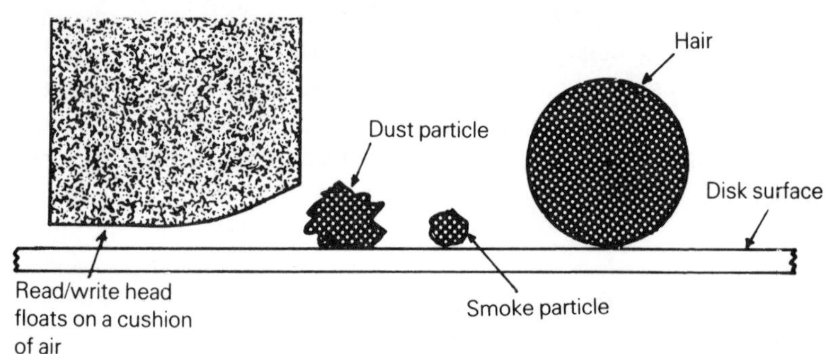

controlled environments known as 'clean rooms', which require air-conditioning, filtering and special discipline in the handling and storing of disks. Although still in use, rigid disk packs are rapidly being phased out in favour of the Winchester disk, which does not require such a controlled environment.

The Winchester disk drive overcomes this problem by being contained in its own clean room: the disk and drive are housed within a sealed container, free of any minute debris which could cause a crash. Winchester disks are not affected by environmental conditions and have been widely adopted in the industry. Although more expensive than floppy disks, they have greater capacity, quicker access times and are much less subject to wear or accidental damage. The term *Winchester* strictly speaking refers to a particular design used by IBM; an alternative term in common use is the *hard disk*.

Optical disks

Optical disks are now a reality after many years of anticipation, and look certain to become widely available at ever-falling prices. These devices are designed to carry vast amounts of digital data on a small disk with all the simplicity of current magnetic media, and in a normal non-controlled environment. The results of this activity are likely to have an impact on the production, publishing and distribution of information in several interrelated ways.

Some of the new techniques will affect the storage and processing of data, while others will provide new and alternative methods of publishing the information. There are currently three main categories of development: videodisk, Compact Disk Read Only Memory (CD-ROM), and optical digital data disks. The first two of these are read-only devices for mass replication of standard information: data is recorded in a stamping or moulding process by the manufacturer and cannot be erased. CD-ROM is the computer form of the audio compact disk used in music systems. A single disk has a capacity of roughly 650 Mb, and is suitable for the publishing of large quantities of data that does not change very often – reference works such as encyclopedias, directories and specialised dictionaries are ideal for CD-ROM media.

Computer manufacturers are just starting to distribute software on CD-ROM (Sun Microsystems being a pioneer in the field), and several type manufacturers are distributing digital font libraries the same way. An interesting development here is 'pay-as-you-go', first introduced by Agfa, which offers a disk with a complete font library, but encrypted so that unique codes are needed to gain access to any of the fonts. Clients purchase a disk for a nominal sum, and then use a telephone hotline to buy access codes to the fonts they want. As such methods of software distribution are convenient for the manufacturers, they often encourage their use by offering the necessary CD-ROM disk readers at lower than normal prices.

Although more standardised than floppy disks, CD-ROM disks are still subject to format variations, so some disks may not work with particular computers. There are several sub-variants of CD-ROM, such as CD-XA and CD-I, intended for home entertainment and multimedia applications.

Optical digital data disks allow users to store their own information, rather than buying it in pre-published form. The WORM (Write Once

Read Many Times) is a disk on which data can be recorded by the user, but which cannot subsequently be erased; long-term archival storage is one application. WORM drives are less standardised than CD-ROM, and several physical sizes are available, including recordable CD-ROMs.

Erasable optical disks are intended for the same applications as a standard magnetic disk: data can be recorded, updated or deleted at will, and disks can be re-used. These disks are becoming more widely available for standard computers as well as dedicated graphic arts systems. With typical capacities of about 600 Mb, they are particularly useful for storing large file volumes such as digital colour photographs.

In optical disk technology a focused laser is used to record data by altering the physical properties of minute elements on the surface of the disk; different methods involve the application of heat, magnetism or a combination of both. A lower-powered laser is used to read the disk by detecting the changes thus caused by the reflection of polarised light. The disk is protected at all times against dirt and accidental damage by a laminated cover; as there is no contact between disk and recording head, wear and disk crashes are virtually impossible, and there is no need for a special 'clean' environment.

The advantage of the optical disk over conventional magnetic media is storage capacity. Sizes vary, but a typical 12-inch disk might hold as much as 1.5 gigabytes (1500 megabytes) of information; in addition, several disks can be housed in juke-box arrangement to give even greater capacity. Storage of this level is required as soon as illustrations are included in the digital information to be recorded. A page of text in A4 format, for example, may contain, including control codes, 6000 bytes of data. A halftone photograph which covers the same area of 100 square inches, and which is to be output at high resolution, would require 9 million bytes of information! Even with the use of data compression techniques to try to reduce this figure, the storage demands of graphics are still huge. For this reason, most typesetting projects which involve large numbers of illustrations are currently handled conventionally, with pages of text output with windows into which illustration films are stripped manually. The advent of the erasable optical disk is expected to change this situation radically.

The chief drawback to optical disk storage is access times, which are not yet as fast as with magnetic media. Until this is solved optical disks will be limited to archival tasks, rather than the 'live' storage and virtual memory functions of magnetic hard disks.

SEQUENTIAL ACCESS DEVICES

Sequential access devices store information serially and must search for it strictly in order. Retrieval times are therefore much slower than those of random access devices and depend on the position of the required data relative to the recording head. Paper and magnetic tape are examples of this kind of storage device.

Paper tape

Early phototypesetting systems used punched paper tape to record keystrokes and drive the typesetting machine in slave mode. The numeric values which represent characters and typographic instructions are recorded as combinations of holes punched in a number of channels across the tape by a perforating head attached to the keyboard. Teletypesetting code (TTS) is a six-level code originally designed to drive hot-metal linecasters; it provides 63 (2 to the power of 6 minus one) binary codes. Other paper tape systems use ISO seven-level or ASCII codes.

Perforated paper tape was used by typesetting houses as a way of capturing text on off-line keyboards, is now obselete, and has been replaced by floppy disks and magnetic tape. Although inexpensive, paper tapes are slow and cumbersome when compared with magnetic media. The paper tape must be re-reeled for data to be retrieved, and it cannot be overwritten; corrections must be keyed onto a separate paper tape and merged to produce a third, and correct, tape.

Magnetic tape

Magnetic reel-to-reel tape has long been used in mainframe computers for the storage of massive amounts of data. It is often supplied as input from database installations, but can also be used to drive typesetters directly. Because it is very economical in storage, magnetic tape is also used for archiving finished jobs which need to be retained against future updates; when required, this tape is downloaded back onto the typesetting system. Jobs containing very large amounts of data, such as digitised halftone illustrations, are sometimes held on magnetic tape. As the tape has to be reeled backwards and forwards to access data, retrieval times are relatively slow, and any data stored on magnetic tape for typesetting must be ordered into correct sequence prior to the start of output. This can be a time consuming and expensive task.

Magnetic tape is sometimes used in cartridge or cassette form in small portable keyboards based on microcomputers; the same restrictions on access apply as with reel-to-reel tape, and floppy disks have largely replaced this application.

6 Text input

Text entry into a typesetting system can be performed in a variety of ways and the input method chosen by the publisher will be governed by the following factors:

Complexity Does the job to be typeset consist of straightforward keyboarding, with relatively few changes of typeface or size and simple layout, or does it involve complex typographic formatting, mathematics or tabular work?

Size How many keystrokes are involved?

Frequency Will the job be repeated at regular intervals, or is it a 'one-off' piece of setting?

Presentation Will the job be supplied as hard copy, typed or written on paper, or does it already exist in some other form, such as on disk or tape? If the latter is the case, is it held as raw text, which needs to be formatted and organised into pages, or is it already in page form?

End use Is it intended to update the job at a later stage for a revised edition? Is a reissue in a different format or typographic style planned? Or is the final product to be a set of bromide paper or film galleys or pages?

All these considerations will affect not only the initial choice of typesetter used for any particular project but also, in a detailed way, the arrangements made between publisher and typesetter for supply of copy, and the method of input chosen for the data capture. One useful distinction which is immediately clear is that between traditional methods of data capture, where the typesetter is responsible for keying the text from hard copy, and the increasingly common acceptance by typesetters of copy or complete pages created by authors and publishers and held on some form of magnetic storage medium. There are considerable advantages in economy, accuracy and speed of schedule in the direct input approach, but there are also technical and publishing problems to be overcome if these benefits are to be fully realised. This topic is examined in more detail later in this chapter in the section on interfacing word processors with phototypesetters.

The different approaches to data capture can be summarised as follows:

1 Keyboarding by typesetters from hard copy typescript.
2 Scanning of hard copy by an optical character recognition device.
3 Interfacing word processors and the supply of data on magnetic media by author or publisher.
4 Output of complete pages from an author or publisher's electronic publishing system.

KEYBOARDING

Despite the huge attention focused by the media on the arrival of single keying and the imminent demise of the typesetter's compositor, the keying of text from typewritten copy is, at present, still the most common method of data capture. Hard copy offers maximum flexibility in a 'non-coherent' environment, where material is supplied at irregular intervals by a random number of different and constantly changing authors who, even if they own microcomputers, inevitably use different makes of machine or software, with a greater or lesser degree of discipline, and who all lie to a large extent beyond their publisher's and typesetter's control. Add to this vision of potential chaos the extremely low prices which can at present be negotiated with supplies for straightforward typesetting, take into account the problems of how to enter subsequent copy-editing corrections and design mark-up onto the 'magnetic typescript', and it is then easy to understand why the news that 'the author's done this one on computer!' is greeted by the publisher's production staff with less than rapturous enthusiasm!

This is, of course, the blackest scenario. There are plenty of relevant publishing and typesetting situations which can be planned in advance to realise the full benefits of single keystroking, and these have grown as the technology has become more standardised and its application more generally understood. The considerations which identify a project as suitable for this approach are outlined later in this chapter. It is true, however, that for many general typesetting applications, the keyboarding of copy by the typesetter's compositor remains the most economic and practical method of getting data into the typesetting system.

Input terminals

The design of the text input terminals can vary greatly, but generally contain a standard set of functional components. These are a keypad layout containing both alphanumeric and function keys, a display screen to show the operator the copy just entered and a storage facility to hold the captured keystrokes until they are ready to be passed to another part of the typesetting system. Keyboards are distinguished as *counting* or *non-counting*, according to whether they are capable of performing hyphenation and justification routines on the text as it is entered. Current practice is to use counting keyboards throughout.

Early input terminals were simply termed 'keyboards', and were often purpose-built by the typesetter manufacturers. Nearly all current models use standard microcomputers such as the Apple Macintosh or the numerous IBM PC compatibles, with specialised software and expansion boards fitted as required. Although no longer made, Linotype's APL is still in widespread use: this was based on the Apple IIe computer.

The two main advantages of using such 'standard platforms' are the low cost of the hardware that results from volume manufacturing of machines; and the flexibility of a software-based product; multi-function microcomputers can support not only typesetting programs, but also any other application software running under the same operating system, such as word processing, database or general business and accounting packages. These programs can also be easily updated as new software is released.

Keyboard layout

The layout of most keypads is usually based on the conventional QWERTY design found on typewriters. This is in fact an anachronism, as the QWERTY layout was specifically designed to limit keying speeds in order to prevent the mechanical basket of typewriter keybars from becoming entangled, but the layout is now firmly entrenched despite claims to faster keying speeds and greater ease of operation by the manufacturers of non-QWERTY layouts.

A typesetting keyboard must be able to produce not only a complete range of alphanumeric characters, but also the commands necessary to determine the relative size and position of those characters, and to

The layout of a typesetting keyboard with QWERTY keys in the centre surrounded by separate blocks of dedicated function keys and programmable keys arranged in logical groups.

transfer the data, once keyed, to other parts of the typesetting system. Early keyboard designs tended to use dedicated keys, with one character or function per key, to perform these multiple requirements; the Monotype hot-metal keyboard, for example, used a bank of 334 separate keys to access – in one size and face only – the seven alphabet range of characters, figures, punctuation marks and associated control commands. Contemporary layouts have moved towards the replacement of the dedicated keypad with a greatly reduced number of keys and a series of control keys which, when depressed simultaneously with an alphanumeric key, perform a special function. This results in a keyboard of much simpler design, with all keys within easy touch-typing reach of the operator, but means that the keyboarder must remember a large number of different keystroke combinations. Some of the professional typesetting terminals based on standard microcomputers now offer an extended keyboard with more dedicated keys. Any keyboard design must strike a compromise between the advantages of a simple layout and the ease of dedicated keys. Whatever the design, control keys are normally grouped in blocks around the sides of the QWERTY keys, with the control functions most commonly required placed in the most convenient areas for touch-typing.

The functions of a keyboard designed for text input into a typesetting system can be summarised in the following categories:

Word-processing functions

All alphanumeric characters, including punctuation marks and figures, are keyed from the standard layout. Modern keyboards have profited from the rapid development of powerful microprocessors, and now full word-Pprocessing functions can usually be accessed from most keyboards. Function keys are used to select, delete, move around, replace or insert individual characters, words, lines or blocks of copy. Modern microcomputer practice favours the use of a hand-held mouse for many control and selection tasks: this is easy to learn, but experienced users complain that removing the hand from the keyboard slows them down. Consequently, software manufacturers are increasingly building in keystroke equivalents to the use of the mouse.

Character strings – words or parts of words – can be defined by the operator and then automatically sought out and replaced in the text by alternative versions; this is known as a global search and replace routine.

Typographic functions

The function keys on the keyboard can also be used to record typographic information relating to the typeface, size, interlinear spacing, measure and justification mode (ranged left, ranged right or centred) of the job in hand. Alternatively, the information can be entered as a series of character strings distinguished from the main text by their position between unique pairs of symbols, such as {*command*}. This typographic formatting can however equally well be applied at a later stage, when the job is passed to the front end system, and it is often more convenient to leave this task until the last possible stage. Typographic formats are often distinguished from text on the display screen by the use of reverse video or half-intensity characters; the commands are stripped out automatically when the job is output by the typesetter.

F34 H18 L18 M24 6 QC F32 H36 L36 A18 Text Input
QC F1 H10 L12 A30 Text entry into a typesetting system can be performed in a variety of ways and the input method chosen by the publisher will be governed by the following factors: QL F3 A6 Complexity F1 □Does the job to be typeset consist of straightforward keyboarding, with relatively few changes of typeface

The first edition of this book was originally keyed on a Linotype APL 230 terminal. This is how the opening to this chapter would have appeared on the monitor. The codes are as follows: F - Font number (F34 denotes Avant Garde Bold, F32 Avant Garde Medium, F3 Times Bold and F1 Times Roman); H - height or point size; L - leading or line feed (in points); M - measure (in picas); QC - centre (applies to copy immediately preceding the code); A - advance (extra interlinear space); QL - quad left; [] - em space.

Some of the formats required to effect complex changes in typography can be very involved; if particular formats are required repeatedly within a job, they can be defined and stored under a much smaller and easier combination of keystrokes. The operator has then only to key this simple combination to access the entire sequence of typographic instructions. This process is known as creating a user format, or user-definable format (UDF). In straightforward bookwork the formats are few and simple; there might be one format for the main text and a second for the extract matter. In more complex work, formats are used in a much more sophisticated way.

FMT7 | F1 H10 L12 M24

A string of typographic commands stored under a user format. Keying the format call FMT7 would access Times roman 10/12pt set to a line length of 24 pica ems.

A UDF directory discloses what chain of typesetting instructions lies hidden behind each individual format; these can be easily accessed and updated as necessary.

Macros are another kind of shorthand notation used at the keyboard. Macros are activated by a single keystroke, and may control command strings which access pi characters, superscripts or fractions.

User formats and macros reduce typesetting instructions to a minimum, and can lead to considerable savings in time and reductions in error rates.

System functions

These functions relate to the input terminal's position within the overall typesetting system; depending on the system configuration they may include the writing of the captured keystrokes to storage – either internal memory, disk or tape, the passing of the file to another terminal within the system for inspection, editing or formatting, or the transfer of the completed job to a proofing device or an output typesetter.

One important fact that should be clear is that the number of keystrokes required to produce a typeset job is not the same as the number of characters finally typeset. The proportion of control keystrokes to typeset ens will obviously vary with the nature of the job, but it is not unusual for complex directory-style work to carry an overhead of 30% extra keystrokes or more. This can have considerable implications for the estimating of typesetting projects: when a job is quoted in terms of a 'price per thousand keystrokes', it should always be made clear exactly what is meant, and what overhead of control keystroke is anticipated: the difference can be costly!

All modern text input units offer the facility for writing completed jobs to store, and even the smallest and most ephemeral pieces of setting are now normally recorded onto a storage medium for filing after output. Revisions to the original text can then easily be made by calling up the relevant file.

Any of the storage media described in detail in Chapter Five can be used to hold the keystrokes once they have been captured, but by far the most usual form of storage in modern units is provided by floppy disks. The advantages of the floppy disk lie in the speed of access to any predefined data, the flexibility of correction and the ease of transfer or copying of data.

Once the text has been keyed, it is written to disk. It can then be transferred to any other terminal within the system for editing or formatting.

Displays

'Blind' keyboards, where the operator has no opportunity to inspect copy as it was keyed, are no longer a part of current typesetting systems, and even limited 'marching' displays, which show only the last few characters keyed, are now mainly found only in specialist keyboards; these include ultra-portable units where considerations of

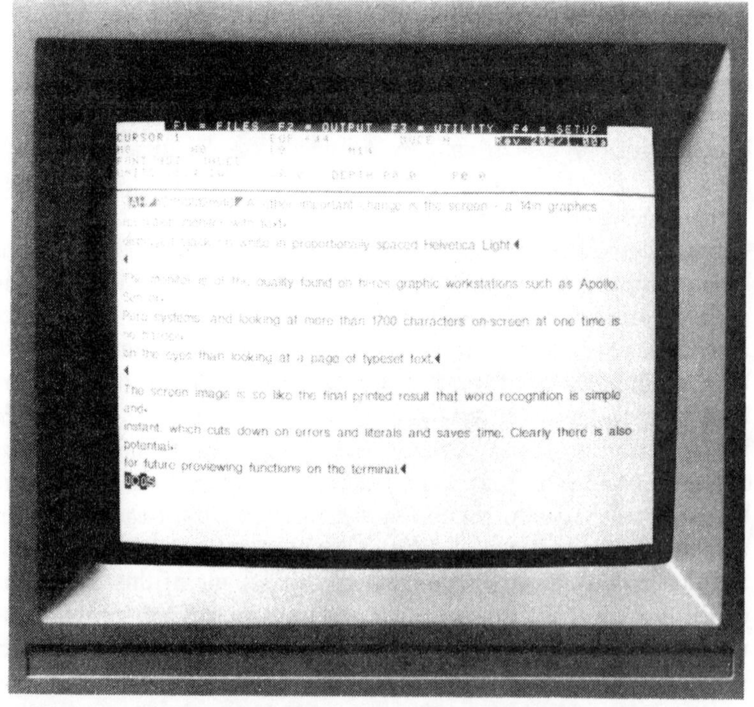

The screen of the APL230 terminal showing status information in the top window and a typographic format within brackets at the start of the text itself.

size and space make anything more sophisticated impossible. More conventional terminals use a VDU (visual display unit), which is most commonly a CRT monitor screen. This can display a variable number of lines of text, generally dependent on the size of the screen. Copy on professional typesetting terminals is often displayed in monospaced characters of a single typestyle, although the current trend is towards a more realistic representation of actual typefaces on the screen; the major application of this type of display is currently in electronic page make-up, and these devices are discussed in detail in Chapter Seven.

Depending on the individual design, some monitors may represent special sorts – accents from exotic foreign languages, or less common mathematical symbols, for example – by a code rather than by the actual character which will be typeset in the final output, due to the limited character set which can be displayed on the screen.

In addition to the text being set, the screen usually displays, as a guide to the keyboard operator, information relating to the status of the job, including the name and number of the file being created, the number of the characters keyed so far and the space remaining in the file.

Counting/non-counting keyboards

Simpler designs of input terminals handle text in the form of continuous word strings; although the typographic formatting can be entered along with the text, it is not possible for the system to calculate and nor, therefore, for the screen to display, the line endings which will be created in the text. Copy keyed in this mode is known as unjustified or UJ copy, continuous copy, or – but never within earshot of the keyboard operator! – idiot copy. The hyphenation and justification (h&j) of the text is performed either by the typesetting system's computer, a page make-up system or, usually to a less satisfactory standard, by the control computer of the output device itself; this latter option is less preferable since line-ending decisions made by the phototypesetter's logic are first seen only on the final output. Terminals of this design are called *non-counting*, and were generally cheaper to buy and faster to use than *counting* keyboards; they were ideal for economic capture of straightforward bulk text. Typesetter manufacturers no longer make non-counting terminals as their raw text input function can be handled equally well by off-the-shelf word processing software and standard microcomputers.

Counting keyboards are more sophisticated. Information about the set width values of all characters in all typefaces and sizes held on the system is either downloaded onto the keyboard unit's own memory store, or accessed on-line from the system's minicomputer. In either case, the information allows the hyphenation and justification of the text to be performed by logic within the keyboard unit as the copy is keyed. The line endings and hyphenation points are displayed on the operator's VDU screen, and the operator can override any line ending or word break he considers unacceptable. Text entry by this method is obviously potentially slower and therefore more expensive than with non-counting keyboards and is most suitably reserved for specialist uses.

Current applications include complex directory work, where it is an advantage for the operator to be able to review the progress of the job, and typographically demanding work where the hyphenation and justification logic of the computer may need to be frequently overruled.

OPTICAL CHARACTER RECOGNITION

Optical character recognition (OCR) machines have been used in data processing and banking for over 20 years, but until relatively recently they have made little impact on the typesetting industry. An OCR device operates by scanning a beam of light across a page of copy which has been typed in a special face; the optical signals reflected from each character in the copy are analysed and compared with a corresponding master image contained in the unit's memory. As each character is 'recognised' it is converted into digital codes acceptable to the typesetting system.

Early machines were both expensive and limited in the small number of faces they could read; with these early devices, copy for scanning has to be typed in one of the number of specially designed machine-readable fonts: Courier 12, Perry OCR and OCR-B are examples of frequently used designs, which must strike a compromise between ease of recognition by the scanning device and acceptability to the human eye.

abcdefghijklmnopqrstuvwxyz
ABCDEFGHIJKLMNOPQRSTUVWXYZ

Linotype OCR-B, a typeface specifically designed for optical character recognition.

Typesetting commands are handled by special codes typed into the copy; if errors are made in the course of this typing, a series of special correction keys on the OCR keyboard can be used to delete and replace individual characters, words or lines. The digital codes output from the OCR machine can be used to drive a typesetting machine direct, but it is more usual for them to be written to disk or tape for subsequent retrieval and checking. Speeds can be as high as 300 characters per second with well-prepared copy, while error rates as low as 1 in 10,000 characters are claimed by some manufacturers. All aspects of performance are ultimately related to the cleanliness of the copy input for scanning; for general typesetting applications, the cost of the necessary meticulous copy preparation can outweigh the advantages of high-speed scanning.

A major development in OCR came with the introduction of the Kurzweil Data Entry Machine (KDEM), which was designed to overcome the limitations implicit in the need for specially prepared copy as input for traditional OCR machines. The KDEM could be programmed to recognise any typewriter font or typeset face. A sample from the printed input copy was presented to the machine for scanning, and the characters were analysed into combinations of loops, curves, straight lines and other shapes, with reference also to size and position. An operator verified each character as it was analysed, after which the information was stored in the unit's computer memory.

Modern optical character readers are often termed ICR (intelligent character recognition), and can recognise a wide range of fonts without pre-programming by analysing the characteristics of individual letterforms. These systems are increasingly supplied as software programs to be used in conjunction with a low-cost desktop scanner – some can even analyse characters directly from a telephone-line facsimile signal. Difficult or unknown characters are flagged for the operator to correct, and some ICRs can learn unknown letterforms for subsequent use.

Having been captured, a text file can then be reformatted for output in a different typographic style – for example, as a new edition of a book or paperback version – or can be treated as a database file for subsequent manipulation and updating. The obvious applications are for printed works which were originally set by hot metal, phototypeset using outdated technology or for which the original data capture records – tape or disk – no longer exist. Magazines and newspapers which use direct input will often use OCR/ICRs to capture contributed material such as freelance articles or readers' letters.

In practice, there are limitations to the abilities and relevance of optical character recognition machines for typesetting. Some of these are technical, and concern the unsuitability for scanning of some types of printed copy: newspapers, poor photocopies, facsimile printouts and some computer printouts may prove difficult for the machine to read, while unevenly or faintly printed pages, broken or battered letters and small sizes of type can all create problems for the scanner, especially in recognising the distinction between 'confusion pairs' of characters such as 1 and l, 0 and O, f and £, 7 and ?, or 5 and S. Any need for frequent operator intervention to check and correct errors may quickly erode the economic advantages of the system.

It should be clear from the above, that it is a fallacy to expect to be able to dispense with proofreading for text captured by OCR. Even with ideal copy, no OCR machine can be guaranteed to produce entirely error-free results, and thorough reading of proofs is essential.

Some of the latest ICRs can preserve page formatting instructions, but more often than not the text will need to be reformatted on an editing or page make-up terminal. Editing copy on screen is much more expensive, line for line, than straight keyboarding of new data, and for jobs with a complex structure, or a large number of corrections, the amount of work which is subsequently necessary may well affect the economic viability of OCR scanning.

Optical character recognition, although it has increased in reliability since the earliest experiments, is still far from becoming a common method of inputting text into typesetting systems. The economic viability of the process for any particular project is ultimately affected by the error rate and the degree of operator intervention required, and this becomes apparent only during the scanning of the live copy itself. Unless accuracy rates of well over 90 per cent are achieved, it is generally more economical to rekey the copy from scratch than to edit the scanned OCR/ICR version.

Voice recognition

After years of prediction, a handful of prototype page make-up systems have been demonstrated which can perform certain functions by voice recognition. The days of authors reading their copy out loud into their computers are still some years away. Experience so far has shown that even for devices working with a limited vocabulary, very advanced software is needed to enable the machine to distinguish between homophones, and to predict words from the context in which they occur. Those successful devices which are now available have a fairly restricted range, with small, user-defined vocabularies designed for specialist applications: control of industrial production processes, using isolated 'words' clearly separated by spaces, is one example. Any voice-input system used in a typesetting context would require a very extensive vocabulary for text input, although it is possible that a restricted range of recognisable commands could be used for the input of control codes into a typesetting system.

Vast amounts of money have been invested in research into more sophisticated voice-input systems, and developments are bound to be of interest to the typesetting industry. The limited text input systems on the horizon are currently being proposed largely for sufferers and potential sufferers of RSI (repetitive strain injury), the painful tendon and muscle damage which afflicts some keyboard users.

THE WORD-PROCESSOR INTERFACE

A major development in recent years in the area of data capture for typesetting has been the increasing pressure for the acceptance of text keyed by authors and supplied to publishers and typesetters on some form of magnetic media. The impetus for this has come both from the increasing access which authors in institutional and business environments have to word-processors, and, more recently, from the availability of low-cost multi-function personal computers. For a relatively modest financial outlay, authors now have within their grasp all the flexibility of powerful word-processing software for the preparation of written material and the supply of final clean text on floppy disk. The use of word processing (in the sense of both dedicated machines and the increasingly common use of word processing programs running on micros) will continue to accelerate and increasingly motivate publishers to acknowledge and meet the challenge posed by the 'electronic manuscript'.

Indeed, the widespread availability of cheap, easy to use page layout software has prompted many magazine and newspaper publishers to leapfrog the 'single keying' phase and advance directly to supplying completely formatted pages to a typesetter for output. The supply of raw text and statistical information for subsequent formatting is more relevant to book publishing, plus the preparation of directories and financial reports from database material.

It is technically not usually necessary to re-key copy that has been supplied in electronic form, whether on cassette tape, reel-to-reel tape or floppy disk. This basic statement of fact is immediately subject to a host of qualifications concerning technical aspects (which machine was used to input the text, which machine is intended for output, and how will the data be transferred between the two?), industrial relations considerations (is the typesetter in a position to accept the text in machine-readable form?) and questions relating to the publisher's role (how far is the author's computer literacy and keyboarding skill to be trusted, how will the typographic codes and copy-editing corrections be inserted, and to what extent are the publisher's staff competent to control subsequent processing of the job?). But the fact remains that there are now only rarely technical restrictions on the acceptance of copy in electronic form, thanks to the greater standardisation of hardware and software between business and typesetting applications. The degree to which the benefits of single keying are realised depends on the level of understanding and advance planning which the publishing company can generate between itself, its authors or journalists and the typesetter.

For the publisher the advantages of the electronic manuscript can be grouped under the main headings of improved schedules, improved accuracy of data, alternative publishing opportunities and, most of all, reduced typesetting costs. The degree to which these are relevant varies with the detailed circumstances of every project, and in some instances none of them may be applicable, in which case conventional re-keying is the correct solution. All other things being equal, however, text accepted on magnetic media should lead to improvements in proofing schedules, not only because re-keyboarding by the typesetter is eliminated, but also because the original keystrokes produced by the author do not suffer from introduced errors at subsequent stages. Similarly, the fact that a publisher is willing to accept text in an electronic form from an author automatically implies that the original keystrokes are considered sufficiently accurate to make the exercise worthwhile; there is little point in processing a text riddled with keyboarding literals which will need heavy and costly correction at a later stage.

Depending on the complexity of the structure of the project, the electronic record supplied by the author may be suitable for treatment as a database; once captured, the text can be formatted for output in varying typographic styles and can be manipulated, updated or used to provide 'spin-off' publications. It may be possible to combine elements from different jobs to provide completely new publishing opportunities.

These possibilities may all be of value to a publisher, but in most cases are probably considered to be secondary benefits; the major advantage associated with the single-keystroking process is the reduction of typesetting costs. These savings have been much vaunted by the promoters of single keying and in the early experimental days wildly optimistic figures were often quoted. It is a fallacy to expect that any disk can be fed into any typesetting system and produce immediate and perfect typeset output. There are costs involved in the processing of magnetic media which do not arise in conventional keyboarding, and while these can be expected to be lower in total than with a traditional approach, they must nevertheless be brought into the equation. There are also hidden costs, in terms of overheads, incurred in the extra planning and monitoring which is normally required with a job supplied on magnetic media; if the job is not well planned, these hidden costs can soon outweigh the more immediately visible savings.

It is difficult to quantify the savings which can be made through the adoption of single-keying procedures. A basic guideline is that the more planned and 'coherent' the environment, the greater the benefits will be. Maximum economics can be achieved when the greatest possible number of people responsible for originating copy can be trained in the use of compatible elements in a well-designed system. The practical illustration of this ideal is the newspaper: a large percentage of the copy is actually created by the paper's own journalists and need be keyed only once, using text input devices which are an integral part of the overall editorial, pagination and composition system. Text is immediately acceptable to any part of the newspaper system without the need for any conversion or translation. The cost equation is relatively simple: any savings can be crudely calculated as the difference between the costs currently involved in the re-keying of copy by typesetting staff, and the sum of the capital investment required for new equipment, written down over its anticipated life, plus the expense of staff training.

With magazines, the savings of single-keying were less tangible, as smaller staff levels and a higher reliance on contributed copy from outside made large centralised computing and database systems less

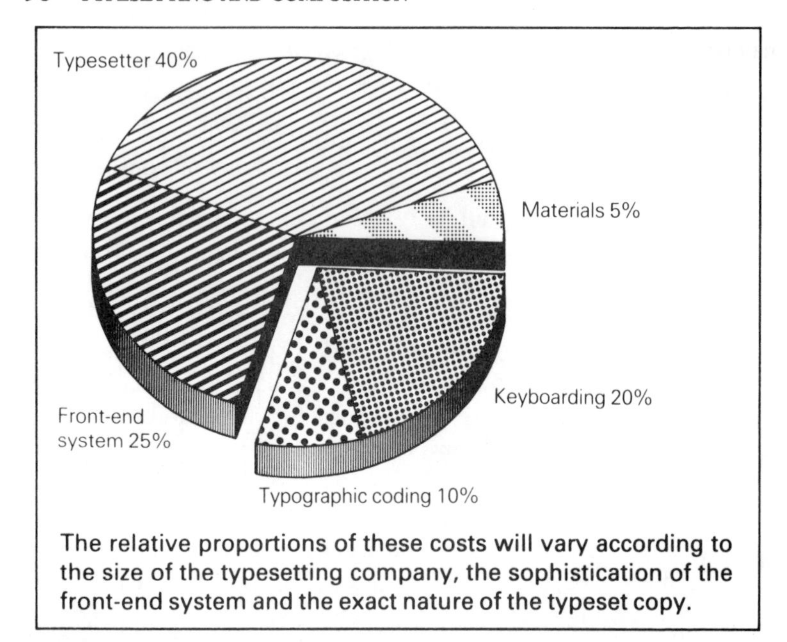

Typesetting costs: the use of text supplied on magnetic media may generate savings in keyboarding and typographic formatting costs.

relevant than relatively more expensive distributed processing networks. Most large magazine publishers resisted direct input until it became feasible to make up whole pages on site, reducing their outside typesetting costs in effect to the cost of the photographic output material plus a typesetter's handling charge.

If the concept of accepting text in pre-keyed form is broadened to cover copy supplied totally by outside contributors or authors, as in book publishing, the problems become even more complex. The technical, industrial-relations and publishing aspects of single keying, examined in more detail below, all affect the degree of savings which may be possible. Typically, the overall typesetting costs of a straightforward non-fiction book can be split into the fixed costs of the typesetter, materials, text keyboarding and typographic formatting. The last two operations are generally accepted to comprise 30% of the total costs and are the areas in which savings can be effected by using an author's word-processed text.

The most suitable projects for acceptance in electronic form, and on which the maximum savings can be made, are those in which the text may be defined in one of the following ways:

1 **High-volume, or repeated at regular intervals** It is rarely worth incurring the expense and overheads of trying to interface the author's word processor for small amounts of copy and for one-off jobs, unless these are very competently prepared.
2 **Simple** Tabular and mathematics work can be handled effectively on a micro, but it is more difficult to do this than to process straight text. This does not necessarily rule out such jobs from conversion; depending on the amount of tabular or maths setting relative to the total extent, it may be feasible to leave holes in the output as if for illustrations, set the complex matter elsewhere, and strip it into the text output at a later stage.
3 **Keyed in a reliable and consistent form** It is advisable to use test samples of the author's work for trials before going live on the actual text.
4 **Likely to require minimal or no revision** This is not the same thing as the quality of keyboarding, and refers to the editorial nature of the job itself; it is best to avoid accepting on disk jobs which are known in advance to require updates before being typeset in the final form. The disk, when supplied, should be clean and final.

If a job fits these criteria reasonably well, or equally importantly does not conflict strongly with any single one, then the next stage is to consider the practical problems of providing the data in a form acceptable to the typesetting system.

The industrial relations question

The two UK trade unions most closely involved in typesetting have been the National Graphical Association (NGA) and the National Union of Journalists (NUJ). The NGA has now merged with the other main print employees' union, Sogat 82, to form the Graphical, Print & Media Union (GPMU). These unions represent a large percentage of the keyboard operators and journalists working in the industry, although neither can claim full membership among eligible staff. The move towards single keying led inevitably to conflict between employers wishing to maximise savings in production costs and unions fearful for the employment prospects of their members, and also created tension between the NUJ and the old NGA as they manoeuvred for the power to represent and control the new input technology. The struggle was most intense in the newspaper industry, where the potential benefits of the coherent electronic publishing system were thrown into sharper relief by the urgent need to replace obsolescent technology and the desire to abolish restrictive working practices. All national and many major provincial newspaper groups have introduced some kind of electronic composition, with a transfer of part of the keyboarding process from NGA members to journalists. Magazine publishers are also following down the same path. After years of opposition, the NGA, with some reservations, effectively accepted this situation as a *fait accompli* during the latter half of the 1980s. With NGA objections muted, the NUJ (traditionally a 'softer' union) quickly reached accommodation on the terms and conditions of using 'new technology' with most publishers.

The NGA's successor, the GPMU, thus faces a decline in its power base within the typesetting industry, with a reduced number of members and a consequently reduced income from membership subscriptions. The union is not convinced by the argument that new 'information technology' will automatically produce new employment opportunities within the industry, nor that any jobs so created will in any case be relevant to their members. Experience so far indicates that their suspicions are well-founded, although a major growth of single keying and direct page make-up coincided with the particularly heavy industrial recession of the early 1990s, so it is hard to determine which was the true cause of many job losses.

Typesetting for book publishing has so far been less affected by industrial relations problems than other areas. In part this is due to the difficulties facing publishers trying to establish systems which will handle copy from a large number of outside sources; there is not yet the same impetus to transfer the processing of keystrokes in-house as in newspaper or magazine publishing. This may change, however, as the technical and logistical challenges of processing the author's own keystrokes are met and overcome; there are already scientific and legal publishers who operate their own electronic editorial systems, and this pattern will probably spread. Ironically, one factor which holds this process back is the very one that would otherwise speed its progress: the introduction of cheap but powerful micro-based keyboards and terminals has enabled typesetters to maintain price levels for traditional keyboarding and typesetting at rates only slightly above those charged almost a decade ago. The survival of this 'soft' market in general typesetting will be an important factor affecting publishers' attitudes towards the feasibility of in-house systems.

Technical problems

Material supplied on magnetic media must be transferred to the typesetting system in an acceptable form before it can be further processed. There are two aspects to this transfer: the physical transfer and the conversion of the software.

Physical transfer

There are no industry standards for floppy disks. Some of the varying factors are as follows:

Size 3, 3½, 5¼, or 8 inches

Number of sides Single or double.

Recording density Single, double or quad.

Sectoring Hard or soft.

Formatting The arrangement of information on the disk surface.

Recording speed Some disks revolve at different speeds depending on which areas are being read.

All these physical discrepancies must be handled in such a way that data can be presented to the typesetting system in a uniform and consistent manner.

Software conversion

This is sometimes necessary because the keyboard of a microcomputer cannot adequately represent all the characters and functions that can be accessed from a typesetting terminal's keyboard, and because the code structures used by the word processor or microcomputer may be different from those of the typesetting system. As data transfer has become more common, publishing software has increasingly been provided with 'drivers' for popular word processing programs such as Microsoft Word or WordPerfect. At the same time, many word processors now give a choice of formats that they can write files in. By choosing file formats carefully, it is often possible to achieve a direct file transfer without conversion. Even so, it is still common for tabulations to be lost during the transfer from one program to another, so additional conversion work is required. A conversion process must be capable of handling the following tasks in order for the data to be comprehensible to the typesetter:

Code conversion Transmission codes are designed to achieve communications compatible between different computers. The most common code used is ASCII, but EBCDIC (Extended Binary Coded Decimal Information Code) also occurs. In these codes, each alphanumeric character and function is represented by a numeric value; machines using a 7-bit value have up to 128 such codes, and these are usually standard, but greater variation occurs in models with an extended set of 256 characters, where the allocation of codes to some of the less common additional characters may be arbitrary.

Special characters Typesetting keyboards provide the user with a range of standard characters which includes a variety of fixed spaces, accents, signs, mathematical characters and fractions. This is far greater than that available on most micro keyboards. Although some micros may have a selection of such characters acceptable through special keystroke combinations, the range is not as extensive, and the way in which they are assigned codes may differ between models. Characters which even on a typesetting keyboard need to be accessed from a special pi font provide even greater potential for discrepancy; micro users may well resort to inventing their own codes for these, using unwanted characters from the set available. Translation tables are required to cater for these characters.

Command code conversion Most word processors cannot simulate all the typographic functions of typeface, size, interlinear space, justification mode and measure that can be accessed by a program specifically designed for phototypesetting. Those codes used on a micro to approximate typographic functions, such as bold, italic, indents, underling, tabbing and centring must be either converted into proper typesetting commands or deleted from the data. This is not as easy as the conversion of the alphanumeric character set, since different manufacturers of typesetting machines have adopted different codes to define the various typographic functions.

Typing and typesetting conventions Differences exist between the use of certain identical keys on a word-processor keyboard and a typesetting keyboard. The hyphen key on a word processor keyboard, for example, is used both to break words and to represent a dash in punctuation; dedicated typesetting keyboards have extra keys to provide dashes of different lengths, and the hyphen is never used for this purpose.

Similarly, on many micro keyboards both opening and closing quotation marks are represented by the same single character; typesetting keyboards use different characters for single or double, opening or closing quotes. Some publishing software incorporates 'intelligent quotes' allowing them to substitute the correct form by reference to its position in a word.

Again, while most micros now make provision for the distinction between 0 and O or 1 and I, typists familiar with older-style typewriters lacking keys for 0 and 1 may persist in the use of the same keys for both letter and figure.

Typesetting codes The insertion of codes which control typographic formatting of the copy can be incorporated into the keying of the original text, or can be left until the raw uncoded text has been transferred to the typesetting system and then performed at a VDU terminal. This latter option can be expensive, and as the aim of the interfacing operation is to eliminate the expense of keyboarding it is more logical to attempt to include typographic codes at the initial data-capture stage. The problem this ambition poses are discussed later in this section under the heading *Publishing considerations*.

The physical and software conversion of data can be achieved in a variety of ways, depending on the machines and the coding structures involved at each end of the interfacing process. The most common options are discussed below.

Direct compatibility

The increasing standardisation of microcomputers and the ability of software to generate and recognise standard data formats has greatly eased the compatibility problems that used to afflict direct input. If the typesetter should be using older equipment without this facility, then it may prove viable to provide the client with software or even complete terminals that can write in the required format.

Optical character recognition

Text from the word processor disk can be printed out and scanned by an optical character recognition machine to provide input to the typesetting system. This is not so much a solution to, as an escape route from the problems of interfacing the word processor with the typesetter: the reservations made earlier with respect to conventional OCR scanning still apply and once the text is in hard-copy form it may in any case be preferable to incorporate any typographic commands and text corrections that are relevant, then re-key the copy in a traditional way (negotiating a special 'keen' price from the typesetter in view of the cleanliness of the keying copy provided!). The advantages of interfacing magnetic media with typesetters lie in creating as direct a link as possible between the original keystrokes and the final output; a printout of the text, however used, at once implies extra processes and costs, and is best avoided except as a final option.

Media conversion

Media converters are microcomputers which are programmed to read the structure and content of floppy disks, and to translate the data into an alternative format for output. The conversion program is loaded from the inbuilt hard disk, then the floppy disk holding the content from the word processor is inserted and the data is read off it. The data is held in memory while the conversion software is reconfigured to the desired format, and the data is then output either by direct cable connection to the typesetting system, or more usually to a floppy disk in a structure and code compatible with the typesetting system. The media converter has separate disk drives to enable it to accept the various different sizes of floppy disk.

Early media converters were capable of reading only a limited number of formats and also required much of the programming necessary for the conversion process to be written by the operator; they were therefore rarely cost-effective for single disks or small amounts of copy. With the newer devices, conversion programs are supplied as standard software packages and are updated as new word-processing formats are released onto the market by manufacturers.

The machines are relatively expensive to install, and successful operation requires a degree of experience; this has led to the growth of a commercial service of disk conversion offered by specialist bureaux and typesetters, which publish lists of the numerous makes of disk which can be accepted and the typesetting formats which can be output by their multi-disk readers. These lists are not, however, exhaustive: there will always be some disk types which cannot be converted in this way, either because the disks are too new, obsolescent or simply esoteric. Word processing software can often be the subject of revision even between machines or programs carrying the same name, and the conversion program will have to be periodically rewritten to maintain its accuracy. The list of formats from a conversion bureau should not therefore be accepted as proof that a disk can be read; a trial disk should always be checked before the live data is presented. As with all conversion processes, it is essential that full technical details and a printout of the contents accompany any disk.

The best selling range of conversion systems at present is supplied by InterMedia. Most of these are based on PC computers (the SPS and MMC series), but there are also InterMac versions for Macintosh models with the NuBus expansion slots. The choice of platform is largely irrelevant, as the systems can be configured to read and write in virtually any format. Both versions are available in several levels of complexity, ranging from a relatively simple dedicated 'bridge' system that converts one predetermined format to another, up to elaborate models which can be fitted with several disk or tape drives of different formats, and including extensive disk conversion routines plus the ability to allow the operator to write custom conversions.

Data communications

While floppy disk formats suffered from the lack of standards, data communications have become increasingly standardised because of the requirements for common connections to join electronic devices together. Networks such as Ethernet and LocalTalk, plus communication ports such as RS-232C and SCSI control the cables, plugs and voltages used in the physical connection between equipment.

For data communications to work, the *protocols* of the transmitting and receiving devices must be matched; the protocol governs the synchronisation of the stream of signals, the direction of transfer, and the error check and recovery procedure. Data can be transmitted in asynchronous, synchronous or bisynchronous mode.

In asynchronous mode, the data is transmitted as a sequence of bits with start and stop bits surrounding each character, so that the receiving unit can tell where each character begins and finishes. The signals defining each character may also include a parity code to confirm that no data has been corrupted or lost during the transmission.

Synchronous data transmission sends information as a continuous stream of bits at a speed dictated by timing devices at each end of the interface, with start/stop codes defining blocks of data rather than individual characters; it is a faster method of communication.

Bisynchronous transmission describes the simultaneous sending of data in synchronous mode in each direction.

The speed of transmission is measured in bits per second, or *baud*; any figures quoted include the codes needed to co-ordinate the transmission as well as the actual data transmitted. The higher the transmission speed, the more powerful are the error-recovery mechanisms that are needed to preserve the integrity of the data.

Data sent out through the RS232C port of a microcomputer will be received sequentially, irrespective of the way in which the data may be formatted on the floppy disk; the deciphering of the disk structure performed by media conversion devices is thus avoided, and data can be sent to the typesetting system. Although physically transferred, the data will still, however, contain word processing codes, which need conversion into codes acceptable to the typesetting system before the data can be processed further; a translation or *interface program* is normally used to perform this task. This can be a completely automatic process, with codes being deleted or substituted by software, but in some cases manual intervention at a terminal may be necessary. Translation facilities for popular models of microcomputers are offered as a service by specialist bureaux.

Data communications between a micro and a typesetting system normally employ one of the following methods:

Networking The word processor and the receiving typesetting system are physically connected by cable, with communications software which handles the transmission and reception of the data. As this method requires the word processor and typesetter to be physically fairly close – generally within the same building – this method is usually only used for in-house typesetting operations.

Text retrieval or 'milking'. Data is played out through the RS232C port of the microcomputer to a portable collection device known colloquially as a *milking machine*; cassettes of tape or floppy disks are used to store the data. The device is then taken back to the typesetting installation, connected by cable and the data is downloaded into the system. Milking machines or text-retrieval terminals are useful where the keying source and the typesetter are geographically remote, although the amount of data has to justify the costs of bringing the machine to the microcomputer; if large and regular amounts of copy need to be transmitted, a milking machine can be left permanently plugged into the micro, and the cassettes or disks sent by mail to avoid this expense.

The increasing use of common disk and data formats has largely overcome the need for milking machines.

Telecommunications A modem enables data to be sent at high speed over the conventional telephone network. As the telephone is designed for analog transmission, it is not possible to send data in digital form. A *modem* (MOdulator/DEModulator) is used to convert digital data to analog signals for telephone transmission, and the receiving modem retranslates these signals back into binary codes.

Very fast modems are now available which can operate at up to 9600 baud, though they need 'clean' telephone lines to operate satisfactorily. With standard lines, errors caused by normal line noise often cause the modems to slow down dramatically to a rate at which reliable transmissions can be made.

Acoustic couplers work on the same principle, but are less sophisticated than modems; sending and receiving units are connected by the use of cradles into which the telephone handsets are fitted. Transmission is slower and more prone to corruption by interference noise than with modems.

Modems are perfectly satisfactory for sending text files, which are generally only a few tens or hundreds of kilobytes in length. To keep transmission times (and therefore telephone charges) to a minimum, it is often possible to use a data compression program, which will remove redundant or duplicated information from the file. Compression ratios of 2:1 or 3:1 are commonly achieved with text.

Page make-up programs now allow pictures and graphics to be placed alongside text in a file, and it may be necessary to send these completed pages to an output bureau. Graphics, particularly halftone photographs, have enormously greater file sizes than text. For instance, the whole of the text for this book occupies about 600 k and fits easily on a single floppy disk with plenty of room to spare, and would take about 20 minutes to send via modem. A typical 60 × 100 mm photographic halftone as reproduced in this book would occupy about 400 k if handled in electronic form. Thus just three photographs occupy twice as much disk space as the whole of the text. Colour and higher halftone screen rulings multiply these figures dramatically. A full-page A4 colour image at typical magazine halftone quality will occupy at least 9 Mb (9000 k), and would require many hours of modem transmission.

Modems are impractical for sending such large files, and the common practice is currently to save them onto a hard disk cartridge and physically transport it.

However, digital telecommunications are now possible, and these allow large files to be sent very quickly. ISDN (Integrated Services Digital Network) is an international standard for transmitting digital data, and is available from all British Telecom digital exchanges. ISDN lines are available in multiples of 2 or 30 lines, each capable of transmitting 64 kilobits (8 kilobytes) of digital data per second. An ISDN 30 installation can thus transmit 30 × 64 kbits per second. Therefore an ISDN 2 installation would take just over a minute to transmit each megabyte, and an ISDN 30 just over four seconds. ISDN requires that a dedicated line or lines have to be installed, and a node unit, similar in appearance to a modem, is required to accept the data. ISDN transmits digital data directly, with no need for a modem, and can therefore send very large volumes of data at high speed.

Electronic mail These services provide subscribers with a 'mailbox' on a remote computer which can be written to, and read from, by a personal computer. To access data, a user of electronic mail needs a microcomputer, communications software, a telephone line, an acoustic coupler or modem, and a printer to record in hard copy form data accessed and displayed on the monitor. Messages or copy are sent to the mailbox protected by a special code, allowing only the subscriber to access his data.

Electronic mail allows different computers to communicate via modems, with copy transmitted and collected at times most convenient to both sender and recipient; there are obvious advantages for material which has to be transmitted across different time zones. However, the speed limitations of modems still apply. A further use of electronic mail is to access remote database or information services for instantaneous and absolutely up-to-date business information.

Various electronic mail systems are in operation, including British Telecom's Telecom Gold, Easylink from Cable and Wireless, and CIX (Compulink Information Exchange).

Publishing considerations

Once the technical problems of converting the data have been solved in one of the ways described above, the text will have been successfully transferred to the typesetting system. Before it can be proofed or output, however, all the typographic commands which will govern the text's final appearance must be incorporated. The degree of typographic formatting necessary at this stage depends on the amount of planning which was possible between author, publisher and typesetter before the initial keyboarding commenced. If no consultation was possible and the copy was keyed 'raw', the word-processed text can still be used but intervention will be required at an editing terminal of the typesetting system to insert typographic coding. This is a slow and expensive operation and unless the text is designed to be straightforward in appearance, with few headings, changes of face, different sizes or other variations, prohibitive costs will probably be incurred.

The key to direct and economic use of the author's keystrokes lies in the planning and requires the use of some kind of generic coding system which is designed to overcome the discrepancies of coding existing between different computers. Such a system provides a set of standard commands which can be entered by the originator of the data to access particular characters and functions, and which are automatically translated by the typesetting system into typographic formats. Concepts such as 'main-head typeface and size', 'B-head typeface and size', 'text face and size', 'extract type size', or 'measure' can all be allocated simple codes to be keyed in their relevant positions at the same time as the text, for conversion by a translation table into the specific typographic details required for the job. The successful design and consistent use of such a code system helps facilitate direct typesetting from the original word processor keystrokes.

Coding systems

A variety of different coding systems has been proposed. Typographic mark-up languages transfer the commands used by the typesetting system itself, in simplified form, to the initial keyboarding; the author enters at the micro keyboard codes such as <m24>, <fl>, <p10> to denote a measure of 24 ems, type face 1, in a size of 10pt, for example. Although this kind of typographical mark-up might be acceptable to people familiar with typesetting terminology, most authors find it difficult to use, especially in complex work, and its practical applications are therefore limited.

Another type of coding system aims at to define the structure of a text by reference to the elements of the document and their relative position within their hierarchy. The Standard Generalised Mark-up Language (SGML), developed in the USA and published as a Draft International Standard in late 1986, breaks down the text of any document into logically defined parts; every separately identifiable concept within a piece of text is described by reference to structure. The different coding of elements does not neccessarily imply that they will have a different typographic appearance: the approach is designed primarily to prepare information for mounting on a database. This may then be used to publish the information in an alternative medium, such as compact disk or via on-line access, or can be manipulated to provide entirely new products. An example of how SGML might be used to classify data for such an application is shown below:

```
<hotel>Seaview Hotel
<town>Margate
<county>Kent
<classification>AA approved
<accommodation>36 rooms
<additional features>12 with bath
<rates>from £16.50
<period>per night
```

The labels may be used both for the application of typographic style and also to classify the varying elements of information in their correct hierarchy in the database. Another generic mark-up system is CALS, a standard required by the US Department of Defense for documentation held in electronic form which accompanies military equipment. US military procurement concerns a great many manufacturers and suppliers worldwide who are therefore adopting CALS for their documentation systems. It looks like becoming a standard for high end corporate publishing.

Coding systems like SGML are very precise in the way they structure data, but they require a great deal of advance planning and powerful computer software to translate their structure into typography; for many straightforward publishing applications this approach is unnecessarily complex.

Of greater relevance to general publishing work are those generic coding systems which are typographically orientated and seek to describe the hierarchy of text and headings that occur in free-form documents; where structural coding defines content, these systems describe form. They are usually easier to apply than structural coding systems, and reflect in many ways the traditional mark-up used by editors and designers to define the various elements of text in hard-copy typescripts.

The most generally accepted system is ASPIC (Authors' Standard Pre-press Interfacing Codes), designed and developed in 1983 by Tony Randall of the typesetting company Electronic Village to facilitate the acceptance of word processor disks from customers. ASPIC was adopted in 1984 by the British Printing Industries Federation (BPIF) as the recognised industry norm for the electronic mark-up of text. It consists of a number of basic, non-technical codes or flags which can be keyed with text and which indicate to the typesetting system any changes in typeface, size, layout or special characters required at a particular point. The system is easily learnt, requires no knowledge of typesetting terminology and is very flexible: text coded in ASPIC can be input to a typesetting computer via any microcomputer or word processor. ASPIC can be used before any final decisions about typographic style have been made, and the ASPIC codes can therefore be incorporated by an author into his copy during keyboarding.

ASPIC codes can be summarised in three categories:

Essential ASPIC is a short list of codes for general applications, including codes for headings, paragraph indents, and changes in type style between roman, italic and bold.

Standard ASPIC caters for addition font changes, including small capitals, indented text, changes in justification mode, space for illustrations, and typographic characters such as dashes and quotation marks.

Supplementary ASPIC provides codes for miscellaneous characters, such as asterisk, dagger, paragraph sign and other frequently used signs. It also includes three sub-categories:

Language ASPIC: accents and letters of the Greek alphabet.
Mathematical ASPIC: maths signs, symbols and fractions.
Tabular ASPIC: codes to define, call and terminate columns.

Almost all codes in ASPIC consist of lower-case letters enclosed in square brackets: everything within these delimiters is a code, everything outside them is text. ASPIC is essentially mnemonic, and can be learnt easily; anyone regularly keyboarding work should become fully conversant with the codes in a very short time. To work effectively, ASPIC must be used consistently; even where an equivalent is available on the micro keyboard to access a certain character, the ASPIC code should still be used.

The full list of codes, together with a more detailed description of ASPIC, can be found in the booklet *The ASPIC Handbook*, obtainable from the BPIF.

This coding system can even be applied to some desktop publishing systems. Programs such as Ventura Publisher, Aldus PageMaker and QuarkXPress can be set up to incorporate *stylesheets* which are functionally translation tables for codes embedded in word processed text. Any pre-arranged coding system can be set up between the word processor user and the desktop publishing facility, including many of the ASPIC *Essential* and *Standard* codes. Although DTP stylesheets cannot cater for all special characters, some of these are already handled automatically by the programs themselves.

Advance planning (text only)

Any material which is to be supplied to a typesetter on disk or tape should be the subject of rigorous discussion – *before* the work is started. Disks which arrive out of the blue may destroy much of the potential benefit of single keystroking, and the advance discussions should involve all parties: author, editor, designer, production controller and typesetter. This requires a fundamental shift in the traditional attitudes and linear relationships between these various people.

Desktop publishing output has different but equally important requirements and is discussed later.

The following points form a master checklist for the production controller responsible for arranging typesetting from textual matter supplied on disk:

1 Is the job suitable for processing from disk? Tabular and mathematical setting require a considerable amount of extra skill at both keyboarding and conversion stage; a conventional re-keying from print-out may be a preferable option in some cases.

```
[h1]"CLASSIC' CARS[1c][1x][h2]The
Ford Zodiac[1c][2x][t1][b]Born in
the late '50s, the Ford
[bi]Zodiac[b] and its lower-
specification sisters the
[bi]Zephyr[b] and [bi]Consul[b],
are not long enough in the tooth to
have achieved true veteran
status.[][r]Nonetheless, these
elderly ladies are often to be
found displayed by their proud
owners at rallies and county shows
up and down the country.]]
[h3]Reliable[1c][3x][t1]Powered by
the very reliable if somewhat
unspectacular Ford 105E engine [md]
a "classic' in its own right [md]
the [i]Zodiac[r]'s 2.2 litres
proved adequate to haul the
vehicle's 1[p123] ton kerbside
weight without undue effort.[]
```

'CLASSIC' CARS

The Ford Zodiac

Born in the late '50s, the Ford *Zodiac* and its lower-specification sisters the *Zephyr* and *Consul*, are not long enough in the tooth to have achieved true veteran status.

Nonetheless, these elderly ladies are often to be found displayed by their proud owners at rallies and county shows up and down the country.

Reliable

Powered by the very reliable if somewhat unspectacular Ford 105E engine — a 'classic' in its own right — the *Zodiac*'s 2.2 litres proved adequate to haul the vehicle's 1½ ton kerbside weight without undue effort.

ASPIC in operation, showing (top) *text as keyed with ASPIC codes in position, and* (bottom) *as output from the phototypesetter after translation of the codes into typographic commands.*

2 Is the client likely to prove reliable in his keyboarding and his computer 'housekeeping'? A badly organised electronic manuscript can present infinitely more problems than its paper equivalent. Try to discover if the client has produced earlier and similar work in this way; if doubts exist, contact the previous publishers and profit from their experience.

Never be pressured into attempts to convert electronic copy that is for any reason unsuitable, just because the client has used a word processor for convenience or feels that 'new technology' provides its own justification; you are the one who will have to sort it all out if it crashes around your ears!

Diplomacy is the keyword here; jobs have been re-keyed from print-outs before now with the client blissfully assuming that the production was breaking new ground in typesetting technology!

3 Does the client expect to share financially in the savings which may accrue from the avoidance of double keying? If so, is he or she aware of the probable sum involved? There is a great deal of misconception surrounding the extent of the savings which can be made, and the likely figure should be clarified in advance to avoid later misunderstandings.

4 Proofing and correction of the copy will still be necessary, unless the client is willing to accept total responsibility for the accuracy of the text. Who will pay for any literals or copy-editing changes which are necessary to the text supplied on the disk? Is the client prepared to accept the disk back and incorporate any changes required? This requires tact: not all writers take kindly to being asked to correct their own spelling and grammar! If the typesetter is required to make corrections, the cost can perhaps be offset against the client's share of keyboarding savings – but the wildly differing costs of the two kinds of keying will have to be explained in advance.

Even more critical are those situations where incorrect keying may cause data to become corrupted, or disordered files may entail the extra costs of sorting before the data can be retrieved. The typesetter and client should agree in advance who will bear the responsibility, and costs, for any such unfortunate accidents.

5 Work out a detailed arrangement for guaranteeing the security of the data. Ensure that the client retains a back-up copy of any disk

supplied, in case the disk goes physically missing or the data on it is corrupted or lost during transfer. Back-up disks must be absolutely accurate and up to date.

If the job is to be stored on disk for future updates, decide who will be responsible both for storage and for any costs arising from this.

6 Ask the client to provide the following technical information at the earliest possible stage:

a) Details of the exact make and model of word processor or micro which is to be used, and the operating system and wp program version under which the work will be created; the formatting and coding of data can vary dramatically between different models of the same machine.

b) Details of the magnetic media used – cassette, disk, or reel-to-reel tape. Floppy disk is the most likely form in which text will be provided by individual authors: the size, number of recorded sides, sectoring, recording density and internal format may need to be specified if this is an unusual format.

c) A test file to show exactly which character is produced by each and every key on the word processor or micro keyboard may be necessary. Peripheral characters are often produced by different keys on different machines, and a complete print-out of all the keys on the author's keyboard in strict order enables a translation table to be adjusted to ensure that the characters typeset are the same as the characters keyboarded.

This file should include all alphanumerics a–z, A–Z and 1–0, followed by peripheral characters identified by name:

. full point
, comma
? query
! exclamation mark
= equals sign

The author should also be asked to give details of any special codes which have been used to denote characters; if an accepted standard such as ASPIC has been rigorously followed, a statement to that effect is sufficient.

d) If the typesetter does not have the correct wp translation driver, it will be necessary to provide a sample of text which uses the control codes of the word processor, so that these can be identified for stripping out in the translation process. This file will show the typesetter how text on the word processor is underlined or emboldened, how headings are positioned, and how the lines and paragraphs are ended.

The typesetter may be able to provide a specially designed piece of copy for this purpose.

7 If generic coding is to be used by the author, a type specification is required at an early stage so that the relevant conversion program can be written to translate the codes into typesetting formats. This implies that the designer of the text needs to be involved at an earlier stage than is traditionally necessary, to decide at least the structure of the work in terms of number and hierarchy of styles of text, headings and extracts; since the final version of the text will not have been written at this point, the requirement for a methodical and organised author becomes even more apparent! As far as is feasible, the final typography of the job should be fixed at this stage, although it is of course possible to amend the typographic values assigned to the generic codes at any time up to final output.

A short test file, using every code that will appear in the final text, should be provided by the author at this stage to be output from the typesetting machine as a check that the translation program works correctly and that the author is using the relevant generic codes in the appropriate places.

8 When the text, or any part of it, is ready to be released by the client, it is essential that a clean, accurate printout accompanies the disk. If the publisher has no facilities for reading or printing the disk in-house, this printout will be used for proofreading and copy-editing purposes, and for marking corrections which are to be made by the typesetter. It is also needed by the typesetter as a check that the data on the disk has been fully and accurately transferred to the typesetting system.

A list of the disks supplied, the files on the disks and the order in which they are to be processed should also be included.

Planning for desktop publishing

The widespread adoption of desktop publishing systems, and the consequent shift in typesetting services to accommodate them, has simplified many of the problems of direct input, while adding a few new ones. Once again, the client and the typesetter (or output bureau) must talk to each other in advance, so each knows what to expect from the other. The checklist in this case is:

1. Establish which program or programs are to be used. In particular make sure that the version numbers of both the software and the computer's operating systems are identical with those that will be used for output. Failure to do so may result in pages which do not match the client's original, or which completely fail to output.
2. Check which fonts the client is going to use, and whether they are compatible with the output system. If new fonts need to be purchased for a specific job, and are unlikely to be needed for other clients, the output bureau may ask the client to pay all or part of the purchase cost.
3. As before, establish the reliability of the client. There is as much if not more to go wrong with ready made-up pages as with coded text. Clients must be aware of the importance of including the source files (such as TIFF, EPS or TGA formats) for embedded graphics, of setting the correct screen ruling for tints and halftones, and also need to understand the difference between spot and process colour separations, and how to achieve them.
4. Most desktop publishing systems include on-screen previewing of the finished results, and proofing devices such as laser printers are widely used. Bureau output services usually assume that the client is responsible for accuracy, and that any file sent can be output 'as is'. Nevertheless, it is good practice for the bureau to check that a file works before committing it to output by previewing it on their own screen, or even making a laser printer proof. This will show up any gross errors, missing or altered graphics files or unavailable fonts.
5. Disks should be accompanied by the client's proof printout, plus a specification sheet. Modem-ed files require similar accompaniment

– this can be sent by facsimile for speed. The specification sheet should detail which files are to be output, which embedded graphics file they require, and whether colour separations are involved. If the job files cover several disks, the contents of each disk should be detailed. If not agreed in advance, the specification sheet should also detail the fonts used, plus output medium (film or paper), and if film, further details (positive or negative exposure, right or wrong reading, emulsion side up or down). It's also a good idea for the client to specify the intended film size, so a page formatting mistake does not result in the exposure of unnecessarily large film areas.

6 Clients should keep back-up copies of all files until the page has at least been output satisfactorily and passed for press. The output bureau should also keep the client's file for a short period after the job has been output to allow for loss or damage of the page at subsequent production stages – if longer term storage is required by the client, terms should be negotiated.

Theory and practice

In the ideal scenario, the number of stages through which a typescript must pass is drastically reduced. Disks that include page assembly information or generic codes for typographic formatting can in theory be sent direct to a typesetter for output as bromide paper or film.

In practice, things are not so simple. Where author and client (in the form of the publisher) are separate, as is common in book publishing but rare elsewhere, it is essential to have some intermediate stage between author and typesetter, to provide the point of input for the traditional publishing skills of copy-editing and styling, the elimination of errors in the text or inconsistencies in the coding, the application of a design specification and the checking of the compatibility of the data supplied with the proposed typesetting system.

Many of these operations are typical publishing tasks and the logical place for this interface seems to be the publisher's office. Publishers are, however, traditionally reluctant to invest in expensive equipment, and may not wish to employ or train people with the required skills. Many publishers have therefore preferred to employ specialist bureaux to act as the intermediaries between author and typesetter; the disks supplied by an author are forwarded to the bureau, which is responsible for checking the compatibility of data and writing the conversion program for the disk. The publisher meanwhile carries out the copy-editing, proofreading and design functions on a hard-copy printout from the disk. This updated printout is then supplied to the bureau, which incorporates any corrections marked by the publisher at the same time as checking and correcting the generic coding of the text. If the disks supplied by the author do not contain generic coding, it can be entered by the bureau. The bureau then produces a new and correct disk, together with an updated printout, which can be further checked by the publisher as required before being passed on to the typesetter for output. This system can accommodate the 'one-off' author, who does not have to be taught how to insert even the simplest codes into his text.

7 Front-end systems

It was once possible to define typesetting systems by broad categories, reinforced by reference to the names and equipment of specific manufacturers. This is increasingly difficult as systems become more flexible in operation and modular in design, and a more useful distinction nowadays is that between the various component parts of a system and the functions which they perform within the overall configuration.

Basic functions of a composition system can be defined as data input; page assembly; and output. The difference between traditional typesetting and modern electronic page composition systems is the order of these elements. With traditional typesetting, page assembly took the output from typesetters and cameras and literally stuck them together. Electronic page assembly places the elements together on-screen and then outputs them all together.

Data input primarily means the keying of raw text, but can increasingly include scanners for graphics and OCR capture. Data input and electronic page composition functions take place on systems which are collectively known as the *front end* of a composition system – the output unit(s) acting as the *back end.*

To be strictly accurate, any equipment used for entering data into a system can also be considered part of the front end system, including outside sources, but the term generally just refers to equipment within the typesetter's premises.

A single manufacturer may be responsible for a complete front and back end installation at a typesetting company, but this is no longer anything like as common as it once was. Many suppliers of very powerful front end systems – Miles 33 or Xyvision, for example – do not build output machines themselves, and neither do the suppliers of low-cost desktop publishing systems. Many 'independent' front end systems include drivers for one or more makes of typesetter: Linotype's CORA typesetting language is also a favourite, as this allows access to a number of popular typesetter models.

Back ends have become even more interchangeable since the

widespread adoption of the 'device-independent' PostScript language. Any PostScript front end can drive any PostScript back end, so the question of which output device to buy is more and more a matter of price/performance rather than any necessity to buy from a single manufacturer on compatibility grounds.

A front-end system normally consists of a number of terminals, a computer and various software programs for text-processing functions. The size and distribution of computing power within the front-end varies according to the sophistication of the overall system. All terminals used for the input, editing and correction of text will have their own computer power to some degree, but in addition a central processing unit (CPU) or file server is sometimes required to perform specialist tasks at high speeds. These functions may include fast and automatic hyphenation and justification of text, the administration of files within the system, the sorting of large volumes of data into predefined order, complex composition such as mathematical or tabular work, automatic pagination and the storage and manipulation of the vast amounts of data associated with the electronic processing of graphics. The CPU which performs these computer-intensive tasks can be part of an integrated front-end, such as the typesetting systems built by manufacturers like Atex, or SII, or a general-purpose mainframe or minicomputer running software which the typesetting company has written itself, or a combination of both.

As microcomputers and graphic workstations have developed to achieve performance levels that would have required minicomputers less than a decade ago, so the use of CPUs is tailing off. Large publishing operations such as newspapers and magazines are increasingly using *distributed processing*, relying on the power of individual terminals for specific tasks, with common access to resources such as fonts and graphics databases contained on networked hard disk units. File server units are used to carry out the housekeeping functions and to regulate data flow around the system.

EDITING AND CORRECTION

Text input and editing used to require separate dedicated terminals. Such terminals have all but disappeared from manufacture with the widespread availability of word processing software on low-cost standard microcomputers. Standard word processors can be used, or adapted software which writes directly in the typesetting system's code format.

The Linotype APL230 terminal which can be used for either text input or editing and correction.

Nevertheless, many typesetters still use dedicated text input terminals which suit their needs perfectly well. Many of these are based on standard microcomputers themselves, but variously fitted with special keyboards, screens and interface boards. On a dedicated terminal, the keyboard includes a combination of alphanumeric keys for text entry, programmable keys for storing the user-definable formats of frequently used keystroke combinations, dedicated keys for editorial functions, and system command keys to access files from memory and activate functions such as hyphenation and justification. These keys are usually grouped into separate blocks, with colour-coded keytops for ease and speed of operation.

Linked to the keyboard is a monitor to display the text that is being worked on; between 12 and 30 lines of about 80 characters are usually shown on the screen, with a number of lines reserved for control information. The job can be scrolled up or down, according to the screen memory available in the terminal, to provide fast access to any part of the file; in addition, some systems make use of line numbers to enable the operator to jump straight to the required position in the file.

Terminals designed primarily for editing and correcting bulk text normally use a monospaced typeface, in a single size of 14 or 18pt, displayed green or black on white, with typographic codes distinguished by 'reverse video' or half-intensity characters. On some systems, all such commands can be suppressed by a single keystroke to allow the operator to view only the text of the job being worked on. As the function of these terminals is the fast and efficient processing of large volumes of text, there is no requirement in the displays for any representation of true typeface or typesize.

Correction of text by an operator at a terminal is performed by the use of dedicated editing keys which allow individual characters, words, lines and blocks of text to be deleted, copied or moved within the file; text can also be added in either 'insert' or 'overstrike' mode. A cursor controlled from the keyboard is used to define the point in the text at which changes are being made. If the original copy has been keyed without the inclusion of typographic coding, the formatting of the job is also performed in this manner.

Editing terminals are normally used to carry out all the corrections necessary after a typeset job has been proofread by the customer. The skills required in editing on screen differ from those needed for keying high volumes of data at continuous high speed, and most typesetting companies therefore have a specialist department for such work. This is also the place where any corrections arising from the typesetter's own reading are made before proofs are sent to the customer.

Traditionally all work was read by the typesetter's own highly skilled staff and passed back for correction, so that the customer's proofs were, to the best of the typesetter's ability, completely clean. Today, however, pressure for reduced costs has eliminated the actual correction process for many straightforward types of work, and proofs which are sent to the clients are frequently unread by the typesetter; clients are expected to mark both their own ('author's') and the compositor's errors. There is an obvious risk involved in this. At the very least someone, whether typesetter or publisher, should 'scan read' the proofs to pick up any major disasters caused by forgotten font changes or transposed job files. For regular work, particularly in magazine publishing, it is often the practice for a 'page rate' to be negotiated, in which a certain level of author's corrections is assumed and is incorporated in the overall charge. Page rates can often include a pre-agreed number of halftones and any special headline setting that might be required.

Any corrections to a job before proofing are made to the original disk or tape, and are therefore automatically incorporated in the job file. Corrections after proofreading can be keyed in the same way onto the original file, and this is normal if the amendments are anything other than very light; clean bromides or film of the affected galleys or pages are then output. If the corrections are minimal, however, it can be cheaper for the typesetter to key these lines as separate patches and strip them into the original setting by cut-and-paste techniques. In such cases, the original file of the job held by the typesetter will not hold the corrections made after proofing unless the typesetter is specifically instructed to carry these back onto the file. With ephemeral or periodical work this may not be a matter of great importance, but if there is any chance at all that the job will later be re-accessed and re-output – in a revised version, or in a different format – then the corrections should either be carried back to the job or it should be noted on the publisher's records that the file is not clean.

Corrections manually patched into the original bromide paper or film can suffer from density problems unless the chemical processing of output produced at different times is closely controlled: the correction lines may appear darker or lighter than the surrounding setting. There is usually little the printer of the job can do, in either platemaking or machining, to overcome this problem, and it is essential therefore to check the corrected work for evenness of density and image weight before the camera-ready copy is accepted from the typesetter. With the spread of automatic processing, this problem is fortunately now less common than it used to be.

The accuracy and straightness of manually stripped correction lines depends to a great deal on the skill of the paste-up artist, but it is possible to minimise the risk of tilted or bowed lines: a block of two or three lines of film or bromide paper is physically much easier to handle and position than a single narrow strip and even if a correction can be accommodated within a single line, the typesetter will probably prefer to set a patch which includes the affected line. The improved speed and accuracy of paste-up should more than justify the small increase in typesetting costs involved.

Where the client has supplied fully assembled page files, it normally proves cheaper for the client to perform the correction and send a revised file for output as a completely new page, rather than require the output bureau to alter and re-output the original file or to produce and strip in a patch.

In addition to the basic text-editing functions, systems may offer a choice of the following more refined editing facilities.

Search and replace routine

Most word processors and editing terminals have the ability to perform search and replace routines. The operator can define a sequence of characters and spaces – often up to 60 characters long according to the system – and the computer is instructed to search the job files for occurrences of this particular character string. The system can operate in discretionary mode, calling up these strings onto the monitor for the operator to check and manually change the text as necessary; or it can function automatically, replacing the defined string wherever it is found with a second defined sequence of characters.

The process has several editorial applications, and can be used to:

correct inconsistencies or misspellings from the original copy:
e.g. *search for* Smith, *replace with* Smythe

implement editorial changes of mind:
e.g. *search for* Common Market, *replace with* European Economic Community

It can also be used in a planned way by the typesetter to:

save the number of keystrokes:
e.g. *search for* EEC, *replace with* European Economic Community

avoid the risk of keyboard spelling errors:
e.g. *search for* XX, *replace with* polytetrofluoroethylene

This type of routine is also used to convert text keyed on a word processor using a generic coding system such as ASPIC into files of typographically formatted text: the search and replace process implements the replacement of the generic codes [h1], [t1], etc., by commands which the typesetting system can understand through recourse to a set of translation tables written for each particular job.

Edit tracking

This facility is found on more powerful front-end systems, including those supplied by Atex and Xyvision. The system records in memory any lines in a file which are edited or corrected at any one stage during the life of the job; these lines are then marked both on the terminal screen display and on the hard-copy proofs. A system of different marks is used in the margin of the text to differentiate between changes, insertions of new copy and deletions from the text. Both the terminal operator and the customer can then easily identify for re-reading those lines which have been amended, leading to improved accuracy and time savings in the proofreading cycle. On jobs with multiple proof stages the system automatically removes marks entered at an earlier stage, and highlights only those areas affected by the most recent correction stage.

Spelling checks

A spelling check program works by comparing each word in a job file against a dictionary resident in the central computer memory; if a certain word is not found in the dictionary, the system presents it as 'unknown' for review by an operator. Some word processors can optionally run simple checks in the background, producing a bleep whenever an unknown word is typed. This is useful as a spelling monitor but can be annoying when (correctly) typing work with frequent technical words that the dictionary does not contain.

The dictionary can often be expanded by the user: if words presented for review are correctly spelt, and have appeared only because they are new to the spelling-check program, they can be added to the dictionary and will be available for subsequent checks.

A limitation to the usefulness of these programs is that they cannot distinguish between incorrectly spelt words and the incorrect use in a certain context of correctly spelt words. In a phrase such as 'I was at there party but he was not their', all the words would be verified as correct. Equally a mis-spelling that created another word that was correctly spelt (such as *tree* accidentally spelt *free*) would not be detected. Grammar checkers are now available which can detect context as well as spelling, but so far they are not as convenient in use as spelling checkers, as they are not built directly into word processor programs.

HYPHENATION AND JUSTIFICATION

Hyphenation and justification (h&j) of text was one of the first applications of computing in typesetting. The logic invoked by the earliest programs frequently produced very poor word-breaks and loosely spaced text, often resorting to letterspacing words to fill out lines; when compared to the operator-controlled h&j of hot-metal composition the results were not impressive. The computer programs now used are very much more powerful and sophisticated, and different approaches to hyphenation and justification can be adopted according to the specific type of work being produced.

Hyphenation and justification can be performed at a counting input terminal at the same time as the original copy is keyed, with the operator reviewing each individual line ending and overriding it as necessary; this interactive method is suitable for complex or tabular work, when it is important to know whether or not copy will fit within a certain measure.

In straightforward composition it is more usual for the h&j process to be performed after capture of the original text, either semi-automatically at an editing terminal, with operator intervention to correct line endings as required, or fully automatically in background mode. Automatic h&j can also be performed by the computer within the typesetting machine itself, fed by unjustified data, but in this case there is no opportunity for the word breaks to be checked for acceptability before output, and so it is more normal for h&j to be treated as a front-end function.

To perform h&j the computer must have access to the unit set widths of all characters in each size for every typeface used in a piece of text. Depending on the system design, the information can either be accessed on-line from the central processing unit, or downloaded to a terminal on disk. The system is also programmed with information which defines the standard word space preferred in a line, and the minimum and maximum word spaces permitted; default values for these will exist within the system, but these can be adjusted by the typesetting company to their own different specifications, or for the particular requirements of individual jobs.

When running the h&j program, the computer records and adds, for each line, the widths of the characters in the typeface and size in which the text is formatted, together with the number of word spaces keyed, and subtracts these from the total number of units of widths in the measure of the line. When this total is exceeded and the next word space is keyed, indicating the end of a word, the line is 'overset', and the computer makes a line-ending decision. It can do this by reducing the width value of all the word spaces in the line, within the limits defined by the minimum permissible word space; if the line will fit without reducing the word space value beyond this limit, then the line justifies. If this is not possible, the final word keyed in the line is excluded and the word-space values are increased; if the line fits without exceeding the maximum allowable word-space value, then the line again is justified. If neither of the above attempts produces a justified line, then the computer can, if so programmed, increase the amount of space between all characters in the line, tighten the fitting of all characters, or tighten the fitting of certain predefined combinations of letters only; these last two options are sometimes described as *character compensation* or *kerning*. All such adjustments to inter-character space need to be handled with great care and within tightly controlled limits if the results are not to become visually obtrusive. More usually, the program will turn to hyphenation to fit the line.

Hyphenation programs are based on logic created from the sequence and frequency of occurrence of certain combinations of characters within a given language, usually reinforced by listings of common prefixes, suffixes and 'root words'. When called upon to hyphenate a word, the computer analyses the character combinations using complex algorithms or sets of defined computerised rules, and splits the word accordingly. This logic is not, however, totally efficient and often breaks words in unacceptable places: 'translate' may be split correctly as 'trans/late' and 'manslaughter', unacceptably as 'mans/laughter'. To cater for words which do not hyphenate satisfactorily under logic, the program uses an 'exception dictionary' to list all such words and their acceptable break positions; when called upon to hyphenate any word, the program first searches this dictionary, and only if the word cannot be found in it will the software resort to logic to decide the break position. It follows that the quality of typesetting which can be achieved on any system is affected by the size and relevance of the h&j program's exception dictionary. These can vary between a few thousand words, which may not be sufficient for quality composition, and much more powerful dictionaries like the one found in the Miles 33 PENS systems, with a standard one million character capacity. Exception dictionaries are supplied for different languages and for specialist applications such as legal or medical work; in addition, most professional systems offer the facility for operator-defined words to be added to the dictionary as they are found. Regrettably, operator-defined facilities are rarely found in desktop publishing systems.

The parameters which define the preferred, minimum and maximum permissible word spaces can be varied by the typesetter to suit the requirements of particular jobs or customers. As the standard of hyphenation and justification produced by a typesetting system is crucial to overall quality, and can vary so widely between different systems and typesetters, any specification from a publisher should include reference to the word-space parameters expected. This can often form part of a publisher's 'house-style' document.

Other variables which can be controlled include the minimum size of word which may be hyphenated, the minimum number of characters allowable before or after a word break and the maximum number of consecutive hyphenated lines which may appear.

Operators can also insert discretionary hyphens into specific words to indicate where the word should be broken if hyphenation proves necessary, and can similarly apply 'forbid' commands to keep particular words intact; these might include proper names, dates, sequences of figures or words which already contain a grammatically necessary (*hard*) hyphen.

Although speeds do vary according to the combination of type size and measure being set and the sophistication of the hyphenation program used, hyphenation and justification can be a very fast operation. This enables jobs to be cast off to fit a certain extent with great flexibility: a job can be h&j'd in background mode, and the number of lines that the job makes can be telephoned to a customer for approval; the specification can be modified as necessary and the job re-run to give a new extent. This is particularly useful for book publishers, who need 'even workings' (printable sections) of 16 or 32 pages.

After proofreading, any lines which are corrected will need to be re-hyphenated and re-justified; this can often be performed interactively by editing or page make-up terminals as corrections are keyed. If for any reason the typographic specification of a job must be changed after the first hyphenated and justified proofs have been produced – to accommodate extra material without increasing the overall extent, for example – it is preferable to try to make the necessary adjustments by alterations to the interlinear spacing or to the number of lines per page. Neither of these changes affect the h&j of the original text, while any change to the typeface, size or measure involves a new h&j pass: this may be easy for the typesetter, but necessitates a complete re-proofing and re-reading of the job. This option is not normally available in magazines and newspapers which are built to a rigid grid structure, as varying the column depth or leading would show up.

Hyphenation and justification programs are now extremely sophisticated, and capable of producing acceptable results in most situations. The best h&j software struggles, however, if the type specification is unrealistically demanding: the relationship of type size to line length is crucial in avoiding excessive word spacing or over-frequent hyphenation, and the skill and experience of the typographer has a vital role to play in the production of evenly spaced and flowing text. If doubts exist about the suitability of a given type specification, a specimen piece of setting in the correct typeface, size and measure should be requested from the typesetter so that the resultant hyphenation and justification can be assessed; it is not always necessary to have copy specially keyed for this purpose, as typesetters often hold special files of dummy material which can be quickly formatted and output to the correct specification.

One of the biggest complaints normally directed against desktop publishing is the quality of its h&j. In fact the best DTP programs such as Quark XPress or Advent 3B2 have facilities that are as good as some dedicated typesetting systems, and produce excellent results in the right hands. The difference, apparently, lies in the DTP operators, who frequently do not have the training or experience to override the computer's line break decisions.

Indeed, writers who use page layout systems or counting direct input programs have a unique advantage. They can rewrite their sentences interactively to avoid poorly justified lines and bad word breaks; typesetters cannot do this as their job is to reproduce faithfully the words given to them by their clients.

AUTOMATIC INDEX GENERATION

In the conventional production of a typeset book or technical manual, the index is compiled by a specialist editor working on a set of page proofs. Indexing cannot be completed until all corrections have been incorporated on these proofs, and the subsequent setting, checking and approving of the index can cause a lengthy delay to production at a most critical stage of the schedule. The longer and more complicated the text, the more the manual indexing cycle holds up printing and binding, and the greater the delay to both publication and the publisher's return on capital.

Automatic index-generation programs are designed to overcome this problem. The list of index entries is compiled from the typescript, not from a set of page proofs, and page numbers are automatically assigned to the index items during the pagination process.

Indexing can be a typesetting system function, but it is also built into many electronic publishing systems designed for corporate in-house publishing. The Xyvision and Interleaf systems, which are widely used for technical documentation, incorporate sophisticated automatic indexing. Even some of the 'long document' desktop programs include this feature now – Ventura Publisher is a case in point.

There are several ways of defining words that are to appear in the index; these can be marked on the typescript using a highlighter pen or some other system agreed with the typesetter; as the original text is keyboarded, the operator flags these words with delimiters for extraction into a separate file. Alternatively, separate sheets of index copy may be prepared, with reference markers keyed into the main text to connect the index items to the point in the text at which they must be referenced; the index copy is then keyed into a separate file. Another approach involves the indexer in the preparation of a list of index terms which is keyed into the system; the computer then searches the main text against this list, and all occurrences of these words are detailed for editorial review; with this method the indexer works to some degree in isolation from the text, and it may prove difficult to assess the relative importance for indexing purposes of every occurrence of the words which the computer finds.

When the main text is paginated, the index flags or references are automatically extracted, matched to the relevant terms held in the index file, and allocated page numbers according to the position of the flags in the composed pages. The index terms appear at this stage in folio sequence, and must be sorted into alphabetical order and processed with *match-and-drop* routines to remove the repeated index term from each entry:

blackbird, 37	*becomes*	blackbird, 37, 42
blackbird, 42		

In a similar way, *match-and-replace* programs remove redundant main index terms from entries, replacing them with space, ditto marks or dashes as required:

warbler, garden	*becomes*	warbler, garden
warbler, willow		——willow
warbler, wood		——wood

Once the index text has been processed and sorted, it is typographically formatted according to the required specification, and from this point on follows the same path as conventionally produced indexes.

Many different sorting levels can be used to enable indices with hierarchical structures to be created; thus a guide to motor vehicles could be sorted by specific model of car, within type of car, within country of origin, within price range, etc. Most systems support the generation of several indices of this type simultaneously.

The concept of automatic index generation is very attractive, but it requires all the disciplines of conventional indexing, as well as considerable pre-planning at an early stage; it is easy to 'over-index' by marking too many common words on the typescript. A thorough reading of the first index proofs is needed to catch those instances where the same items have been indexed in different ways because of different wording in the text:

Orville Wright
Wilbur Wright
the Wright brothers
the Wrights
these intrepid pioneers

are all references to the same item, and will have to be recognised as such for absorption into a single index entry.

Provided that the variations between manual and automatic indexing techniques are understood and can be accommodated, there are considerable scheduling savings to be made through computer-assisted indexing processes, especially in multi-volume work where the creation of indices in the normal way could cause delay to the overall production schedule.

MATHEMATICS COMPOSITION

Complex maths setting requires specialised programs to be run on the front-end system. Maths programs must be able to cope with multilevel equations and expressions, and powerful software, in conjunction with special keyboards, is used to simplify the keyboarding of the most complex work. The emphasis lies on speed of access to multikeystroke symbols or commands; some systems offer a choice between large keyboards with up to 400 dedicated keys and a more conventional editing layout using multi-keystroke commands to access the range of characters required. Special fonts can be defined to include the combination of figures, symbols, Greek letters and pi characters which may be necessary.

Common features in maths programs include accurate control over the positioning of superior and inferior figures, the weight, length and placement of rules, the centring of denominators and numerators, the horizontal alignment of multi-line equations, the sizing and positioning of such multi-line characters as brackets, parentheses and integrals, and the automatic breaking and spacing of equations.

For pagination, elements such as equations can be treated as 'no-break' areas by the automatic paging program.

TABULAR COMPOSITION

With specialised tabulation programs the most complex tables can be set without difficulty. The keyboard operator can either specify the measure for each column in the table, or use the software to calculate this: by keying the longest line in each column in the correct typeface and size, the operator allows the system to convert the number of units taken up by each line into picas and points. This measure is then stored on a tab format, along with the other typographic details of typeface, size, style of justification (ranged left, centred or ranged right), gutter space between columns, and vertical rules as required, for the entire width of the table. This avoids the need for much repetitive re-keying: the operator need hit only the tab key, followed by the relevant setting copy for each column in turn across the table, to range copy as specified under the format.

Additional features include the use of vertical tabs, with the program automatically justifying the table to the depth of the longest column, automatic alignment of figures at a decimal point or comma, and controlled positioning of 'straddle' heads over multiple columns. Both horizontal and vertical rules in a variety of weights can be generated from the keyboard, fitted to both the measure and depth of the table; vertical rules can be defined so that they break on either side of straddle heads. Depending on the capabilities of the typesetting machine, geometric shapes, tints, solids and reversals may be included in the job, enabling complex business forms work to be produced.

Some systems can handle tabular work of up to 80 column widths, and the terminal operator is able to scroll the monitor screen left to right and up or down to view any particular area of the job. Many tabulation programs offer a 'hide' mode in which all tab and typesetting

```
TAB1M10L TAB2M1L TAB3M5C TAB4M1L TAB5M11R
TAB6M5L TAB7M1L TAB8M4C TAB9M1L TAB10M3R
CT6 Manufacturer TAB TAB Model TAB TAB Price ET
CT6 Petersen TAB TAB Kleenrite TAB TAB £89.95 ET
CT6 Hauser TAB TAB HX300 TAB TAB £75.00 ET
CT6 Renard TAB TAB Premiere TAB TAB £68.95 ET
```

Manufacturer	*Model*	*Price*
Petersen	Kleenrite	£89.95
Hauser	HX300	£75.00
Renard	Premiere	£68.95

A tabulation format and its use in a table. The tabulation parameters, which may be established anywhere in a file preceding the first point of use, specify the tab number, its width and the justification style. [TAB6M5L] defines Tab 6 as a measure of 5 picas, ranged left. In the example above, 10 tabs (including those to create gutters between text columns) are established. The table displayed uses tabs 6 to 10, established by the Call Tab 6 command [CT6}. Thereafter, the next tab in sequence is called by use of the [TAB] key until the End Tab [ET] is introduced.

commands are deleted from the screen to allow the operator a clearer appraisal of his work.

As mentioned before, tabulation is frequently a weak point in the transfer of data from word processing programs. However, some electronic publishing systems can import numerical data directly from spreadsheet programs such as Lotus 1-2-3 or Microsoft Excel, and format them automatically into tabular setting, which saves a great deal of time and effort.

AUTOMATIC COLOUR SPLITTING

Work which is to be printed in two or more colours on the same page requires a separate film negative or positive for each colour at the platemaking stage. Typesetting and electronic publishing systems are increasingly incorporating sophisticated colour handling and separation features. Some of the latest typesetting systems have colour handling features which are practically indistinguishable from the electronic page assembly systems used by colour reprographic houses.

The conventional way of producing these films is for the bromide or film output from the typesetter to be duplicated; a retoucher then carefully masks or paints out with opaquing fluid the image from each film which is not to print in that particular colour, and separate plates are then made for printing. This manual method is very effective when the colour split is simple, with the separate colour images limited in area and well spaced from each other in the page design; the masking out of the unwanted image is then a rapid process. If the colour split entails a large amount of closely registered work with individual words, for example, picked out for emphasis in a second colour within the text, then the facility for automatically generating colour-separated bromides or films direct from the output setter can prove very cost- and time-effective.

A copy-editor or designer marks on the typescript, or on a set of proofs, the items to appear in the different colours of the job, and the keyboard operator flags these items with start and finish delimiters; the program then translates these markers into instructions for the imagesetter to output separate pieces of page film, each carrying only the image required to print in that specific colour. At the page make-up stage, any rules, borders, tints and register marks can be added to the different separations and the film output can then be ready for platemaking without the need for any intermediate manual work.

If the designer is working with a direct input page make-up system, such as many desktop publishing programs, then the colour of any page element, including text, rules and tints can be specified on-screen. The better DTP programs give a choice between spot and process colour separations – for example, if red is to be printed as a separate colour, then this can be specified as a spot colour separation, but if the job is to be printed in the four-colour process, then red needs to be defined as a combination of yellow and magenta elements. Some systems also allow the designer to specify colours from common reference sources such as the Pantone Marking System, with the choice of outputting these as spot colours or as automatically defined process colour references.

When this facility is used, special proofing arrangements are normally required: a conventional 'all in one' proof is needed for normal reading purposes, while a second, separated proof must be checked to ensure that the colour split has been correctly performed. Some laser printers can be used to produce shades of grey to indicate colours; lower cost colour page printers can also provide useful proofs so long as absolute colour fidelity is not required.

TYPOGRAPHICAL REFINEMENTS

Most manufacturers of typesetting systems offer software options which allow variations to the standard typography produced by the system. The burgeoning PostScript type and graphics software market has also produced specialist type manipulation programs.

Automatic kerning programs enable the space between certain pairs of character to be reduced to prevent the appearance of loose fitting; 'To', 'Aw' and 'Wa' are typical examples of the awkward combination of letters which can be adjusted with this software. The program holds in memory a record of all the particular combinations of characters between which space is to be tightened, and the amounts by which this is to be done, expressed in units of set width; this figure differs for each kerning pair in each typeface, and also varies in proportion to the body size of the type. When the automatic kerning program is invoked, the computer searches the text for these combinations and reduces the space between the characters accordingly; this occurs before the text is hyphenated and justified.

To away ATA KG

To away ATA KG

Text set with and without automatic kerning between specified characters.

The overall character-fit of a particular piece of text can also be altered by using the program to either add or remove space in fractions of a unit between all characters; this gives the setting an overall tighter or looser appearance, and is described by the terms 'track adjustment' or 'character compensation'. Such flexibility can prove useful when previously set copy must be matched exactly for correction lines.

A further option, a vertical justification facility, allows the left-hand edges of lines to be optically, rather than mechanically, aligned, compensating for the design features of individual characters.

The general tendency in most modern phototypesetting systems is to set more tightly than was usual with hot-metal type, and the manufacturer's 'normal' spacing may as a result already be quite closely fitted. To complicate the issue further, different typesetting systems all have their own preferred 'standard' values. Text designed for reading in short 'takes' can in general tolerate tighter character-fitting and word-spacing without readability being affected than can type meant for continuous reading; the individual typeface design, and the size and measure in which it is used, are also important. If the standard character-fit of a typeface is to be altered from the norm, specimen setting in the correct face, size and measure should be checked in advance so that the visual effect of the changes can be properly assessed.

The fonts used with desktop publishing systems are coded with default kerning values. Some DTP programs can override these values, and it is in turn possible for the operator to override the DTP values, either on-screen or by re-setting the kerning tables. Where this facility is not available, there are specialist programs which can modify the fonts' own kerning pair values – examples are Letraset's LetraFont, Altsys' Fontographer and URW's various Ikarus versions.

Critical setting of small amounts of text, such as required for display setting, can be achieved with great accuracy by using some graphics programs such as Adobe Illustrator, or type manipulation programs such as Letraset LetraStudio or Brøderbund TypeStyler.

DATABASES

The term database is often loosely used to describe any file of information which is held by a computer in such a form that it can be retrieved and/or corrected. With modern typesetting systems and the availability of cheap storage facilities most data will be held in this way by the typesetter for at least a short period of time, but this does not imply that the information can be treated as a database.

A database consists of a store of related information structured in such a way that it can be interrogated, sorted and processed to create alternative or amended versions of the stored data. Thus the text of a novel that may be held on disk and can be corrected and reformatted for output as a paperback edition is not a database, and is more properly described as a datafile; a holiday guide that gives information about different geographical areas, hotel facilities, sporting activities, price lists and contact addresses would probably best be constructed as a true database, to allow the rapid updating of the various elements (prices, addresses, etc.) or production of spin-off publications (by local area, price range, etc.). Catalogues, directories, timetables, price listings and parts lists are all prime examples of potential database applications. Information is structured by category in records, each containing different fields (e.g. names, addresses, telephone numbers, prices); information can then be updated or sorted automatically by reference to its record or field position within the database.

The creation of a database for typesetting is a specialist task, involving computing power separate from that of a typesetting system, and there are as a result a limited number of suppliers experienced in this field.

The typesetting of a database may, if the job is to be newly created with publication in printed form as a specific objective, involve the planning of the database structure itself or may require the adaptation for typesetting of an existing structure. Databases are often held on computer by the organisations responsible for the data, who may themselves take on the task of updating it prior to typesetting: in these circumstances, the typesetter must be consulted to ensure complete compatibility of the magnetic medium on which the data is to be supplied. This may be reel-to-reel magnetic tape, for which a specification needs to be agreed to include recording density, block sizes, record lengths and coding structures (ASCII, EBCDIC or ISO). Input may, however, also be via floppy disks or via keyboards from hard copy supplied.

When planning a database, it is essential to have the fixed objective of using it to publish certain specified information in an agreed form; if these aims are not clearly defined and planned at the outset, the incomplete or incorrect structure of the resultant database may severely limit its value and prove expensive to correct at a later stage. It is usually helpful to discuss plans in advance with a typesetter well-practised in database manipulation, in order to benefit from other people's experience. Once the structure is decided, the bulk data can be captured by the typesetter, who may well subcontract this part of the job to one of the many bureaux which specialise in database coding and structuring. The updating process thereafter is a less onerous task, and maximum flexibility and accuracy of information is achieved if this can be performed by the publisher's own staff; disks or tapes containing the updated information can be supplied to the typesetter for automatic integration into the master files. If the publisher has no facilities or prefers not to get involved in this part of the production cycle, a decision must be taken about the frequency with which takes of corrections and revisions should be supplied to the typesetter; random updating with information corrected as it changes, will prove very expensive but corrections should not be allowed to accumulate beyond the point where the extent of the re-keying jeopardises the integrity of the database: a compromise must be reached somewhere between the two extremes.

Data processing is required to manipulate the information in such a way that different elements of the data can be combined, selected or extracted according to predetermined specifications. Programs to incorporate these routines are designed or adapted from existing software by the typesetter and individually tested for errors before being run as a complete suite of programs; included in this software is the typographical formatting of the text and page layout. Specimen runs of pages should be checked in advance until absolutely correct, not only for data manipulation routines but also for typographic style.

The advantages of a computerised database are enormous. The structured nature of the information allows corrections and updates to be made more economically than with conventional rekeyboarding and make-up techniques, and the ease of revision allows schedule-critical publications such as catalogues and listings to be as accurate as possible on date of issue. Spin-off products can be created by the selective extraction and re-ordering of information from a limited number of records, giving added value to the stored data; in addition, the information may be suitable for publication in non-print orientated media, like on-line databases or CD-ROM. For these reasons, the information should ideally always be held in neutral form – that is, independent of any coding specific to the typesetting system; field codings should be distinct from typesetting commands, allowing the latter to be stripped out of the data if necessary without destroying the database structure. The database can then be supplied on magnetic tape in a neutral form acceptable to other computers for reformatting as required.

Neutrality of the database also provides its owner with the insurance of being able to remove it from any particular typesetter if necessary, preventing him from getting locked in to one supplier. The contract between publisher and typesetter should emphasise this requirement. For typographically demanding work, it may also include an obligation for the typesetter to maintain, during the life of the contract, specific typefaces or levels of typographic quality.

The security and insurance of a database are of prime importance. The publisher should make clear who accepts responsibility for the security of the information and, if this is the typesetter, should ensure that adequate measures are taken; charges for these arrangements should be quoted and agreed in advance. Most typesetters operate a security system that includes the regular backing-up of data, so that any information lost due to computer crashes or other accidents is limited in scale.

A copy of the data should be held in fireproof conditions at a location separate from the typesetter's premises, and should be updated at regular intervals; sometimes a third copy of the data can be held by the publishing company.

The data should be periodically examined for any possible deterioration of the magnetic media, and copied onto new disks or tapes as necessary; the typesetter should perform this function as part of the normal security and safety checks.

These measures may sound rather drastic, but they are a small price to pay to avoid the corruption or potential loss of the entire database. More detailed information concerning the responsibilities of the typesetter can be found in the booklet *Customs of the Trade for the Manufacture of Books*, issued by the BPIF.

ARCHIVED FILES

It is easy to be seduced by a technology that allows data to be so easily stored and re-accessed into adopting this 'smart' solution for every job, regardless of suitability. Many straightforward typesetting jobs do not, however, need to be held in any form other than the film stored at the printer and a well-documented production file, while even those jobs which at first sight seem to be prime candidates for archiving and retrieval may sometimes be just as simply, and more cheaply, handled in more mundane ways. Before deciding on the method of storage to be used for any file of data, it is important to decide exactly what, if any, future use is expected for the information and to what extent it will be rewritten or updated; remember, in this context, that simple statements like '5% update' can be interpreted, according to the degree of cynicism at work, as the resetting of every twentieth page or the correction of every twentieth word; the '5%' figure will be the same in each case, but the resetting costs certainly will not be! Before placing a job which requires periodic updates with any typesetter, check that it can handle these updates to the file in the required way.

Most typeset work is written to disk by the typesetter as a matter of course, and stored for a limited period of time before being discarded. Any special instructions regarding the archiving of data must be made clear when the job is keyboarded, so that corrections made after proofreading may be included on the stored job. By definition, most ephemeral setting does not need keeping in any form once the camera-ready copy has been turned into film by the printer. Much straightforward typesetting falls into the same category; if there is no re-use for the data planned at the outset, it is pointless to incur the storage charges which the typesetter will levy once the standard period of free storage has expired. It is worth considering, however, that modern front-end systems store typographical formats of jobs in such a way that they can readily be changed to allow the text to be output in different forms; paperback, large-print or luxury editions of a novel for example can all be created from a single file by changing the format strings which govern typeface, size, interlinear space and measure. To control which jobs should be disposed of or kept in storage, some form of checklist of titles is needed, and should be regularly reviewed by the publisher's editorial and production staff.

Information which is to be updated and published at regular intervals can be handled in a variety of ways, depending on the anticipated level of correction. At the one extreme, the update level may be so great that the job, although intended for repeated publication, cannot economically be archived and re-accessed for correction at all, but demands a complete new setting for each edition. The point at which this becomes necessary will vary for each particular job, but as a general rule once corrections affect 40% of the 'ennage' of the total job it will probably prove more economic to start again and re-key the work, using the amended edition as setting copy. This may allow a typesetter with a less sophisticated and therefore cheaper system to be used, thus further complicating the economic equation.

At the other extreme, the corrections may be so light that they make the accessing, correcting and re-output of complete new pages unacceptably expensive; no-one (except perhaps an unscrupulous typesetter!) will be happy with a situation where a job has to be called from memory, scrolled, edited and output as a complete new page of bromide or film merely to accommodate a change to a single figure or word. It makes better economic sense to handle such minor corrections as patches and paste them into the original camera-ready copy. This method works well until the camera-ready copy starts to show signs of age, at which point it will need replacing by a complete re-keying and re-proofreading process; the expense of this operation may well affect the economic viability of the edition which has to bear these costs. One alternative solution is to choose a typesetting system which allows files to be edited and updated while limiting output to only those lines or areas of the file defined by the operator; typesetting costs are minimised, but the integrity of the data file is guaranteed, and new camera-ready copy can be produced as required without any additional keyboarding costs.

Between these two extremes lie correction levels which enable the storing of jobs on file to be economically justified; for projects where regular and moderate updates to existing material are required, the concept of a data file which can be accessed, edited and selectively re-output will prove both economically and administratively worthwhile.

PAGINATION

Most front-end systems offer some kind of facility for transforming files of text into pages before output to the proofing or typesetting device, but the complexity of work that can be handled and the ease and speed with which the pagination process is performed varies from system to system. In the most basic pagination processes, an operator calls up the files of text onto the screen of an editing terminal and counts off the requisite lines per page, using the cursor to enter page-break commands at the appropriate point, while more powerful systems allow blocks of type, illustrations and other graphic elements to be displayed and moved freely around the screen. Desktop publishing systems generally fall under the latter category.

Manufacturers of composition front-end systems have historically and for very good reasons approached pagination from two different angles. Long documents with some overall regularity of style and page layout, such as journals, non-illustrated books and directories, are most effectively and economically handled by automatic or 'batch' processing; interactive area-layout programs are designed for the creation on screen of pages with individual design requirements, as in brochures, newspapers, magazines and heavily illustrated books. An easy way to appreciate the difference between the two is to consider automatic methods as splitting files *down* into page, and the interactive approach as making individual elements *up* into page. The most sophisticated pagination systems combine the best features of both automatic and interactive processes into very flexible and powerful systems capable of handling both styles of layout within a single document.

Automatic pagination

Manual cut-and-paste techniques, using bromide paper or film output from the typesetter, were for a long time the accepted way of converting galleys of text into page form. Although manual pagination may seem laborious, experienced paste-up artists can work at quite high speeds if the setting and page design allows. Even today, paste-up can still prove faster than interactive electronic page assembly, particularly for one-off jobs. Electronic assembly comes into its own for lengthy batch pagination, and for regular, highly structured pages such as newspapers and magazines, where it is worth setting up many of the commonly used page features in advance.

With complicated jobs, the pages are often laid out initially by a designer or artist cutting and pasting up photocopies of proofs, who will take responsibility for solving any page-break problems. These page layouts or 'dummies' will be followed by the paste-up artist to produce high quality camera-ready pages using bromide originals. In-house use of composition systems cuts out the dummy and paste-up stages, and allows the artist to produce final pages ready for output as a whole.

There are many kinds of work for which manual make-up is the preferred approach, either because the job is too short to justify the use of an automatic program, or for reasons of pure economics: many small typesetting companies, handling a mix of different work, find it cheaper to employ versatile paste-up artists than to invest heavily in the computer hardware and software required for automatic pagination, and can offer publishers compelling economic arguments in favour of manual paste-up! There are therefore few firm rules about the viability of automatic processing: many typesetting establishments use a mixture of computerised and manual methods, according to the requirements of individual jobs. But when a suitable job is handled by a powerful and effective automatic program, the speed of throughput can be very impressive.

In an automatic batch pagination program, all the rules for page make-up of a job are defined in advance and input into the computer; the text is then processed against this pagination specification and, provided that the program has sufficient flexibility to compose all pages within the set parameters, the job is paged completely automatically. The pagination rules are derived from the publisher's or designer's specification for the appearance of the page, together with a set of parameters which allows the program the flexibility to adjust certain elements of the page as required to achieve a fit. This might include the ability to re-hyphenate and justify blocks of text to save or make lines or to alter the spacing between certain items. It is essential that the system be allowed some flexibility of this sort in the program to enable it to handle pages, or groups of pages, which cannot be composed within the limits of a rigid specification.

To set up a batch pagination program, the design specification is entered into the computer via a menu on the screen of a terminal; the following outline shows the elements of page design covered by the System 400 from Miles 33, one of the most comprehensive automatic pagination programs.

Page dimensions

The operator defines the standard page layout, including page depth, number of columns (if more than one) and measure, width of gutter in multi-column work, width of column for side-notes, position of running heads and feet, and any 'reserved areas' (e.g. for later insertion of illustrations).

Choice of positions

These specifications cover the automatic position of tables or illustrations on the page, whether they are actually present in the file or treated as reserved 'windows' of space into which the illustrations will later be manually stripped.

Tables and illustrations may be placed at the top, bottom, or centre of a column, or in *situ* where referenced in the text.

The system can be instructed to leave an area of white space for an illustration or to define position by a ruled box, and can include captions or reference numbers to identify the illustration.

Tables may be allowed to break at the foot of a column or page, in which case the box and headings are automatically repeated at the top of the next column.

Footnotes can appear in single column or straddle multiple columns; long footnotes break automatically over to the next page. Footnote reference characters can be defined in order of hierarchy (superior figures or signs *, †, ‡, §, etc.). The space between footnotes and text can be defined, with or without the use of a rule.

Side-notes may be positioned as shoulder notes, adjacent to the text references, and can be aligned on either the ascenders or baseline of the text, on either side of the page.

Running heads and feet

A standard text, for example the title or chapter title of a book, may be specified for recto and verso pages. Alternatively, text may be extracted from each individual page to form dictionary style running heads or feet; this text might be the first or last heading or headword that appears on the page when the job is paginated. If required, the copy can be abbreviated, capitalised, italicised or set in a completely different typographic style to the main text.

Continuation headings can be automatically generated from the text to appear at the top or foot of the page.

Folios are automatically generated in sequence, to appear in the style and position specified.

Page-break control

Widow, orphan and *stump* lines can be avoided if so specified.

Headings can be defined to have a minimum number of lines of text appearing beneath them before the foot of a page or column, or above them at the top of a page or column.

'No-break' areas can be designated to prevent any specified blocks of text (tables, mathematical equations or verses of poetry) being split at a column or page boundary.

Short pages can be specified to include a minimum number of lines of text at the head of the page (e.g. at the end of chapters).

To assist with the fitting of text into any specified page design, the system can be programmed to vary the amount of vertical space between different elements of the page in any of the following positions.

- ☐ Between illustrations or tables and text or captions.
- ☐ Between footnotes and text.
- ☐ Between paragraphs.
- ☐ Between lines of text in equal increments.
- ☐ Over the total page of depth.
- ☐ Wherever white space exists in the page.

For each of these possibilities, a series of increasing values, coded from 1 to 10, can be set by the operator, acting on the publisher's instructions, to create a hierarchy of preferences describing those places where space may be allowed to vary from the original design specification. Higher values are set for those areas where space can acceptably be changed, and a value of 0 if used to define options which are absolutely forbidden. The resulting table of preferences is described by Miles 33 as a 'Tries Table' and is automatically brought into operation by the pagination program to solve problem pages.

Great care should be taken by the publisher in specifying the design of pages for automatic pagination processes and in trying to foresee the possible consequences for pagination of the various features of the design. Individual jobs may all bring their own particular requirements, but some basic preferences can usually be summarised in a house-style document to avoid having to repeat them for every job (with the risk of forgetting a crucial one!).

The least obtrusive area in which to allow extra space to fall is usually around illustrations, between footnotes and text, and on either side of headings; space should be increased proportionally above and below headings or captions, and not in units of equal value, to maintain the position and status of these elements relative to the surrounding text.

Overall page depths are conventionally allowed to fall one line short or long, as long as the facing pages of a spread are treated equally, and always bearing in mind the opacity of the paper on which the job will eventually be printed.

In quality bookwork, vertical justification of pages by increasing or reducing space between every line is usually avoided as the overall colour of the page is affected by what is in effect a change to the interlinear spacing.

Other automatic pagination programs control page design by the use of similar menus or job plans, with a series of min/max values defined for certain variables in a preferred order; the specification for the Miles 33 PENS pagination program lists 62 elements which can be controlled by the operator, and which default to standard values if not otherwise specified. Overall sets of parameters can be stored as page styles on most systems for recall as and when required for similar jobs.

If none of the variations allowed under the job's pagination specification permit an acceptable page break to be made, most batch programs can resort to re-hyphenation and re-justification of the text on the page to try to save or force a line, and thus facilitate a different break point for the page. Miles 33 PENS systems, for example, can employ up to 16 sets of variable spacing parameters in a defined sequence to adjust the spacing within a page. Another option instructs the program to review a certain number of previously composed pages to find alternative breaks on these pages, and thus allow an acceptable break on the problem page.

Automatic processing of this kind is extremely fast (less than two seconds per page for simple work with the Miles 33 System 400) and very economical for long documents with consistent page styles. Book and journal publishing are prime market areas for automatic pagination systems.

When jobs consist of a collection of highly individual pages or contain a large number of integrated illustrations, even the most powerful batch programs cannot, however, always offer a total solution; some degree of interactive intervention into the automatically processed sequence of pages is necessary. Before the 'combination approach' adapted by some modern systems is discussed, it is important to consider the applications and operation of interactive make-up terminals.

Interactive area make-up

Interactive page assembly programs are by definition more flexible than batch pagination. With interactive processing, the operator is involved in the detailed layout of individual areas or pages. As the operator plans each page at a layout terminal, the computer calculates and displays the results of the decisions on a monitor. A lot of repetitive tasks can be avoided by setting up 'master pages' which contain commonly used elements. Items suitable for incorporation in master pages would be: the page size itself; the main text area (which might be divided up into columns if necessary); folios; running heads; outer rules and boxes; and crop marks. Different master pages can be created and called up as necessary: for instance, master pages for a magazine may be set up as news and feature styles, in a choice of single right, single left or facing double-page spreads. Styles for text attributes can also be created in advance and stored: for instance the typeface, point size, leading, and h&j characteristics could all be stored under the single word 'text' and called up as required. Other candidates would be different headline styles, captions, footnotes and so on.

Interactive make-up implies the use of terminals with screens which display, in as close a form as possible to the final output, all the typographic and graphic elements of the page. To show an exact replica of every difficult typeface in its true size and correct position requires considerable processing power; the screen is driven, like a low-resolution imagesetter, as a raster device, with a bitmap of pixels drawn on the screen to create the image. The acronym coined to describe such screen displays is WYSIWYG (What You See Is What You Get); the screen image shows real type, with every detail of the typeface, size and position exactly as it will be produced by the output recorder. Many dedicated composition systems and virtually all desktop publishing systems have provision for WYSIWYG display. Originally this took the form of a separate preview function, and sometimes required an additional computer and screen to the main text entry and editing terminal. Another variation on the theme is the split-screen terminal, where text is edited in monospaced characters with embedded typographic commands in one half of the screen, and displayed in real fonts and with codes suppressed in the other, as with the Compugraphic Power View 5 terminal.

Many current systems work in WYSIWYG mode permanently, letting the operator work constantly with an on-screen prediction of the finished appearance of the page. Text is displayed in the actual typeface and size in which it is formatted, with command codes suppressed; any typeface held on the system can be represented faithfully, together with all accents, signs and logos and pi characters. Any editing changes to the text are displayed 'in real time', with simultaneous re-hyphenation and re-justification as necessary. Slanted, condensed, expanded and kerned type can be created interactively on the screen, and point size, measure, interlinear space and indents can all be increased or decreased to fit layouts.

The operator generally defines the boundaries of the page, and the position of all type and graphics, by means of a puck or mouse on a graphics tablet connected to the terminal. Moving the mouse causes the cursor to describe the same movements on the screen; functions can be selected from on-screen menus by the use of buttons or keys on the mouse. Irregular shapes can be drawn freehand on the tablet and type flowed in to fill the shapes, or positioned in blocks by the plotting of x/y co-ordinates.

Some screens have high resolutions of about 100 pixels per inch, which allows type to be clearly legible in sizes as small as 7pt. Standard microcomputers generally have lower quality screens – the popular Apple Macintosh has 72 pixels to the inch – but any area can

A WYSIWYG screen showing all page components including photographs. This is from the DPS-Typecraft PageSpeed *newspaper software, on an Apple Macintosh II.*

be enlarged for ease of viewing, or reduced to allow a better overview of the entire layout. Some programs offer the facility to display small type in block form, rather than real type fonts; this reduces the processing required and gives faster repainting times. Grid sheets created by the operator can be overlaid on the page as an exact check of the position accuracy of the layout, and the area in view on the monitor may be scrolled in any direction to allow easy access to any specific place on the page; this facility is needed for make-up of large areas, such as newspaper broadsheet pages. Rules, boxes and other shapes can be created on the screen, while any previously digitised graphics may be called up from memory and included in the layout.

The aim of WYSIWYG displays is to allow operators to compose pages of complex text on screen and check the accuracy of their work before outputting it to proofing or setting devices; time and materials can both be saved if the operator can be confident of results before the page leaves the system. Codeless page assembly systems, coupled with WYSIWYG displays, also provide greater ease of use to newcomers to composition, who do not need to learn complex codes.

In newspaper composition these electronic layout terminals are seen as a solution to the problem of tight deadlines and the need to have a fully digital version of the paper for transmission to geographically remote printing plants. Complete pages of text and illustrations, including display advertisements, may be assembled at high speed, with final editing and copyfitting adjustments made on the layout screen and, after approval by the editor, sent as complete composed pages for proofing, setting or digital transmission without the need for any further manual intervention. Magazines also have many of these requirements and can also take advantage of electronic page assembly.

Whether these displays are easier for trained operators to work with than conventional screens which show typographic coding embedded in the text probably depends on the preferences of the individual operator and the purpose for which the terminal is used. The influence of desktop publishing systems with codeless WYSIWYG displays is increasingly felt by the typesetting industry. However, once the initial learning curve is surmounted, most operators grow frustrated with a completely codeless operation, because the action of selecting menus with a mouse can be much slower than making a couple of keystrokes; many programs now offer keyboard equivalents or 'shortcuts' which can optionally be used in place of the mouse.

Automatic or interactive?

Of the two methods described, automatic pagination is apparently more attractive in principle, since the work is performed at high speed by computer without the need for intervention by an operator. Fully automatic processing is only really feasible, however, if the job is of a sufficient size and of a sufficiently repetitive nature to allow the benefits of computerised processing to be realised; any work which has traditionally required the services of a skilled designer to handle the layout of individual pages is likely to prove beyond the scope of a batch program. If such jobs need to be handled automatically because of the high volume of pages or the tight production schedule involved, many unacceptable pages may be produced by the system; the 'no-break' nature of illustrations may detach references from the pictures, force them out of sequence or create pages that simply cannot be composed within the parameters set for the page design. These errors will not become apparent until the pages are proofed out, at which stage changes must be made either to the copy, the position of illustration references or the pagination program rules in an attempt to solve the problems. The job must then be re-run through pagination, causing delays to the schedule and extra processing costs; there is also no guarantee that the corrections made will not cause pages which were composed successfully on the first run to be broken in an unacceptable way on the second pass. This 'ripple pattern' is a common effect of pagination programs that rely completely on automatic processing, although some programs can be set to limit ripple effects to a few pages.

The more sophisticated pagination systems such as Xyvision or Miles 33 Oasys overcome this inflexibility by including some means of interactive facility. These systems can be used to compose exception pages which are recognised as lying beyond the scope of the automatic program, and for which it is simply not cost-effective to try and establish formatting. The interactive facility is also needed to incorporate changes made to the work after proofing and checking, due either to editorial revises or to unacceptable pagination. In both systems, the operator can call up any specific pages to the screen; changes to text or layout on these pages can be made and displayed in real time on the screen, with automatic re-hyphenation and re-justification. Once the operator is satisfied that the page is correct, the page or sequence of pages to be recomposed can be defined to the system, limiting the repagination process to a specific area of the job, and thus eliminating the danger of a ripple effect. The Xyvision system can define this recomposition area as a page, column, paragraph or even a single line, as necessary. No new errors can be introduced into previously approved pages, and proofing, reading and setting times and costs are all reduced.

Manual make-up

Although automatic pagination programs and interactive page make-up terminals are increasingly common within typesetting systems, many kinds of work are still made up into page by hand; the typesetting machine produces galleys of text on film or paper, which are assembled into page form with other text elements such as headings, folios and footnotes, and any line or tone illustrations required. For straightforward work such as non-illustrated books, the paste-up artist follows a basic page-layout specification like those used in automatic pagination processing; more complex make-up may require individual layouts to be supplied by the designer, using proofs pasted up onto pre-printed grids of the page.

Manual make-up can be performed with either film or paper; most typesetting machines have the flexibility to output negative or positive film, or bromide paper.

Illustrations can be either conventional film negatives or positive, or paper prints, depending on the quality demanded by the final printed job.

Film make-up, although more expensive than paper, has traditionally been considered to give a higher quality of final printed image: not only does film have greater resolving power than conventional bromide paper, giving a crisper edge to the image, but the actual output from the typesetting system is used for platemaking. Pages made up in bromide paper require an additional camera stage to produce films for platemaking, with the consequent risk of further loss of definition. This is especially relevant for jobs with illustrations of critical quality, where as few intermediary stages as possible should be allowed to intervene between the original illustration and the final image printed on paper. There are, in addition, limitations to the tonal range which can be achieved with paper prints of screened halftone illustrations.

These issues are just as relevant to electronic make-up as manual methods. But the advantages which paper make-up offers in speed of assembly and low material costs have led to its predominance in manual page make-up of both text-only and illustrated work; film make-up is increasingly confined to the insertion of high quality, often colour, illustrations into pages of text which have been assembled in paper and shot to a one-piece film.

Film

Films used in typesetting hold the exposed image in an emulsion on one side of a thin carrier film; the emulsions have high photographic speed and contrast to ensure a dense, black image with clearly defined edges. To maintain image sharpness, films must always be used during contacting or platemaking processes with the emulsion in contact with the surface to which the image is being transferred: failure to do this may cause the image to be slightly thickened or thinned by the light passing through the thickness of the carrier film between the emulsion and the contact surface. Occasionally it may however be necessary to intentionally 'shoot through the back', as the operation is known, and if it is done with care, type and line work should not be affected; halftone quality will, however, be noticeably degraded, and this process should never be used for illustrated work.

Film is always specified by the way the image reads relative to the emulsion surface. For printing by offset lithography, film must be wrong-reading emulsion-up; when the emulsion is facing upwards, the image is laterally reversed (right-reading emulsion-down specifies the same film). This is so that the film, when laid in contact, emulsion-down, with the printing plate, will produce a right-reading image; this will be transferred to wrong-reading on the blanket of the printing press, and offset to a right-reading image on the printed paper:

Image on film (right-reading emulsion-down)
↓
Image on plate
↓
Image on blanket
↓
Image on paper

For letterpress blockmaking (including photopolymer plates), and the uncommon direct-litho process in which no offset blanket is used, the film image must be wrong-reading emulsion-down to produce a wrong-reading block or plate; which prints a right-reading image directly onto the paper.

These considerations apply equally to positive or negative film. Note that terms such as 'right-reading' only have relevance when the position of the emulsion is also specified.

Wrong-reading film is also sometimes called reverse-reading, but this can lead to confusion when written abbreviations, such as r/r e/d or w/r e/u, are in use, and the term wrong-reading is therefore preferable.

Positive film is easier to work with than negative, since a black image on a transparent background enables the make-up artist to control the visual positioning of all the elements of a page very accurately and rapidly. In manual film make-up, positive working is therefore normal where large numbers of different text elements or illustrations are to be combined on the page, and, for the same reasons, for process colour reproduction work. This holds true for most printers in the United Kingdom, Europe and the Far East, but in the USA even four-colour work is invariably made up in negative form, and the specifications of any film to be supplied to American publishers or printers should therefore be carefully checked.

Where film make-up of type into page form is used, the various pieces of film are assembled on a carrier sheet of acetate or polyester, using pressure-sensitive tape or transparent cement. The make-up artist works over a film grid of the page layout taped onto a lightbox, registering the page elements against this master. As the final emulsion surface of the film must be flat, and exposed, to ensure a good contact with the printing plate, make-up is done in wrong-reading form, with the emulsion upwards. As an alternative, to protect the emulsion from the risk of accidental damage and to allow the artist to work in right-reading form, the films can be assembled emulsion-down onto a thin carrier film using a low-tack adhesive; once make-up is complete, a heavier and permanent carrier film is applied with high-tack adhesive to the top, non-emulsion side of the assembly, and the thin carrier peeled away, leaving the emulsion side of the film exposed.

When films are duplicated, emulsion to emulsion contact is essential to maintain image quality, and this process reverses the original image; contacting a right-reading emulsion-down positive to emulsion-up negative film produces a right-reading emulsion-up (or wrong-reading emulsion-down) negative.

To produce an exact duplicate of a film, two contact stages are normally required. To produce a duplicate set of r/r e/d positives, for example:

Original r/r e/d pos

↓

Contact to r/r e/u neg (same as w/r e/d neg)

↓

Contact to w/r e/u pos (same as r/r e/d pos)

Duplicating films for supply to American publishers and printers can be more complicated due to their use of negative film, and special duplicating (auto-reversal) film may be required.

Proofing of film assemblies is by the *diazo* process, producing contact ammonia prints called ozalids, blueprints or dyelines. Positive films are today often proofed on normal photocopiers. The image definition of such proofs is not high, and they cannot be used to check quality of reproduction, but only the accurate positioning of elements on the page. Cut lines and film-edge lines from the assembly process often show on ozalid and photocopy proofs as hairlines surrounding the individual pieces of film; in most cases these burn out and are lost during the platemaking process, but as a precaution it is wise to ring these marks on the proof or issue a general instruction to the printer to remove any surviving lines from the plate at the start of the press run, something which can be done easily with a special deletion pencil.

Paper

Two kinds of paper used in phototypesetting are described by the generic term bromide paper: *resin-coated paper* (RC) is a high quality material with a high-speed emulsion for conventional processing; *stabilisation paper* contains its own development agent within the emulsion, and is processed by being passed successively through an activator and stabiliser solution. Although the less expensive of the two, the image stability of this paper is not as high as that of RC paper, and the image can fade or discolour with time; it is therefore confined to use for ephemeral, short turn-round work.

Setting produced by strike-on composition methods should be on a recommended proprietary paper, or baryta paper, for best results. Baryta paper is also suitable for new work produced by repro pulls from metal type.

Make-up in paper is carried out by pasting the various elements of the page into position on grids pre-printed with details of the layout in non-reproducible 'litho' blue; when the assembled page is photographed for platemaking, the grid lines are not reproduced. An alternative method involves the use of a master grid taped onto a lightbox, as for film assemblies, with make-up on plain paper sheets on top of this. The adhesives used to fix elements in position include rubber-based adhesives such as Cow Gum, aerosol spray adhesives or, most commonly, wax.

Any correction lines are simply pasted over the original setting; these corrections are set and processed at a different time to the original text, and it is important that the density of image is an exact match. This is normally easy to assess from a careful examination of the made-up pages; any patches which stand out as lighter or darker than surrounding text must be replaced at this stage by lines of a matching density. It is too late to correct differences in density once the camera-ready copy has been shot to film for platemaking.

The accurate positioning of correction patches can be checked more easily at a proofing stage than on the final camera-ready copy, when the different surface levels of the text can hide such defects as bowed, slanting or badly spaced correction lines.

Paper is less dimensionally stable than film, and corrections are easier to handle and position accurately if they are set as patches of two or three lines rather than as single-line strips.

Line illustrations for paper make-up are produced as photographic prints or photomechanical transfers, scaled to the correct size and pasted into the camera-ready copy. Quality considerations determine how halftone illustrations are handled: where average reproduction quality is acceptable, as for instance in jobs where the illustrations are few in number or incidental to the main text, the cheapest method is to produce the halftones as screened photomechanical transfers and paste these into the text for one-shot reproduction of the camera-ready copy. This also applies to pages produced on electronic assembly systems: it is often quicker and cheaper to leave holes for conventionally produced halftones than to invest in the expensive electronic scanners needed to add photographs electronically.

To create a photomechanical transfer (PMT), the illustration original is exposed in the camera to a special negative paper, which is then processed in contact with a receiving paper in a PMT processor; after about 30 seconds the sandwich of papers is peeled apart to give a positive paper print of the original. The chemistry used is of the stabilisation type and so the image will in time deteriorate; no repeat prints can be made from the paper negative, and retouching is not possible. For line illustrations, however, the process produces a perfectly adequate and cheap sized print of an original.

Photomechanical transfers of continuous-tone illustrations involve the use of a halftone screen in the camera; this should not be finer than a 120 line per inch ruling. When pasted into the camera-ready copy of type and line work for reproduction, the screened print is reproduced 'dot-to-dot', with each individual halftone dot photographed as a tiny line image; screens finer than 120 lines produce prints with dots which in the highlight areas of the illustration disappear to white, and in the shadow areas fill in to solid blacks during this process. The best results are achieved from originals with a wide but even tonal range, and with low contrast; even so, the tonal range possible with the PMT process is relatively short, giving a final printed image with a generally flat appearance. Some printers include in their promotional material printed examples showing comparative results achieved by conventional film and PMT processing, and these can be a very useful guide.

When higher-quality reproduction of continuous-tone illustrations is required, the originals are converted to screened film negatives. Blocks of opaque red or black film are laid in the appropriate size and correct position in the camera-ready copy of the text, and when the page is photographed these produce transparent windows in the text negative into which the illustration negatives are stripped with adhesive tape. The page film is then ready for platemaking. This method is more expensive than the PMT process but the reproduction of illustrations is of a far higher quality, and it is therefore the conventional way of producing films for highly illustrated pages.

Proofs of paper make-up are normally produced by photocopying, and any cut lines which show on these proofs around correction patches usually disappear when the assembled page is shot to negative. If the PMT process has been used for illustrations, these will appear in the page proofs. Where illustrations are to be handled by conventional film methods, an extra ozalid proof stage will be necessary after the illustration negatives have been stripped into the text, as a check that they have been correctly inserted.

The approved camera-ready copy should be handled carefully, especially if it has been heavily corrected, to minimise the risk of correction patches becoming dislodged. When sent to the printer for reproduction, and when stored after use, camera-ready copy should be packed between stiff protective boards.

Paper make-up offers considerable advantages over film assembly in the low cost of materials, speed of make-up, and ease of proofing. It is now the most common method of manual page make-up for all monochrome work, even when a high standard of illustration reproduction is required, combining ease of make-up for text elements with the reproduction quality of conventional film techniques for illustrations. A final advantage of paper make-up is that very late corrections, provided that they do not entail new setting, can be handled in the publisher's own office; all that is required is a scalpel, a pot of glue, and a steady hand!

PROOFING

The stage at which first proofs of typesetting are required by a publisher depends to a large extent on the complexity of the job. Straightforward book work, such as fiction, is now normally proofed only after pagination, so that one stage of proofs suffices for the correction of literal errors introduced by the keyboarder, the checking of line-endings created by the hyphenation and justification program and the approval of page breaks; the assumption is that after proofing no major editing charges will be made which might necessitate expensive and time-consuming repagination.

Book and magazine work with large numbers of illustrations may need to be proofed first in galley form, so that any corrections which might affect the final extent of the text can be incorporated before the designer or paste-up artist starts to integrate text and illustrations on the page layouts. The complexity of design and the importance of the relative position of text and illustrations on the page are deciding factors in whether to work with galleys or to save time in the schedule by going straight to page.

In most cases, text is hyphenated and justified before proofs are supplied: the h&j routine can affect the extent of a job by making or saving lines, and it is in any event preferable to check, and if necessary correct, any unacceptable line breaks at the earliest, and therefore cheapest, proofing stage. An exception to this general rule might be when a large database work is being compiled over an extended timetable, with heavy updating expected during its production cycle; to read for hyphenation and justification when the copy will in all probability change before the text is in its final form is an extravagant use of a proofreader's time, and it might be preferable in this situation to check early proofs in an unjustified form.

After corrections have been made, unless these were very light, revised proofs are usually necessary. Sometimes these can be combined with the page make-up stage, so that the first page proofs are also checked for the revisions made to the galleys.

Facsimile transmission of late corrections is widely used by both typesetters and publishers to save the time and expense of couriers for urgent proofs; late amendments made to a completed job can be proofed out via fax for telephone approval or correction by return fax before the film or camera-ready copy is released from the typesetter.

Where the client supplies fully made-up pages on disk to the typesetter, then the client will normally have performed all proofing in-house before releasing the page files. The client should nevertheless request to see either the actual output or a photocopy proof of it, as errors due to incompatibilities between front and back end are by no means unknown. Very detailed proof-reading of the final output is not required, as such errors usually manifest themselves very obviously as missing lines at the end of pages and headlines, or wrong fonts.

Proofing methods

In metal composition, proofs are taken from the actual type which will print the final job, and are corrected by hand after reading. Many phototypeset jobs can be handled in a similar way, with proofs taken from the same image that will print the final job. Bromide output from the phototypesetter is photocopied to provide sets of proofs, and when these are returned, any minor corrections are set separately and manually stripped in to the original setting. Heavier corrections are edited into the job file, and the relevant sections are sent for a second pass through the typesetting machine to produce a new and clean image. Both these correction methods are potentially expensive because they use phototypesetter time and costly photographic materials to create what is essentially a proof image which may well be heavily corrected; there may also be considerable administrative costs involved in the copying and collation of these sets of photocopied proofs. Developments in proofing methods have therefore been concentrated on the search for systems which will provide economic bulk copies without the use of phototypesetter time and materials.

Monitors

It is theoretically possible to proof-read text on screen, editing corrections into the copy in the same operation. Experience shows, however, that this is a slow and inefficient process, giving far less accurate results than conventional hard copy proofing methods.

Line printers

Line printers have traditionally been used by typesetting companies to produce listing of control and validation data for their own internal use. The typographic styles and layouts which can be represented are limited, and the low image quality of the proofs compared to photocopied bromide means that these proofs are rarely suitable for reading by editors and authors. Line-printer proofs are sometimes used, however, when the basic requirements is for a simple list of data without any attempt at simulated typography, as for example in the compilation of database information.

Laser printers

Laser printers combine the potential for full typographic flexibility with the advantage of relatively high speeds and the economy of plain paper proofing, and have become the most common form of non-impact printer used in typesetting. Laser printers work on electrostatic principles, with the image created by a laser beam scanned by a rotating polygonal mirror across the surface of an electrically charged drum. This scanning beam is modulated by digital data to produce a change in the charge on the drum's surface corresponding to the image/non-image information encoded in the data. The image is then printed onto paper by conventional Xerographic means: a resinous powder is applied to the image areas, which is then transferred to paper and fused by heat.

Laser printers can use their own in-built electronics to call type from fonts loaded down into the printer from plug-in cartridges, or from floppy or hard disks. When driven by a raster image processor, they are capable of recreating any image of text and graphics fed to them as a bitmap by the front-end system, enabling proofs with line illustrations and screened graphics to be produced in a low-resolution simulation of the page to be output.

If the composition process uses the PostScript page description language, then a PostScript compatible laser printer can use the same fonts as the final output unit. If the laser printer is linked to a non-PostScript system with a typesetter manufacturer's proprietary fonts, then special versions of these fonts may be needed for the printer – some imagesetter RIPs can be configured to drive a laser printer as well as the film recorder. If these facilities are not available, then it is sometimes possible to use the typesetter's character width and h&j information with a similar-looking font within the laser printer; this gives accurate line endings, but not a completely accurate preview of the final page or galley.

60pt 36pt 24pt

18pt 14pt 12pt 10pt 8pt 6pt 4.5pt

This book is set in 10/12pt Times

Times Italic **Times Bold** ***Times Bold Italic***

Rockwell Light **Rockwell Bold**

Optima Medium ***Goudy Heavyface Italic***

Plantin *Plantin Italic* **Plantin Bold**

Bembo *Bembo Italic* **Bembo Bold**

Baskerville *Baskerville Italic* **Baskerville Bold**

Century Schoolbook *Century Schoolbook Italic*

Eras Ultra Bold **Franklin Gothic Demi**

☆ ☆ ☆ ★ ★ ★ □ □ □ ■ ■ ■

☞ ☏ ✂------------✂ ☎ ☛

Sample laser printer output. In the larger sizes the ragged edges of the curved strokes of characters may be visible, although the printing quality associated with small offset lithography and uncoated paper may disguise these defects to some degree. Note the 'pseudo font' for Goudy Heavyface Italic which is represented by Goudy Heavyface character widths but by a Times sloped roman face.

Most laser printers are geared to producing A4-size output, and while this is acceptable for much general typesetting work, newspapers in particular require larger formats. Laser printers capable of A3 output are growing more common, but are still comparatively expensive. Laser printers and photocopiers up to A1 size are available for very specialised requirements such as map and chart making.

The majority of laser printers use one of a limited number of printer 'engines', such as the Canon or Ricoh devices, and despite 'badge-engineering' to make them appear part of an integrated typesetting system, are therefore very similar in basic capability. It is the controlling systems such as the RIP, the RAM capacity and the hard disk (if fitted) that provide the main difference between laser printers from different suppliers.

Eight to ten copies per minute is a typical rated speed for an A4 300 dpi printer. This speed assumes that all sheets are copies of the same master page, composed predominantly of text; if every single sheet is completely different, and therefore has to be recomposed by the raster image processor, speeds can fall to as low as two per minute, while pages including screened graphics may require several minutes to compute. Once the relevant bitmap has been processed, multiple copies of the page follow at the rated speed.

Laser printers can be used in a variety of different ways. As plain proofing devices, they offer considerable economies to the typesetter because they use plain paper, require no chemicals or processing time and avoid tying up the typesetting machine in proofing passes, freeing it instead for production of final output. A busy typesetting establishment might recoup the cost of a laser printer in under a year through the savings on materials alone.

The resolution of most laser printers is currently limited to 300 dots per inch, compared to the 1000 dpi and over used by typesetting machines outputting text and line only, and the even greater resolutions necessary for output of halftone illustrations. This low resolution shows in the slightly fuzzy appearance of text printed from a laser-proofing device. This means that standard laser printers are not particularly suitable for quality typesetting. They are acceptable for lower quality setting, such as small newspapers (where the absorbency of ink by the newsprint tends to hide the jagged edges) and ephemeral setting. Laser printers can be used for 'emergency' setting (such as last minute corrections) for higher quality applications: by printing out at three or four times the required final size and reducing this on a camera, the resolution is effectively increased to normal typesetter levels.

Specialised laser printers are now available with 400, 600 800 and even 1,200 dpi. Combined with special hard-coated papers, the result is almost as good as that of typesetter bromide output at similar resolutions. However, the nature of the toner powder imaging method of laser printers means that film and bromide output will continue to produce a sharper result for the foreseeable future. Tint and halftone reproduction is very poor even on the highest resolution laser printers for the same reason.

The larger and more powerful laser printers can be used for on-demand printing. Individual copies of documents can in theory be produced at the same unit cost as single copies from a large print run and unlike conventional lithographic printing there are no penalties for the production of small quantities. Some high volume laser printers can now produce collated, wire-stitched books, and can be used with low-cost perfect binding machines to produce good-looking publications. Xerox has introduced a fully integrated publishing system, the DocuTech, which incorporates a 600 dpi scanner/OCR, a fast 600 dpi A3 laser printer, and powerful software which allows untrained users to set up styles and formats for complete bound publications. This all fits in a single cabinet about the same size as a conventional high volume photocopier.

Benefits of short-run printing to publishers include the ability to produce limited numbers of high-value books at a time, or to test the market for a new product by publishing a small number of sample copies of a work; there are also serious proposals to set up methods of printing specialised publications on-demand at facilities like university libraries, by accessing data held on centralised databases. In all cases the publisher avoids the risk of tying up capital in warehouse stocks.

Every single copy produced by a laser printer can be an original, recomposed in a different form by the image processor prior to transfer to paper. This facility can be exploited to provide high-speed overprinting or personalisation of documents for such applications as banking, security printing and mailing shots. When fed with data from a mainframe computer, high volume laser printers, like the Xerox 9700, can produce a series of unique documents in this way at speeds of up to 120 double-sided sheets per minute.

For general informational publishing, where quality of appearance is less important than speed and cost of production, laser-printer output can be used as camera-ready copy for subsequent printing by small-offset lithography. As with newspapers, the limited resolution of the laser-proofed image will probably be disguised to some extent by the use of paper plates and uncoated paper, and the justified setting and potential variety of typefaces will give a finished appearance superior to the alternatives of typewriter or IBM composer setting. Alternatively, the laser output can itself be treated as an original 'published' document.

Driven by typesetting software running on a microcomputer, the laser printer forms a vital part of the desktop publishing systems which exploded onto the scene in 1986, and which enable professionally finished documents to be created quickly, cheaply and without the need for any traditional typesetting expertise. Desktop publishing systems will be discussed in more detail in Chapter Eight.

Other printing devices

Despite their recent leap in popularity, laser printers are not the only form of non-impact printer suitable for the bulk proofing of typeset copy, and it is worth mentioning developments in some alternative technologies..

Some printers use linear arrays of light-emitting diodes as their imaging system, thus avoiding the potential problems associated with the precision movements of laser systems.

IBM produced a printer called the 4250 in the 1980s which used electro-erosion techniques; the writing head created a current above the image areas on a paper coated at the base with black ink beneath a surface of aluminium; in the image areas, the aluminium is vaporised, leaving an image in black against a silver background. Other materials were available, including one which created a negative or positive on clear film, and one which could act as a lithographic printing plate. Resolution was good at 600 dpi and the printer used fonts licensed from Monotype. IBM was working on higher resolutions and PostScript capability until it dropped the project in 1989, and it only ever saw use in IBM computer installations, on the periphery of typesetting.

Electro-erosion technology looks likely to live on however, as it is the basis of a lithographic printing plate imaging system developed by the US manufacturer Presstek and licensed to the German printing press manufacturer Heidelberg. The Presstek system erodes an aluminium coating to expose a polyester layer which attracts ink to form the image area of the plate. Its first application is in a revolutionary four-colour version of the Heidelberg GTO press, which can accept PostScript page files and image them onto plates fitted directly to the press.

Several other technologies are used on high-speed printers for computing applications. These include magnetography, in which rows of tiny pin-point recording heads are selectively magnetised by digital data to create an image area to which magnetic toner adheres, and ion deposition, in which an electrically charged image attracts conductive toner; in both cases the image is fused to paper by the application of heat. These processes are very expensive, and are so far limited to use in high-volume banking and mailing installations.

Ink-jet printers generate images by firing minute droplets of ink in rapid succession between electrically charged plates, which, controlled by data from a computer, deflect the droplets to build up an image on the paper. From early, very crude applications, such as food packaging and newspaper bingo, ink-jet printing is now being rapidly refined into a process capable of resolutions of up to 250 and 350 dpi, which makes it suitable for printers attached to personal computers. Desktop ink-jet printers currently cost around half to two thirds of the price of equivalent-sized laser printers, and have much lower consumable costs throughout their lifetime as the ink is much cheaper than the expensive toner/drum cartridge of laser printers. Some of the highest quality colour ink jet printers, such as the products of Stork and Iris which use the Hertz head technology, produce results good enough to act as digital proofing devices for colour repro uses.

Colour thermal printers are growing increasingly popular. These deposit coloured ink in several passes from a moving ribbon: heated wire elements are used to transfer the ink from the ribbon to the paper in image areas. Some of these printers use just three process colours (yellow, magenta and cyan), while the better quality models also use a black ink. Thermal printers on the market so far have a resolution of 300 dpi and many are based on Mitsubishi-built A4 and A3 'engines'. They are good enough for positional and general colour proofing, but their poor colour fidelity and halftone handling makes them unsuited to high quality repro proofing. They are, however, well suited to producing very small quantities of posters and fliers.

Two other promising new colour printer technologies are dye sublimation and thermal wax deposition. Dye sublimation produces a smooth mix of colours on the printed surface, and is suited to near-photographic results – it was initially used in printers for video systems and electronic cameras. There are now models available to link to personal computers, some with PostScript interpreters. Thermal wax deposition projects a melted pellet of coloured wax ink at the paper which solidifies to give a very dense image. The quality is higher than thermal printing, but not as good as dye sublimation and the best ink jets.

Colour laser printers have taken a surprisingly long time to appear. Those that exist so far have all been based on digital colour photocopiers, which are in effect made up of a flatbed scanner bolted on top of a colour laser printer. The most widely used at present are the Canon Colour Laser Copier 300 and 500 models, which can be fitted with a device called the IPU, a memory buffer and interface to external computers. A PostScript RIP is also available. By using special software, computers can access the copier's built-in colour scanner, and can also send colour pages of text and pictures to the four-colour A3 printer unit.

FACSIMILE TRANSMISSION

'Fax' has long been used as a means of transmitting reproduction copies of photographs between newspapers and agencies, but recent developments in resolution and speed, and the introduction of cheaper units, have greatly increased its potential for publishers and typesetters. Facsimile transmission enables images and text to be scanned, transmitted to another location via telephone or communications satellite and printed to recreate a copy of the original. The document to be sent is placed face down on the send unit, which is then connected by telephone to the receiving unit; once the connection has been made, the original is passed over a line of light-sensitive detectors (CCDs), which analyse the light/dark content of successive thin strips of the image. The information from each strip of the original is processed into code for transmission over the telephone lines to the receiving unit, where it is decoded to activate an electrostatic mechanism similar to a photocopier for reproducing the image.

The resolution of fax machines varies, but even the smallest and cheapest units are capable of regenerating images that allow text to be read and simple line illustrations checked. As a result, fax is rapidly becoming established as an essential part of general office communications; it is particularly suited for the transmission of late corrections or final proofs between publishers and typesetters. Fax machines are extremely easy to operate, and the cost of transmission is that of the telephone time taken to send the document; this may average a minute for an A4 page of copy.

Standard office fax machines produce a poor printout due to their relatively crude print technology. It is possible to accept fax transmissions directly into a microcomputer if fitted with a modem and suitable decoder board. This allows the fax message to be displayed on-screen and printed on a laser printer at a higher quality than the normal fax output. It is also possible to use some OCR software with the electronically captured fax, rather than scanning in a printout. The microcomputer fax boards can also be used to transmit pages composed on the computer without having to print them out first.

Specialised high-resolution fax systems can be used to send complete pages of film via telephone line to remote printing plants. Newspapers can centralise their editorial and composition departments in one place but transmit the paper, page by page, to printing works in different parts of the same country, or elsewhere in the world, allowing simultaneous production of the same issue and avoiding the heavy transport costs of printed newspapers.

The high-resolution facsimile transmission units use laser technology to scan the original films or paste-ups, and convert the incoming signals to laser beams to expose films or even plates at the receiving unit; whole pages of integrated text and tone, including colour, can be handled in this manner, with output resolutions giving potential halftone screen values of up to 175 lines per inch. The *Financial Times* and the *Independent* are two of the many newspapers which use forms of facsimile transmission as a normal part of their production processes. Two of the major suppliers of the specialist equipment in this field are Linotype-Hell and Crosfield Electronics.

The increasing use of assembly systems which can incorporate all page elements, including halftones, is allowing pages to be sent directly to the facsimile receivers, with no need to output them to film and scan them at the transmission end. The facsimile receivers therefore act as remote image recorders.

Transmission via communications satellite works on similar principles but is very expensive, and can be justified only for those applications where speed is of utmost importance; these may include the near-simultaneous production of international business magazines in several world-wide locations. Like many communications technologies, the cost of satellite transmission may well reduce sharply in the future.

GRAPHICS SYSTEMS

Composition systems capable of integrating text and images are not new. The basic technology has been available for some years, but at a high cost premium. The problems facing the designers of systems for handling halftone graphics at workable speed and at screen rulings of 133 lines per inch and over have been centred around the huge amount of computer processing power and digital storage capacity required, and the need for output recorders with sufficient precision and resolution. Early systems were designed for use in colour repro houses, which already contained the necessary image handling skills and precision scanning and recording units.

The falling costs of computer power and the development of suitable laser imagesetters has triggered the development of graphics handling systems aimed at typesetters. Traditional typesetter manufacturers have recently introduced graphics systems which can handle colour repro functions to all but the very highest quality levels, for about half the price of purpose-built repro 'EPC' systems. At the lower end, some desktop publishing systems have been developed which can handle halftone photographs, including colour images. The quality levels are still open to question, but it seems clear that the problems will be solved quickly. Alongside the colour handling abilities are commensurate developments in compressing and storing the high volumes of data which are generated by high quality halftones.

The potential benefits of integrated text and tone output are considerable: if pages can be made up on the screens of graphic workstations and output in one piece from the imagesetter, the labour and material costs associated with the manual stripping of illustrations can be eliminated, the number of proof-checking cycles can be reduced and pages can be finalised in digital form for facsimile transmission and exposure to imposed foils or even to printing plates much closer to critical publication deadlines. This last advantage is of particular relevance to newspaper publishers.

Although the technical problems of of lower-cost colour systems seem to have been largely overcome, the human aspects have not. Obtaining printed colour halftones that match the original photograph is a tricky business, and requires skill and experience from trained staff. Obtaining a colour graphics system may prove to be the easiest part of the process; the headaches will come when trying to find operators who can produce satisfactory results.

Another potential use of graphics systems is as a way of storing digitised illustrations for subsequent retrieval and re-use; publishers can build up libraries of graphics from which subjects can be selected for successive different publications without incurring the costs of repeated picture research and re-origination. One picture library service in the USA already uses optical disks to store images for reference in this way, but it is probably newspapers which will be the first to apply the principle in a production environment. Many papers have installed electronic picture desks which store illustrations in digital form, allowing the operator to review images on a display screen, select, scale and crop a chosen picture and send the digital data to another part of the production system. Other possible uses of the technology include the creation of illustration banks by publishers of part-works or educational children's books and the storing of any illustrated work which is to be reissued in a variety of different formats.

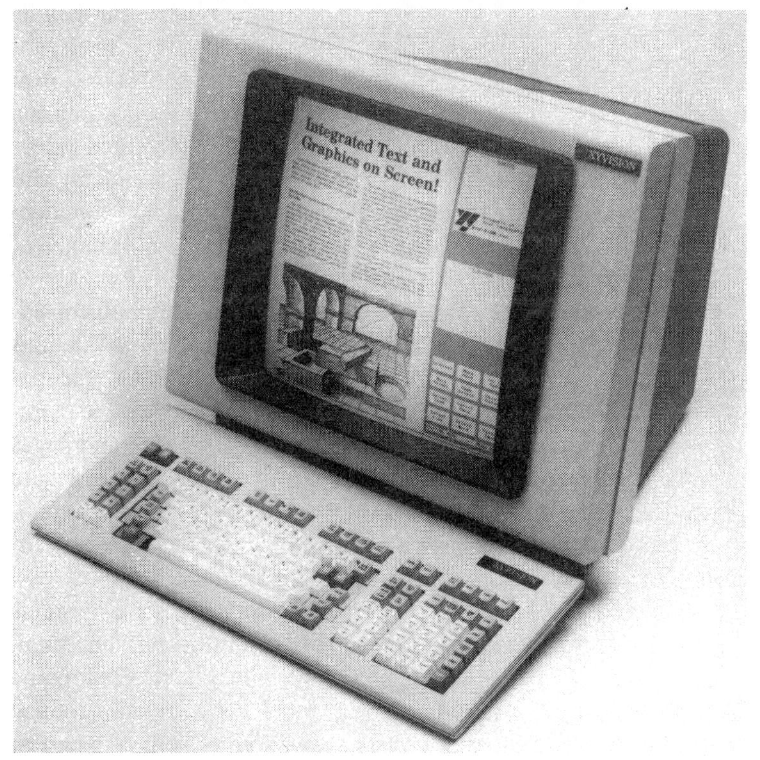

A workstation for the integration of text and graphics; this particular model is controlled from a keyboard.

The basic elements of an integrated text and graphics system are as follows:

1 A scanner to capture line and tone illustrations in digital form, and a typesetting front-end system to supply files of composited text. The scanner may be a colour or monochrome model.

2 High-resolution workstations for the interactive editing of graphics, and the integration of the final image with text files in an electronic page make-up process. The minimum technology for photographic image manipulation is the ability to generate pixels on-screen from 8 bits of information for black and white, and 24 bits for colour. This gives a range of tones which appears continuous to the human eye. Screens which can display photographic results are called *greyscale* monitors. For simple image previewing and placement, full photographic reproduction is not required.

3 Considerable data processing power and computer memory for the manipulation and storage of the information required to hold graphic images in digital form.

4 An imagesetting device of high precision and resolution to output integrated text and tone work at the requisite quality. Particular attention needs to be paid to the film transport mechanism. Some models are prone to stop-start motion which can produce visible banding effects on tints and halftones. Imagesetters to be used for colour tone separations must be capable of repeating multiple separations very accurately, otherwise incurable misregister can occur on the printed results.

Scanners

Just as text processing systems convert words into a digital database, scanners convert continuous-tone and line illustrations into files of digital computer data to form a graphics database; images can be recalled and reconstructed on screen for editing and integrating with text prior to output on film. The device most commonly used to input monochrome illustrations into a graphics system is a flatbed scanner. Originally these were large devices which required skill to operate, made by companies such as Dainippon Screen, Du Pont, Fuji and ECRM (Autokon).

The operator programs the scanner to produce the best possible results for each original by entering the tonal values of the picture and the degree of enlargement or reduction required, along with an identifying number or tag, via a keyboard and display panel. Several models feature on-line densitometers which read the highlight, midtone and shadow densities of the original into the scanner automatically. Controls are set to regulate the degree of sharpness and any special effects which are to be electronically applied. Some scanning stations include a display monitor on which the results of these adjustments to illustrations can be visually assessed. Line illustrations, continuous-tone photographs, pre-screened illustrations and even colour transparencies can all be handled by the most advanced scanners. Scanned images can be exposed to film or bromide paper immediately and used in a manual page assembly operation, or alternatively the image file can be passed to an electronic page assembly system.

These models are still used for high quality applications, but small desktop scanners costing a few thousand pounds are growing in popularity for medium quality applications such as newspapers and even some magazines. Current desktop scanners have resolutions ranging from 300 to 2000 dpi and scanning areas up to A3. They are intended to work in connection to a host microcomputer running special scanning software. The scanner units generally have self calibration and automatic exposure functions, but otherwise rely on the operator to manipulate the scanned image on the computer screen to achieve the correct densities, sharpness and other variables.

Desktop scanners are also available for colour scanning. Despite their manufacturers' claims these are not suitable for high quality repro use yet, although they can produce the so-called 'good-enough' colour. They are also very useful for capturing images which look good on a computer screen and can be used by designers to achieve high quality visual previews. They can also be used in creative graphic arts applications, where an image is to be retouched to the point where the initial colour fidelity is not critical. Small CCD rostrum video cameras are also used for previewing purposes; these are cheaper than flatbed scanners, and an image can be captured instantly rather than taking a couple of minutes, but the image quality is not so good.

For high quality colour work, the big repro drum scanners are unrivalled by desktop scanners. They produce a better density range tthan flatbed scanners, in addition to being highly productive. Lower cost drum input scanners are starting to appear. Designed to work with

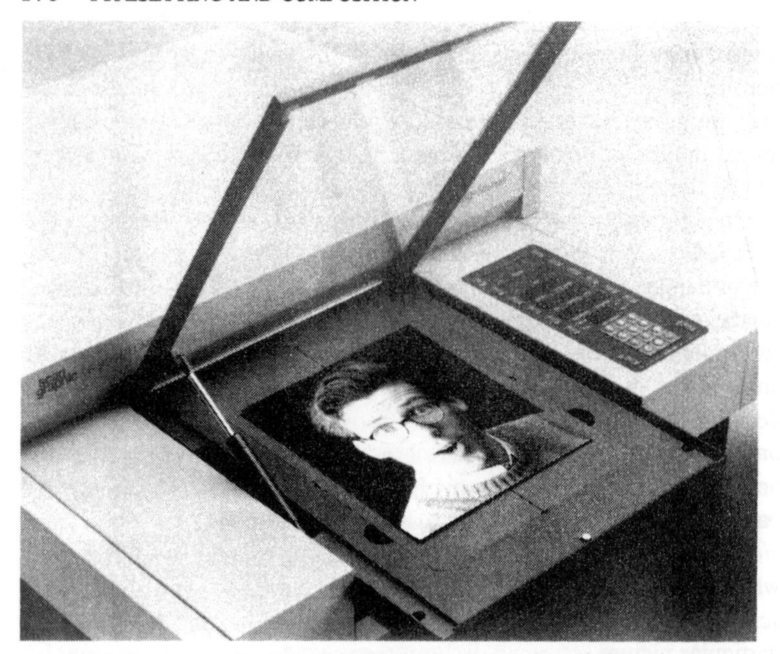

A flatbed scanner for digitising illustrations into a graphics system. The control panel is visible to the right of the copyboard.

PostScript based 'desktop repro' systems, they can send image files to microcomputers through their SCSI ports; these can provide top quality scanning for less than half the price of a traditional graphic arts input/output model. Scitex makes a pair of high quality flatbed scanners called SmartScanner and SmarTwo-PS. These produce high quality images and are very easy to use, although their use of CCD image sensors means that they cannot reproduce the same density range as the photomultiplier based drum scanners.

Graphics workstations

These terminals allow an operator to access digitised line art and halftones from store and perform a full range of creative image-manipulation functions, including cropping, scaling and individual pixel editing, displaying the results of these changes interactively on the screen. They can be configured as separate terminals, or as a software function on a multi-function system. Modern systems, such as the Scangraphic Scantext 2000 Commander and the Xyvision Xygraphix system, tend toward multifunction terminals. Lower cost desktop publishing systems can also be configured as very effective graphics terminals. Most DTP programs include the ability to generate simple geometric shapes and to import scanned and similar graphics from other programs. Text can be flowed around regular and irregular shapes such as cutouts.

On a graphics system or software program, once the illustration has been called up from disk onto the screen, processing is controlled by use of a mouse or a puck with hairline cursor and a number of buttons. Image processing functions usually include the retrieval of images from memory, alterations to the tonal values of the highlight, midtone and shadow densities, adjustments to contrast and freehand editing of details of the illustrations. For editing, a number of on-screen tools are provided, generally including a sharp-edged 'pen', a soft-edged 'paintbrush', and an 'airbrush' which can be set for various levels of transparency and edge feathering. Another useful common function is *pixel cloning,* where a small area of the original image can be copied elsewhere. This is particularly valuable for repairing defects such as scratches in the original image, or for extending backgrounds to fit a particular picture format.

The mouse can also be used to carry out adjustments to the cropping of the illustrations, and, if required to 'cut out' the image from its background by tracing round its contours with the cursor. The effects of all these image-editing processes are displayed in real time on the workstation screen.

When the operator is satisfied with the appearance of the screen image, it can either be returned to store for later retrieval and page make-up elsewhere in the system, or can be integrated with text at the same workstation. The mouse is used to plot the x/y co-ordinates for positioning the various text and illustration elements on the page, and can also describe irregular hand-drawn shapes or trace outlines from artwork on the graphics tablet to define areas into which text is to be flowed; type is shown in WYSIWYG form to allow for accurate positioning of the text and graphic elements. The finalised page can be sent to store, or output via a laser proofer or imagesetter.

There is a great emphasis, perhaps influenced by the demands of the advertising world and the capabilities of full-colour page composition systems, on the retouching and creative editing of illustrations. Impressive though these features certainly are, they may be less relevant to most integrated text and illustration work than the ability to control and administer at high speed the vast amounts of data involved

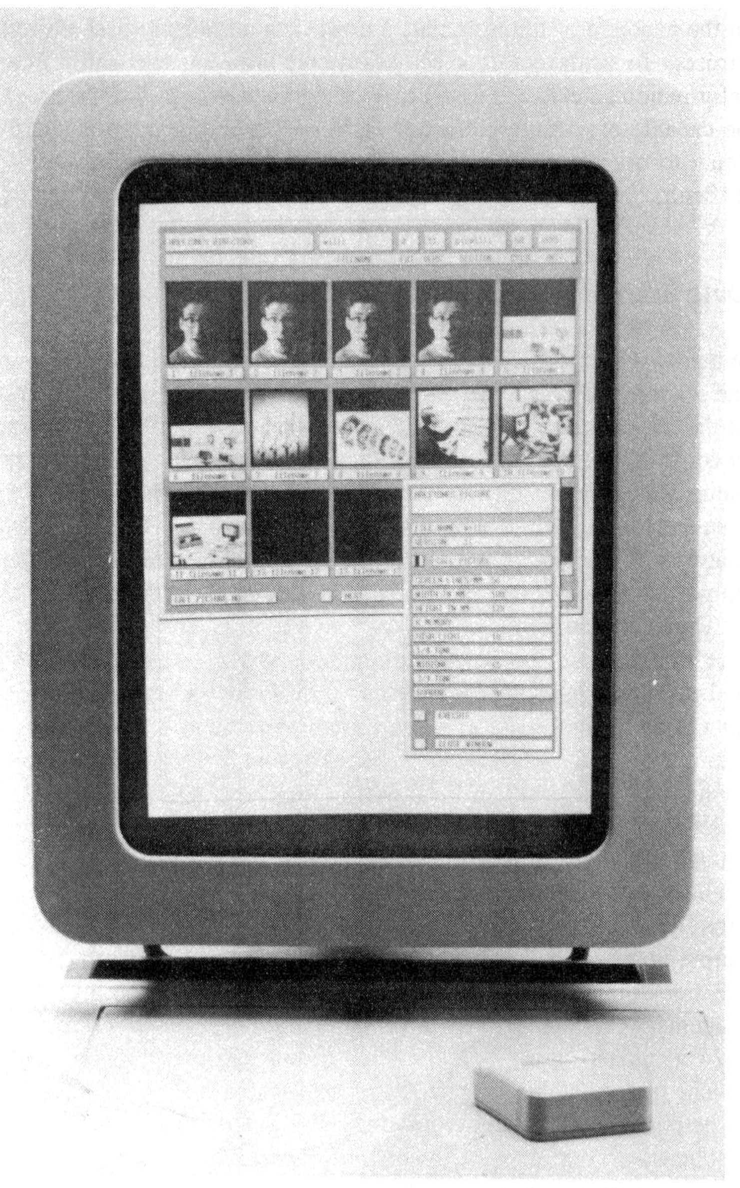

A workstation for the electronic manipulation and editing of digital graphics; the screen is showing a directory of images stored on the system. In the foreground is the mouse used to select options from the menus displayed on the screen.

in the handling of multiple illustrations within the context of a single project. To achieve this successfully, graphics systems must move information quickly and easily between various parts of the system and be capable of sorting and accessing any required data with minimal delay to operating speeds. The amounts of data involved make this difficult.

Data processing and data compression

When an illustration is scanned into a graphics system, the sensors in the scanner detect different degrees of contrast or grey levels in areas of the image, ranging from pure white to solid black. This information is converted into digital form, and each pixel is allocated a numeric value representing the grey level of the corresponding minute image area or sample. Pixels in this context have a different application from that of text display screens or typesetting, where they can represent only black or white, on or off, image or non-image areas.

The quality of image recorded by the scanner depends on two factors; the size and frequency of the scanned samples determines detail and resolution, while the number of digital bits used to quantify the data dictates the number of grey levels which can be recorded. Thus a scanned original is represented by a two dimensional array of pixels, each with a value related to the tonal density of the original at that point. For monochrome images, the pixel is commonly allocated an 8-bit value, giving 256 possible grey levels. Colour images need 256 pixels in each of the three primary additive scanning colours, giving 3×8 bits, commonly called 24-bit colour, to display on a colour screen. For output as colour separations, the red, green and blue additive colours are transformed into the four subtractive process colours (yellow, magenta, cyan, black), which requires an additional 8 bits of storage (32-bit colour).

The frequency of pixels per inch – the resolution of the input scan – is determined by the requirements of the graphics system and the resolution of output required. Practical experience seems to show that an input scan resolution of 300 or even 266 lpi is satisfactory for continuous-tone originals that are to be reproduced, *at the same size*, in a halftone screen ruling of 133 lines per inch, and that a finer input scan resolution does not necessarily improve final image quality; if the original is to be enlarged before output, then the input resolution must be increased to maintain definition, even though the output screen ruling remains the same.

Therefore a monochrome image will require storage space equivalent to 1 byte (8 bits) per pixel, and at a resolution of 266 pixels per inch, every square inch of the final printed image will require 266 × 266 bytes (70.8 k) of storage. Colour images will require four times as much storage to produce the four process colours.

Complex computer algorithms are used to convert the data from the input scan into the form and structure of the screened halftone output dots. The resolution of the imagesetter needs to be at least ten times the value of the halftone screen ruling to achieve a satisfactory quality; to output an acceptable halftone at a screen ruling of 133 lpi, an output recorder must be able to expose the image onto film at about 1500 raster scan lines per inch or more. In practice, film recorders intended for halftone output usually have a minimum of 2000 lines per inch, and the majority of imagesetters on the market can now achieve this resolution.

The volumes of data needed to describe continuous-tone illustrations in digital form vary according to the detail which can be resolved in the final output; images destined for exposure via a laser printer do not require as much data, nor therefore so fine an input scan, as those to be produced via a high-resolution imagesetter. The table below outlines the levels of data required; as a useful comparison to these figures, an A4 page of text might contain approximately 6000 bytes (6 k) of data.

	Laser printer (300 lpi output)		**Imagesetter** (1000 lpi output)	
	Line	*Halftone*	*Line*	*Halftone*
Input scan, lines/inch	300	100	1000	300
Pixels per square inch	90,000	10,000	1,000,000	90,000
No. of bits per pixel (1 [black or white] for line, 8 [2^8 grey levels] for tone)	1	8	1	8
No. of bits per A4 page (100 square inches)	9 million	8 million	100 million	72 million
No. of bytes (=8 bits)	1.1 million	1 million	12.5 million	9 million

Paradoxically, line artwork requires scanning and processing at higher resolution than continuous tone, in order to maintain definition of the line edges; for this reason, halftones input into the system as pre-screened images, in which halftone dots are recognised by the input scanner as individual and minute pieces of line art, require more data than if scanned and processed as continuous tone.

Large volumes of data mean expensive storage, slow access, poor processing speeds and long transmission times. Various techniques of data compression are used to try to reduce the amounts of information involved; the choice of method is determined by the type of images being processed, and the levels of output quality required.

Line artwork can be treated with run length compression techniques: the processor searches for sequences of pixels with identical values (0 or 1), and stores the count of the total value of the row rather than each individual pixel. Thus a row of 16 zeroes could be compressed and stored digitally as 10000, using only 5 bits and reconstituted on output.

For continuous-tone images, one method of data compression simply reduces the number of scanned pixels processed, relying instead on samples of data at minute and regular intervals; in practice, the data discarded is not random information, but data recognised by the processor as redundant. On output the missing data is re-interpolated by the raster image processor, which fills the gaps by intelligent guesswork in relation to the surrounding data. Compression ratios as high as 20:1 can be achieved with this method, although only at the price of some loss of quality; for newspapers and similar applications the compromise may be acceptable.

Several other more complex methods of data compression have been developed, using sophisticated computer algorithms to reduce the amounts of digital information required, and so improve processing and transmission speeds. As faster and more powerful processors become available, new forms of storage are developed and techniques of data compression are improved, the challenges posed by the high speed manipulation of digital graphics will slowly be overcome.

Imagesetters

The different amounts of data required for the processing of an illustration as continuous tone or in pre-screened form mean that halftones are usually screened within the graphics system and not during the input scan.

Screening of halftones may be handled by the raster image processor driving the output recorder which is fed a stream of data describing the image in continuous-tone form, and converts this to screen form 'on the fly' while outputting.

The ideal RIP can also simultaneously accept and process any variation in size, treatment and rotation of type and generate geometric shapes, tints, and patterns from data supplied, building all these different elements into a description of the page before passing it to the output recorder for imaging.

Very powerful and versatile raster image processors are required in graphics systems to perform all these functions at the high speeds required for the output of integrated text and tone pages; if the RIP is not able to keep pace with the speed of the output recorder, the continual starting and stopping of the imagesetter and the consequent interruption to the smooth movement of the film transport mechanism may lead to quality problems in the final film, with bands of varying density appearing; these can be particularly noticeable in halftone images. Some systems screen halftones using a separate processor within the system to try to maintain processing speeds, and some systems maintain dual processors which increase speeds by enabling a RIP to start processing the next page while the previous one is still being output.

The imaging system of an output device designed for graphics requires extreme stability and precision of construction to give the accuracy of output scan necessary for halftones. The polygonal mirror used in many laser imagesetters to scan the beam across the surface of the film must be machined to very fine tolerances, and the spin speed of the mirror and the movement of the film advance mechanism must be rigorously controlled. Various attempts to overcome these restrictions have been made.

Recorders intended for colour separation are built to extra-fine tolerances, with particular attention paid to the film transport during exposure, to ensure dimensional repeatability of the image over four separate exposures. Manufacturers are increasingly using the internal drum type of film recorder for colour, as this holds the film completely still during the entire exposure process.

Examples of internal drum imagesetters are the Agfa SelectSet 5000 (also licensed by Hyphen, Kodak, Monotype and Varityper), the Linotype Linotronic 630, the Purup PE7100 and the Scangraphic 2051 and 2030.

LOGOSCANNERS

Although most manufacturers of typesetting systems hold very extensive libraries of pi characters, new or special symbols may still be required for particular typesetting projects. These can be created as artwork, and pasted into spaces left in the camera-ready copy of the final job, but if the symbols are to be frequently repeated this process can be both laborious and expensive, and it may be preferable to digitise the special symbols into the typesetting system; stored as a series of outlines in the same way as type fonts, they can be sized by software to any required appearing size, and called from memory by a single keystroke. Applications might include company logotypes, trademarks, or symbols for specialist guidebooks and maps; there are great possibilities for designers to add life and variety to typeset work in this way.

Typesetter manufacturers used to supply purpose-built logoscanners which were miniature drum scanners. These have now largely been replaced by standard desktop flatbed scanners. A line image of the symbol to be digitised is scanned from either camera copy or film positive, and the image is displayed on the screen in enlarged form. A range of editing and creative effects can then be applied to the image, using the screen cursor controlled from the keyboard: the symbol may

The Scantext Logoscanner 512, with monitor, graphics tablet and the electronic pencil used for retouching images displayed on the screen.

be condensed, expanded, lightened, emboldened, duplicated, reversed black to white, flipped left to right, rotated, retouched pixel by pixel to clean up or alter its shape, or given outline and three-dimensional effects. Once the image is approved, it can be filed on disk until the job is keyboarded, when it can be accessed by a predefined keystroke.

Similar creative treatment can be applied to any typeface design. The Scantext system allows an operator to call characters to the screen from any font held in the system, and manipulate them on-screen. In this way the design of existing characters can be altered, ligatures can be created for fonts in which they are not supplied as standard, and entirely new typefaces can be invented. Entire libraries of new typefaces based on existing fonts can be created in this way, and stored on disk under new font reference numbers.

Independent software for Macintosh computers is now available to edit and store existing or scanned characters. This includes the Ikarus software from URW, FontStudio from Letraset, and Typographer from Altsys. These can save new characters as part of font sets in the PostScript and TrueType formats: Ikarus will also run on minicomputers and Sun Microsystems workstations, and gives the option of saving in typesetter manufacturers' proprietary formats.

Happy Christmas

A sample of ornamented type created on a logoscanner. The holly pattern was accessed from a decoration held on the typesetting system and used to 'fill' the characters of an outline typeface. The new face was then filed under the name Helvetica Holly.

8 Systems design

There are many different approaches to the design of a modern typesetting system. Some configurations are designed for specific areas of production, and so have particular equipment and run specialist software to cater for a narrowly defined type of work; applications might range from a company inplant unit to a national daily newspaper. Other installations are aimed at a wider mix of straightforward typesetting work, with all-purpose equipment and more flexible software applications.

A typesetting system can vary in size from a single small direct entry phototypesetter to a network of several hundred terminals linked to graphics workstations, digitising scanners and laser imagesetters, The size and purpose of any system determines how the basic functions of text input, editing, data processing and output are performed, but this can also be affected by the particular make of equipment used. Many supplies of composition hardware offer different levels of system aimed at various perceived market areas; as no two views of the market ever completely coincide, it is usually difficult to classify systems into groups of equipment with identical performances. A further complication is that, although some manufacturers offer systems in which all equipment is provided by them as part of an overall package, increasingly the trend is for specialist equipment, such as scanners, laser printers and even software extensions, to be supplied by third parties and incorporated into the configuration around the key elements of the front end; in this instance the manufacturer takes on the role of systems integrator.

Parallel with this move towards modularity of design is the growing tendency to consider the output setter as a slave device, with exposure of the image onto photographic material only one of a number of possibilities for the composed text; other options might include microfilm, on-line database, magnetic tape or compact disk. As the output recorder becomes increasingly divorced from the rest of the system, and is driven in a variety of ways by different front ends, it is becoming more difficult to define a composition system by reference to the output device which it includes.

A further main trend which can be identified in the design of composition systems is the increasing development of typesetting software packages to run on standard personal computers, performing all the composition functions conventionally associated with minicomputer-based systems. The use of standard off-the-shelf machines keeps down the cost of hardware, makes service and after-sale support simple, and also makes available any software running under the same operating system. The IBM PC-AT and its more powerful 386/486 'PC/AT-compatible' and PS/2 successor machines are a popular choice for such typesetting programs. The Apple Macintosh II is particularly popular for both desktop publishing and 'high end' interactive page make-up.

A recent trend has been the falling prices of very powerful RISC technology Unix workstations from companies such as Sun Microsystems, HP-Apollo and Silicon Graphics. These can provide performances significantly in excess of Macintosh and most PC/AT compatibles for the same or only slightly higher prices. Composition and pre-press manufacturers such as Agfa, Berthold, CSI and Scitex have adopted Sun SPARCstation workstations as the basis of powerful graphics systems.

The best composition software designed to run on microcomputers provides all the functions of a dedicated front-end system with very high performance at comparatively low cost. Programs from suppliers such as APT, DPS-Typecraft, Magna, LaserMaker and Talbot Editorial Systems are among the most versatile of this kind. Program features typically include text entry, full editing capabilities, spell checker routines, format libraries for the storage of commonly used keystroke strings, automatic kerning, hyphenation and justification with exception dictionary, and maybe some form of WYSIWYG preview of composed text. Many of these packages also offer page make-up facility although the ease and speed of software, and the degree of flexibility possible in the design of pages vary enormously from one package to another. When edited, the text is composed into a file including the correct commands to drive any one of a wide range of plain-paper laser printers or typesetting devices.

The versatility and user-friendliness of such programs enables small and inexpensive microcomputers to be used as input and editing stations in a professional typesetting environment, with output to a conventional high-resolution typesetting machine.

As desktop publishing systems have improved, so they have been adopted for professional use. QuarkXPress in particular is the basis of systems from several manufacturers, including the Scitex Visionary and Cornerstone colour design systems which can communicate with high end repro systems, and the QED Editorial System for newspapers. A number of third party Quark 'Xtensions' are available which can tailor the characteristics of the main program to suit specific applications, such as newspaper composition or scanner control.

The classification of composition systems has changed radically in the past five years due to the increasing use of direct entry by clients, and as the distinctions between the once separate trades of typesetting and repro become ever more blurred.

The following general categories can, however, still be recognised.

DIRECT-ENTRY SYSTEMS

These machines are no longer made, but many are still in use. In a direct-entry typesetting system the keyboard, monitor, computer and output device are all contained in a single unit. Text is input, edited on the terminal screen, and can then be sent straight to the typesetter unit or, more usually, filed on floppy disk for output at a later stage. The performance of such units is normally quite limited: the microprocessor incorporated into the unit has restricted computing power, and the sorting and sequencing of data may not be possible. Limited storage capacity will probably preclude the merging and updating of complex work, and the hyphenation and justification program may include an exception dictionary of typically no more than a few thousand words. There are limited facilities only for interactive page make-up, and the processing of screened graphics is not supported.

The output unit of direct-entry machines was normally a second-generation device, using negative font masters and photographic principles, but later machines used cathode ray tube technology, and extremely high-quality typography was possible from units such as the Linotype CRTronic.

These systems were designed for the small general typesetting company with a variety of relatively straightforward work, and their main advantage was the low purchase price payable for a complete typesetting

A direct-entry phototypesetter with optional additional keyboards/editing terminals.

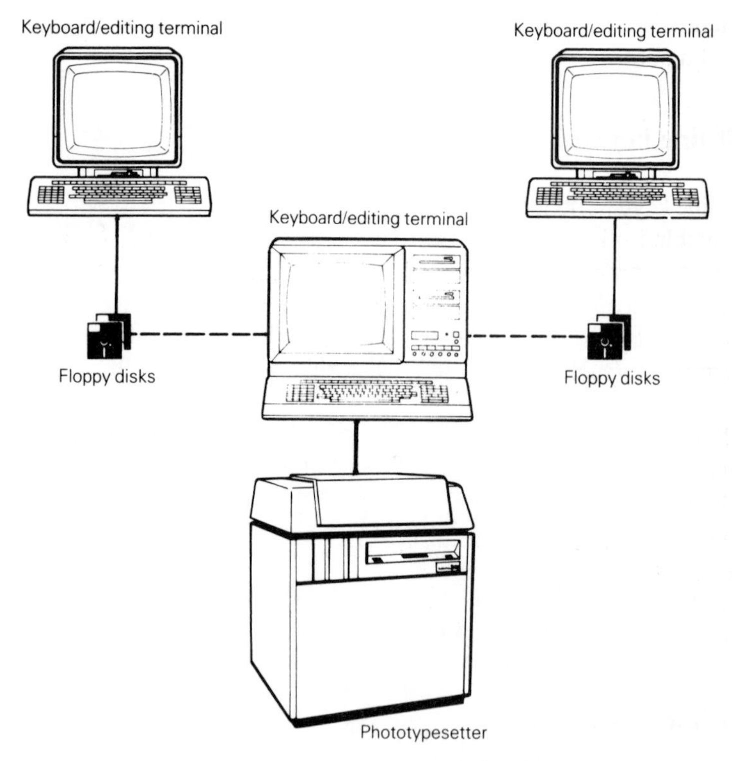

An off-line system: text is stored on floppy disks which are loaded down to an editing terminal to drive the phototypesetter.

installation. Many of these systems can now be expanded by the addition of extra keyboarding and editing terminals, or proofing devices such as laser printers. This avoids the disadvantage of having the output device tied up whenever copy is being keyed or edited, and also allows the typesetting company to expand the size and capabilities of its system as convenient.

DISPERSED SYSTEMS

In this system configuration the component elements of input, editing, computing and output are designed as separate units, not all of which need be physically connected to each other; floppy disk or magnetic tape can be used to transport data between the different units within the system. The most common application of this concept is for the keyboarding of text.

Off-line keyboarding

Off-line keyboarding is used when the nature of the text being captured is suitable for keying on less expensive devices than the system's own interactive terminals; it is often cheaper to input high-volume straightforward text on micro-based terminals and store the keystrokes on floppy disk than to use dedicated input and editing terminals. The keystrokes, which may or may not be typographically formatted at this stage, can then be downloaded into the front-end system for any additional editing and correction, and to be run through hyphenation and justification and pagination routines. Compatibility of floppy disks with the front-end system computer is incorporated by the manufacturer for those terminals which are part of an integrated system; alternatively, word processors can be used to produce ASCII text (with or without embedded codes) onto disks which can be converted to the typesetter's format if necessary.

On-line keyboarding

An on-line system is designed for text to be input at terminals connected directly to the central computer; the operator has real time access to all computer-processing and storage facilities. Keyboarding, hyphenation

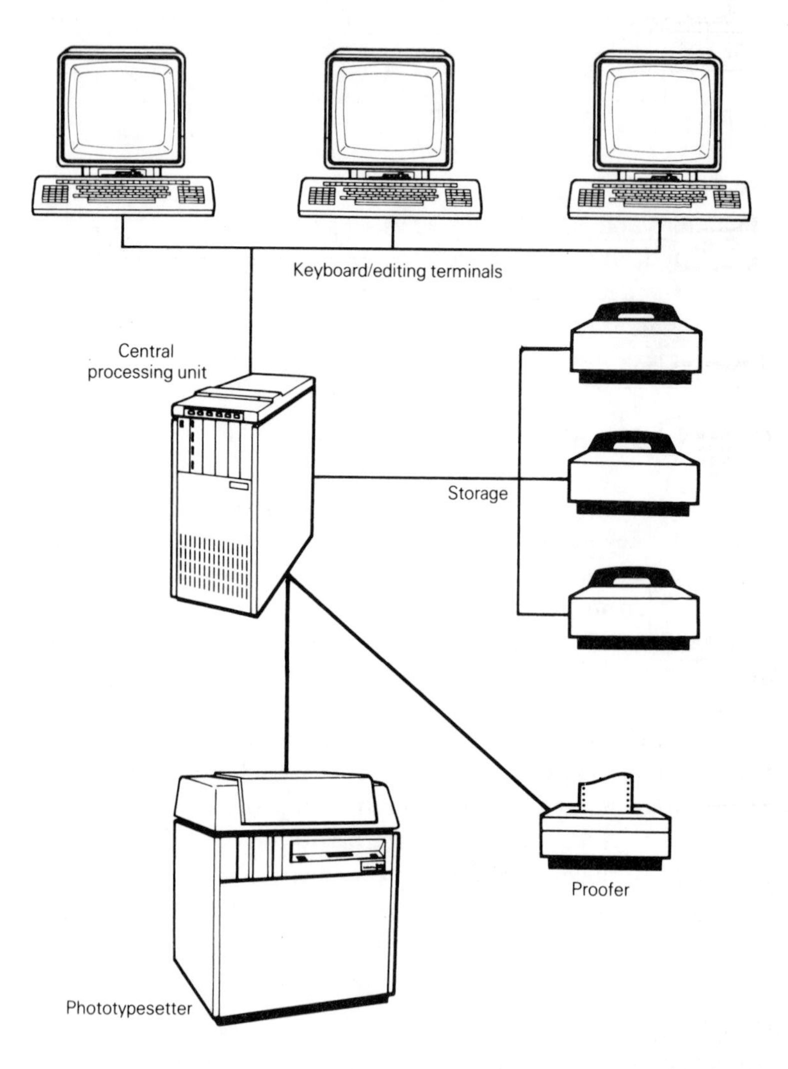

A simple on line system: keyboards have direct access to the central processing unit, and extra storage capacity and a proofing device are included.

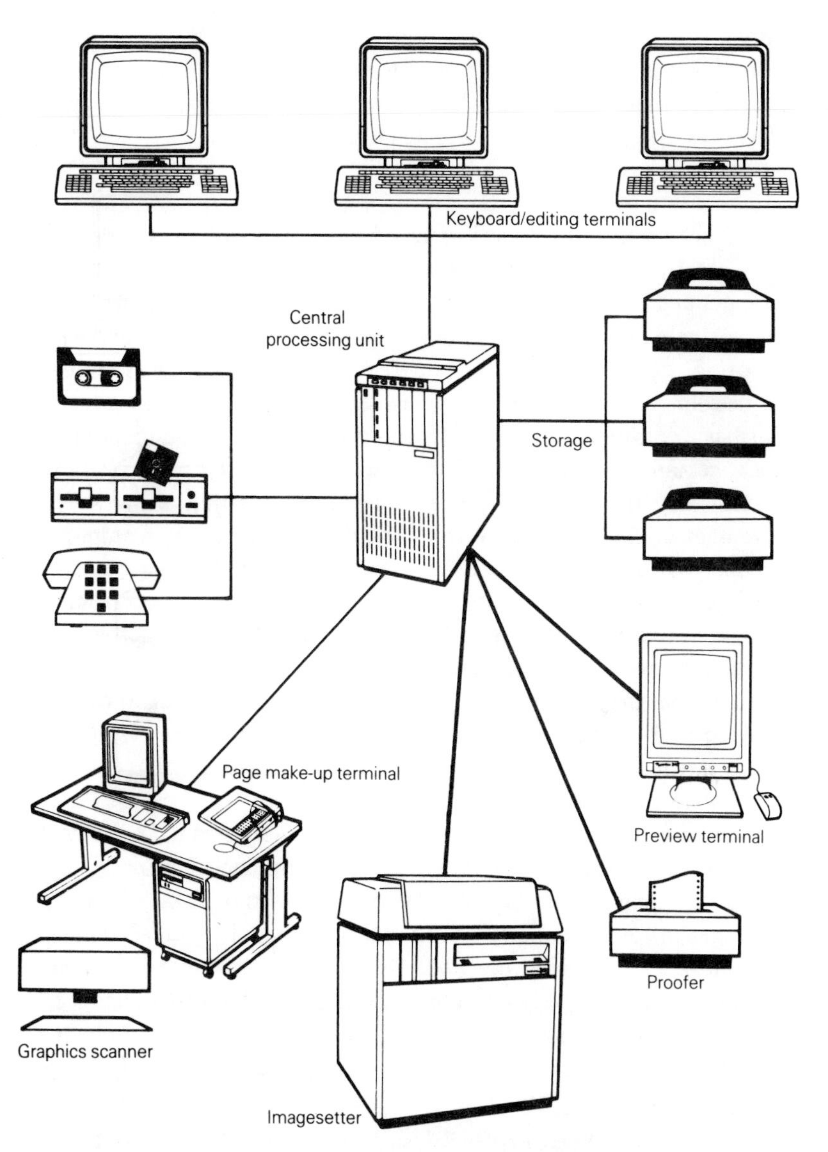

The current 'state of the art': text is input via on-line keyboards or accepted from a variety of external sources. Graphics are digitised into the sysytem and integrated with text at interactive page make-up terminals. Preview terminals and laser printers allow the results to be assessed before work is output via the imagesetter.

and justification and all editing functions are performed interactively, with the results displayed simultaneously on the terminal screen. This application is used for complex types of setting, where the computer's power is needed to assist the operator in making decisions about line lengths or hyphenation, in extensive recall and correction work and in the make-up into pages of integrated text and graphics.

Whether configured for on-line or off-line keyboarding, systems can vary greatly in size. A typical small system might consist of a number of input and editing terminals, a central computer, on-line disk storage and a single output device. In larger systems, a variety of line or laser proofing devices, interactive layout stations, preview terminals, logoscanners, and complete graphics sub-systems may all be added to this basic configuration, together with disk converters and modems for the acceptance of copy from remote sources. The computer operating system may provide multiprocessing capabilities that allow several computer applications to be run concurrently, resulting in improved productivity and throughput. *Multiprocessing or* multitasking systems allow tasks such as automatic pagination or output of a job from the phototypesetters to be performed without interrupting interactive composition at the on-line terminals.

Many on-line systems use 'local area networks' of coaxial cable to provide high-speed links between all the devices in the system; the Miles 33 System 400 can carry up to 128 separate peripherals on a LAN up to a kilometre in length.

The units in such a system may each have their own in-built microcomputer and local storage, with overall system control provided by a central computer or file server; this concept is known as 'distributed intelligence'. A system configured in this way can be increased in size as and when expansion demands the integration of extra terminals, scanners or proofing devices, but without the need to make changes in the basic system design. In addition, functions such as h&j can be performed under a terminal's local intelligence, independently of the central processing unit, and thus without making demands on central computing resources. A further advantage is that, should any part of the overall system fail, the remaining terminals should be unaffected and remain operational.

NEWSPAPER SYSTEMS

Some of the very largest dispersed systems, consisting of several hundred terminals in both off-line and on-line configurations, have been installed by magazine and newspaper publishers. These systems are designed not only for the composition routines associated with conventional typesetting, but also to provide specialist programs for editorial, managerial and financial control – and all at the high speed dictated by critical publication deadlines.

Sophisticated file management techniques are needed for efficient copy-handling functions, which will include the ability to track and record the status of editorial copy throughout the entire system. On-screen directories are used to provide a quick reference to any story held on the system, along with the names of the journalists or editors working on it, the time and date when it was created, its page assignment, and sample lines of text.

As the stories are dummied into page form, the effect of page layout on editorial copy can be monitored and amended as necessary. Full graphics processing of line and halftone illustrations, together with the ability to make up and output integrated pages electronically, may also be supported on the most modern systems, although much newspaper make-up is still currently performed manually by cut-and-paste techniques.

Additional specialist software is required for both the administration and composition of classified advertisements. A typical package will allow advertisers' copy to be entered from a variety of different sources, will automatically check and record the credit status of each particular customer, detail the number of insertions required for the advertisement and pass the relevant information to the accounts department for the automatic generation of invoices. Immediately prior to composition, the program will sort all advertisements at high speed into correct classification and sequence.

The largest newspaper systems also provide complete administrative and financial routines for the paper, compiling statistical reports and management accounts.

The major suppliers of these huge systems in the United Kingdom are Du Pont-Camex (formerly Crosfield Data Systems), Press Computer Systems, ND Comtec, and, above all, Atex.

The market for large systems is limited in size, and the scale of investment required means that most systems, once installed, will have to be paid off over a number of years before being replaced. It is notable that even these large systems increasingly use microcomputers as intelligent terminals, even where centralised computers are still retained for power requirements. Some newspapers with older publishing systems that do not incorporate electronic page assembly are modifying their systems by incorporating extensions to the latest generation of page layout systems on microcomputers.

Not all newspaper publishing operations require systems on such a grand scale, and configurations have been developed for small and medium-sized papers.

One of the most successful micro-based systems is the Mentor package from GB Techniques, which runs on PC/AT compatible computers. Systems can range in size from a single direct-entry terminal to configurations of 200 terminals or more. The systems apply the principle of on-line distributed processing, with all software running in the terminal, improving speed of operation and eliminating any risk of degraded response times at periods of peak use. Different software packages are designed for the functions of simple text entry, editing and copyfitting, control of classified advertisements, and typesetting. Output can be to laser printer, or to a variety of popular typesetting machines.

Much the same philosophy is shown by the DPS-Typecraft newspaper system, which is based on Apple Macintosh computers and a wide range of specialist software. A major user of this system is the London *Evening Standard*, which has pioneered the integration of colour halftones with its micro-based system.

ELECTRONIC PUBLISHING

'Electronic Publishing' is a relatively new term, and can include everything from on-line database publishing using remote terminals to newspaper editorial and production systems. The term is being increasingly adopted to describe the creation of documents using electronic data capture and manipulation for output via either non-impact printers or high-resolution image recorders. This definition aims to distinguish electronic publishing from more traditional typesetting systems, although there is considerable overlap between the two areas and much confusion over the precise terms of the definition.

Within this broad context, 'corporate electronic publishing' describes the use by large commercial organisations of integrated multi-terminal composition systems to produce high-volume documents with integrated text and graphics. A typical configuration consists of a number of workstations grouped around a minicomputer CPU, with an emphasis on the integration of data from different sources, including a range of text processing devices, graphics scanners and computer-assisted design (CAD) workstations. Multitasking system architecture, automatic and interactive make-up facilities and a choice of output devices enable production of documents with fast production schedules and complex revision cycles. Although the hardware configuration of such a system is similar to that of the most advanced commercial typesetting companies, the software is geared to the particular in-house requirements of individual corporations and such systems can be viewed as the very sophisticated successors to in-plant printing departments.

Many such systems have been installed in the USA, with Ford, MacDonnell-Douglas and Boeing among major customers. In the UK the market has been much slower, with ICL's and Westland's purchases of systems from Xyvision being among the few current installations. Other suppliers aiming at this market include Xerox and Interleaf.

At the opposite end of the electronic publishing scale from such corporate systems are desktop publishing systems. These aim at the creation by an individual user of complete documents including graphics, in a user-friendly environment based around personal computers. As these systems continue to grow in sophistication the degree and speed of overlap between desktop publishing and conventional typesetting and printing technology will be of increasing importance to the publishing industry.

DESKTOP PUBLISHING

Although the phrase 'desktop publishing' describes the creation and distribution of documents produced on typesetting equipment small enough to fit on the average office desk, the neatness of the term as a marketing slogan conceals several ambiguities in the concept of what a desktop publishing system actually is, and the applications for which it is suited.

To start with, a definition of 'publishing': when used in the desktop environment, the term covers not the mass production and distribution of information through commercial outlets that the conventional publishing industry understands, but rather the creation of any printed information destined to be read by other people. Desktop publishing can therefore include the production of all kinds of technical, commercial and internal business documentation – manuals, brochures, reports, bulletins, newsletters and even the humble inter-office memo. It can also be used for what are regarded as 'professional' publishing activities, such as the production of books, newspapers and magazines.

Office publishing is not new, and has been performed over the years with a gradually evolving and increasingly sophisticated set of tools. The process of distributing business information had developed from handwriting, via manual, electric and electronic typewriters to the use of word processors coupled to dot matrix or daisy wheel printers, with photocopiers for the production of multiple copies. But until the mid-80s the problem of attractive and professional presentation remained unsolved: word-processing software made it easy to create a clean finished text of a document, but even proportionally spaced output from the most typographically flexible printer is not capable of producing the quality of image needed for many professional applications. Choice of typefaces was very restricted and graphics features extremely limited. Anything for which word-processor quality was not sufficient used to require a phototypesetter, paste-up table, camera, processor, platemaker and small offset press, together with the specialised knowledge to operate this equipment.

What Apple launched as the first desktop publishing system in 1985 (to be quickly followed by a host of other manufacturers) was not therefore a new type of publishing process, but a set of cheap yet sophisticated tools that gave the power to create pages of integrated text and graphics to anyone with access to a small computer. All text composition, editing, graphics manipulation and page make-up functions are performed at the computer, with finished output produced immediately from a laser printer. The user-friendliness of these systems demands no great typographical knowledge or training, with the result that the equipment is being effectively sold to a much wider range of customers than traditional typesetting systems. The factors behind the fast-increasing popularity of desktop systems are both economic and administrative: by retaining control over the keying of the text, creation of graphics, and page make-up, the originator of a document avoids all the costs associated with conventional processes. Some suppliers claim that a desktop publishing system can pay for itself in this way after only a few hundred pages. In addition, any changes to

Interset's Quoin is an advanced typesetting program, here shown running on an Apple Macintosh IIcx.

either text or layout can be made immediately, and reviewed on the computer display screen; once the page is approved, it can be output at once to the laser printer. This output can be used as an original if the total quantity of documents required is small, or for longer print runs the laser output can be treated as camera-ready copy for printing by small offset-lithography. Under special circumstances the disk holding the page information can be transferred to a high-quality imagesetter for output at higher resolution; the desktop system then fulfils the role of a front end, driving an output recorder in slave mode.

Desktop publishing system components

A basic desktop system consists of a personal computer, software for creating text and graphic images and integrating these elements into made-up pages, and a laser printer as output device.

The Apple Macintosh was introduced in 1984 as a graphics-orientated personal computer, with a simple alphanumeric keyboard, and a 9 inch black-on-white screen on which type and images are shown in WYSIWYG form in a bitmapped display at 72 pixels per inch resolution. The user interface is provided by a mouse, which controls the movements of a screen cursor to select options and functions from rows of icons displayed at the edge of the monitor screen; no commands or codes are needed, as the type style, point size, justification mode, interlinear space and all text-editing functions are accessed from these icons with the WYSIWYG display acting as a visual check on the progress of the work. In all aspects of use, the emphasis is on a simplicity of operation that can quickly be assimilated by a non-professional keyboarder. The basic design of the first Macintosh model lives on in the current Classic II machines, though these have substantially more memory and expansion potential than the first model.

The various Macintosh II models, first introduced in 1987 and now available in several shapes and power capacities, were a major step forward in publishing terms. Apart from being substantially more powerful and expandable, they can handle and display up to 32-bit colour, which makes them suitable for professional repro use. Macintosh IIs are also usually favoured for page make-up, as they can be fitted with much larger monitors than the built-in 9 inch model of the Classic SE. Black and white and colour monitors up to 21 inches are available: the latter being suitable to view A3 landscape pages (or a double-page A4 spread) at full-size on the screen. The greater the processing power and RAM capacity of the computer, the faster it can perform alterations to a page. Graphics have the highest power requirements, so users with this requirement usually buy the fastest machine, fitted with as much RAM as they can afford. In 1991 Apple revised its operating system to a new level called System 7.0. Among its improvements is the ability to address virtually unlimited RAM (up to 256 Mb can be fitted internally to some models, and external expansion is possible), and to handle even bigger files by using virtual memory, which uses spare capacity on the hard disk as an additional live memory store. Several Macintoshes can be connected together into multi-user configurations by means of the AppleTalk and other communications networks.

The first desktop publishing system was based on four key items: the Macintosh, the Aldus PageMaker layout software, the Apple LaserWriter laser printer, and the Adobe PostScript page description language. Linotype's far-sighted decision to offer PostScript compatibility for its Linotronic 100 and 300 imagesetters gave desktop publishing an entry point into the high quality typesetting market.

PageMaker has seen major revisions in the years since its introduction, but the essentials remain the same. It is a graphics-oriented page make-up program, designed for the integration of type and illustrations into page, and especially suitable for those pages with a unique design.

The PageMaker software in effect offers a computer simulation of a paste-up artist's drawing board: the user can divide the page according to the required design, displaying a grid of the layout on the screen if needed, and can then position all elements of the page – type, rules, lines, borders and illustrations – by 'clicking' the mouse onto a certain element and dragging it into the correct position. Graphic effects such as tints, patterns and reversals can also be created from options displayed on the screen. The composition abilities of the early version of PageMaker were limited, but the latest version features automatic kerning, automatic hyphenation and justification, a built-in text editor and the ability to handle colour. Facilities for long documents have been added, but PageMaker remains at its best when composing single pages with a relatively loose structure.

The Apple LaserWriter is the device which made desktop publishing a reality. Before the introduction of this sophisticated electronic printer, output from a personal computer was either confined to strike-on devices, or laser printers with limited typographic and graphic flexibility, or had to be routed to an expensive conventional phototypesetter. The LaserWriter allowed users for the first time to produce cheap and immediate output of any page of text and graphics that had been created on the Macintosh screen. Resolution was limited to 300 dpi, but this was adequate for many of the initial markets addressed by desktop publishing. Some LaserWriters are supplied with 13 PostScript outline fonts, each of which can be manipulated into bold, italic, and bold italic forms, and output in sizes between 4pt and 288pt; others are supplied with 35 fonts. Additional fonts can be downloaded as required; there are now some 5,000 PostScript fonts available from a wide variety of suppliers.

What created such an impact, however, when the LaserWriter was introduced, was its ability to output type, line graphics and screened tints in any size and rotation on the page. To do this, a laser printer must process data from the computer into a bitmap of the page prior to output – a function which is performed by a raster image processor within the printer.

Several versions of LaserWriter have been introduced over the years, the current range being based on the 8 ppm LaserWriter II and the 4 ppm Personal LaserWriter, both with a number of specification choices. There is a non-PostScript LaserWriter, the Personal LaserWriter LS, and a low-cost non-PostScript ink jet printer called StyleWriter, both of which use the Apple graphics language QuickDraw and the new

TrueType font format. Other manufacturers were quick to follow Apple's lead with PostScript printers, and today there is a very large choice of models, with resolutions from 300-1200 dpi, and sizes from A4 to A3 and beyond.

Desktop publishing is no longer confined to the Apple Macintosh, and there are plenty of other programs which have followed in the footsteps of the Aldus PageMaker software. The IBM PC/AT computers and their compatibles are popular platforms for desktop publishing, particularly when running the Windows user interface, which makes the PC almost as easy to use as the Macintosh. Popular desktop publishing software includes QuarkXPress, Letraset Ready,Set,Go! and DesignStudio (all for the Macintosh), Xerox Ventura Publisher, and the latest version of PageMaker (for both the Macintosh and PCs). There are also advanced programs which can be used in professional typesetting environments, such as Advent 3B2 (for Unix workstations, PCs, Macintoshes and the Commodore Amiga) Interleaf Publisher (for Macintoshes; more advanced versions are available for Unix workstations), and FrameMaker (for Unix workstations, including NeXTs). There are also a number of low-cost 'entry-level' desktop publishing systems, some of which do not use PostScript; these are at present rarely used in 'professional' graphic arts applications.

Desktop publishing has been accompanied by the development of desktop graphics. Sophisticated drawing and image manipulation software is available, which can generally produce image files which can be incorporated into pages by DTP programs. There are several categories of graphics program.

Object-orientated drawing packages produce line art which will produce a high quality result at any size and resolution, in much the same way as an outline font character. The user produces a series of outline shapes, using straight lines, geometrical shapes, and highly controllable curves called *Bézier curves*. The shapes can be given outlines of any weight and colour, and can also be filled in with different colours if required. Text can be set and distorted within a graphic, and blends of shapes and colours can also be defined. As the images are stored as a series of outlines and fill instructions, the file sizes are relatively small. On output, the printer or imagesetter fills the shapes with the maximum number of image points that its resolution allows, so the graphic is always produced at the best quality available. Typical programs here are CorelDraw, for PCs, Adobe Illustrator, for PCs and Macintoshes, and Aldus Freehand for Macintoshes. They can produce work of excellent quality in experienced hands, and are widely used by professional graphic designers. These images are described in the PostScript language, so they can only be used with PostScript output devices. A variation of these object-oriented packages are the type distortion programs mentioned elsewhere.

Paint packages work on individual pixels of an image. They are easier to use and produce a more natural painted effect than the object-oriented programs, but the quality is dependent on the initial resolution of the image, and a big image will produce very large files as it is 'bitmapped' from the start. Very advanced paint packages are used for high quality retouching of scanned colour photographs. Popular programs here are Adobe Photoshop and Letraset ColorStudio, both for the Macintosh.

Page description languages

In earlier typesetting systems, the raster image processor which drives the imagesetter is interfaced with the front-end system by dedicated hardware and software, using a proprietary computer language. The LaserWriter RIP, however, is driven by a piece of software called PostScript, a page description language developed by a company named Adobe Systems. PostScript is both device-independent and resolution-independent; it resides in the printer or imagesetter, and mediates between the software application of the input computer and the raster image processor in the output device, allowing the computer to add descriptive information about the fonts, point sizes, placement of rules, patterns and tints, and the size, position and rotation of all elements to the page as defined by the screen layout. The RIP takes this page-encoded information and uses font details and graphic manipulation techniques to compute the final bitmap of the page to be recorded by the output device. Because PostScript describes a page of text and graphics irrespective of the resolution of either the input computer's screen or of the output device, it can be used with almost any combination of computer and imagesetter.

PostScript requires that its fonts are written to a particular format. There are several variations of format. Type 1 includes 'hints' which alter the character shape to work in cases where there are not many image-forming pixels, such as small point sizes on a monitor screen or laser printer. Type 3 was the original published PostScript font specification, which third parties could use without paying Adobe a licence fee. This did not incorporate hints. Type 3 has largely fallen from use since Adobe published the Type 1 specifications in 1990. Multiple Masters is a new variation of Type 1 which allows a number of outline masters to be incorporated within the same font (covering variables such as weight, style, cuts), and the user can interpolate these to gain a custom effect.

PostScript fonts require a separate set of bitmapped screen fonts. These only produced high quality images at 'popular' point sizes, and at uncommon sizes they could often become jagged and distorted, though this did not affect the quality of the printed image. This problem has largely been overcome by the introduction of a low-cost program called Adobe Type Manager for the Apple Macintosh and IBM PC/AT computers. ATM uses the Type 1 outline printer font and converts this into a screen display image, thus producing high quality type at all sizes. ATM also removes the need for a PostScript RIP on the printer: however, this only applies to type, and graphics created with PostScript programs still require a RIP for output.

A further variation is Display PostScript, which renders the complete PostScript file (not just type) for display on the screen. This gives an extremely accurate preview and means that there is no need for a RIP on the printer for both text and graphics. Display PostScript requires a powerful machine to operate it and has to be designed into the computer's operation from the start. Although several licences have been taken out, it is so far only commonly available on the NeXT Computer series of Unix workstations.

The ability to send PostScript files to imagesetters offers another application for desktop systems: where the low resolution of a laser printer is inadequate for the final product, the desktop system can be used to create and approve pages before sending them for output at high resolution from a laser imagesetter. This has lead to the establishment of specialist bureaux, equipped with PostScript driven imagesetters, to accept disks of finalised jobs from users of desktop systems for outputting on film or photographic paper. Many existing typesetters and repro companies have also set up bureau facilities alongside their traditional services. This illustrates one further aspect of the way in which the output recorder is increasingly becoming an isolated, slave device, independent of the front end of composition systems.

Although PostScript was not the first page description language, it rapidly became a standard throughout the graphic arts industry due to both the popularity of the Apple desktop publishing system and the ability to output in high quality through Linotronic imagesetters. The majority of desktop publishing and graphics software can now output in PostScript, and many professional composition systems also offer this as at least an option. All imagesetter manufacturers now offer PostScript RIPs (some makes do not offer compatibility with any other standard), and all the major type libraries include at least some PostScript fonts. The major colour repro manufacturers have also started producing links which allow PostScript files to be sent into high-end colour composition devices, or alternatively, to send high quality image scans into PostScript based page composition systems.

Alternatives to PostScript

Today, the only serious rival to Postscript as an output language is PCL, the language for Hewlett-Packard's LaserJet printer, which in its several versions is the best-selling laser printer in the world. The current PCL5 language uses non-PostScript outline fonts based on Agfa's Intellifont format. LaserJets are primarily used in office documentation, and are rarely seen in the graphic arts environments, which are dominated by PostScript applications. At present there are no high resolution PCL5 image recorders.

Fonts are a different matter. In 1989 Apple decided to limit its reliance on Adobe as the supplier of PostScript, and announced that its forthcoming System 7.0 operating system would be able to use an upgrade of the existing Macintosh internal graphics language QuickDraw, together with a totally new outline font format called TrueType. It cross-licensed TrueType with Microsoft, the company which makes the MD-DOS and OS/2 operating systems for all IBM PC/ATs and PS/2s and their compatibles worldwide. Microsoft implemented TrueType into Windows 3.1, a 'graphic user environment' which gives ATs and compatibles a similar mouse, menus and windows operation to the Macintosh.

Printers linked to PC/ATs with Windows 3.1, or Macintoshes with System 7.0, do not need PostScript RIPs: the front end software just needs much cheaper software drivers. Some of the 'device independence' of PostScript is lost, but the new format will also work though standard PostScript devices if necessary.

TrueType fonts differ primarily from PostScript fonts in that they do not need separate 'screen' and 'printer' fonts: the same information is used for both. This saves hard disk space, and also ensures a closer match between the screen and final printed image.

Systems and software

It was once said of the Apple Macintosh that its only disadvantage was that it was not IBM-compatible. The comment is no longer relevant, but it highlights the split between the two major desktop system environments. Although the Apple Macintosh launched the desktop publishing revolution and is favoured in graphic arts and creative environments, its worldwide sales are outnumbered by tens to one by the numerous developments and 'clones' of the original IBM PC. The later PC/AT is essentially a high-speed, high-resolution version of the IBM PC, with added processing power and storage to cope with the demands made by graphics. IBM itself no longer makes ATs, but models using the same hardware 'bus' are made by very many companies worldwide, notably Compaq, which have continued to develop the performance of the standard with use of high speed Intel 80386 and 80486 microprocessors – hence the terms '386' and '486' PCs.

Despite ever-growing performance, the AT standard was long regarded as inferior to the Macintosh for publishing applications, as it was harder to use and not so suited for graphics. This is reflected in turn by the nature of the software available, which tends at the moment to be more comprehensive and innovative in the Macintosh market; as with Aldus PageMaker, new packages are often introduced first for the Apple, and only later moved across to the PC environment. A lot of the weight in this argument disappeared with the introduction of Microsoft's Windows 3.0 environment for the PC/AT in 1990: this makes the computer's operation very similar to that of the Macintosh. Publishing applications are now beginning to appear faster for the PC/Windows environment, and it is possible that the Macintosh may be overtaken in this respect. Apple and IBM are now developing a joint operating system which if successful will eventually work across a range of computer platforms, including IBM's PC, PS/2 and RS/6000 computers, and the Apple Macintoshes.

The power of the Macintosh and the PC/AT standards is such that many composition manufacturers have abandoned building their own computer terminals and transferred their software to operate on these

Agfa's Catalyst is a a professional page layout and colour graphics system running on Sun hardware. The large unit at left is the SelectSet 5000 internal drum imagesetter.

'standard platforms', which offer considerable cost savings. Where microcomputers are still not powerful enough, other composition and repro manufacturers have often turned to the next stage up, the so-called Unix workstations. These generally provide high speed processing, large amounts of RAM, big hard disks, and the ability to work with large, high resolution screens. Most of them use the Unix operating system, hence the label, and increasingly they use RISC (reduced instruction set computing) processing, which is a way of increasing the amount of useful work done by reducing unnecessary or duplicated actions, reducing the need for extremely fast (and expensive) microprocessors. By adopting RISC technology, several workstation manufacturers have been able to reduce their entry-level prices to much the same level as the most powerful Macintosh and 386 PCs.

Important manufacturers of Unix workstations are Hewlett-Packard/Apollo, IBM, Sun Microsystems and Silicon Graphics – Sun is the leader in sales volume. NeXT is a new but rapidly growing manufacturer of Unix workstations, which receives a lot of attention because it was set up by one of Apple's founders, Steve Jobs, and because its use of Display PostScript has obvious potential in the PostScript-dominated publishing world.

Implications

Proponents of desktop publishing claimed that it would lead to the disappearance of the distinction between office products and graphic art equipment. At the hardware level, this has largely proved true: there is now a great deal of commonality between systems. The remaining distinctions are largely a matter of training and abilities, rather than the system capabilities.

Merely to supply the technical means of creating professional images does not automatically transform every user into a typographer or graphic designer. However, professional designers and typesetters have, after a slow start, grown to accept desktop publishing and design. To them the benefits are primarily a greater control over the finished appearance of the work (they can do something themselves instead of trying to explain it to a typesetter or repro operator), the ability to get high quality screen and printed visuals of a concept, plus the ability to modify a job considerably without having to go back to the artwork creation stage every time. Cost reductions are also important, but most professionals rate these behind time savings and increased control.

Desktop publishing systems avoid the costs of the specialised typesetting and repro processes, but in doing so may also bypass the benefits. The skilled disciplines of typesetting work take a long time to acquire, and make a significant contribution to the accuracy and appearance of a finished document; it may prove very frustrating for the user of a desktop system to know exactly what he wants to produce while finding it difficult to achieve.

The relevance of desktop publishing systems for different users thus depends on the level of sophistication required in the final output. Typically, the software systems were intended for the creation of illustrated documents by an individual; all production stages are kept under the control of a single person and the finished pages can be output immediately and at low cost. On the whole they do not transfer easily to large publishing environments where several people are working on the same page simultaneously – these situations require specialised software or considerable modifications to standard desktop programs.

Desktop publishing has paved the way for an increasing use of graphic effects to convey information in visual form. Office publishers are now far more aware of the need for good presentation, and sometimes this has led to the adoption of professionally designed and printed work where no requirement existed before.

If the final document is for limited distribution, laser printers may be used to produce as many originals as are required; for larger quantities, the laser output can serve as camera-ready copy for printing by small-offset lithography. Finally, desktop systems with the relevant software can be configured as in-house editing and design centres, producing low-resolution proofs from the laser printer before transferring the approved document on disk to a high-resolution output bureau.

As more and more clients are taking the basic origination stages of work in-house, typesetters are increasingly used solely for the output of film on high resolution imagesetters. If lower cost laser printers become good enough for use as high-quality originals for halftones as well as text, publishers may well bring these in-house too, and typesetters may find even their high resolution output services redundant. Some publishers, especially in the magazine industry, are already cutting out the typesetting stage altogether, and sending page files directly to repro houses for output to film and assembly with high resolution colour images. The repro houses are obligingly setting up internal PostScript bureaux and adding PostScript links to their high end repro equipment.

With this in mind, typesetters are seeking to extend their services to replace lost business. As publishers obviously want colour integration, typesetters are installing equipment which can handle this – Linotype, Agfa and Scangraphic are among the typesetter manufacturers which have introduced colour repro extensions to their composition systems. The effect is that the once clear-cut distinctions between typesetting and repro are becoming blurred as the functions overlap. Within a matter of years, the separation may vanish altogether, to produce a combined pre-press services industry which handles all composition and image handling functions up to and including platemaking.

Ultimately, desktop repro may mean that it is feasible to bring the colour halftone origination process in-house as well – some newspapers are already trying this. However, the complication of producing good type and, particularly, originating colour is such that there will probably always be room for a service industry to handle this. One could make the analogy that it is relatively easy to learn to maintain a modern car, but so few owners actually want to do this that there is no shortage of business for service garages. So it will probably prove for composition and repro.

9 Working with typesetters

The successful production of any printed work demands a sense of teamwork and co-operation between all the parties who participate in the process of converting a series of ideas into published form. In a full-time publishing operation, the print buyer or production controller's role is to link outside suppliers – typesetter, printer, paper merchant and binder – into this chain. Among these the typesetting company (and increasingly the repro company) occupies an important position in that it is involved, directly or indirectly, with both the editorial and production processes. The degree to which the typesetter can make an effective contribution to the overall production will depend, however, not only upon the mix of skills, experience and technology which he can apply to the project, but also to a large extent on the sense of responsibility and care with which material is presented to him by the publisher.

COPY PREPARATION

In large publishing companies the detailed preparation of copy is the responsibility of specialist staff who can pass the typescript on to the design or production departments for typographic mark-up; in some smaller companies the same person may combine these editorial, design and production functions in one role. At whatever stage it is performed, the thoroughness of the copy preparation and the neatness of presentation of the typescript have a great influence on the speed and efficiency of the keyboarding and the accuracy of the first proofs.

Many book publishers provide written guidelines to outside authors to ensure that copy is delivered in an acceptable form. These apply to work supplied as conventional hard copy, and usually include the following points:

1 Copy should be typewritten, using the same machine throughout the entire text, on one side of the paper only, and with lines double-spaced to allow copy-editing corrections to be added as necessary.

2 All sheets of the typescript should be the same size, preferably A4 for ease of photocopying or fax transmission.

3 Each sheet should contain the same number of lines of copy; these should be typed to the same length, with two spaces only for paragraph indents and no extra space between paragraphs. Ample margins should be left on all sides of the copy to allow room for corrections or typographic instructions.

  Consistent typing of copy will make it easier to calculate the total extent of copy at the cast-off stage.

4 Any handwritten corrections to the typescript should be made clearly and legibly.

5 Footnotes, large tables, illustrations and diagrams should be supplied on separate sheets and their positions within the text clearly marked.

6 Folios should be numbered in strict sequence; any folios deleted must be struck through but retained in the typescript.

  Additional folios of copy should be marked as A, B, etc., and attached to the previous sheet of copy, which should itself be clearly marked to indicate the point at which the extra material is to be included.

7 If the typescript is very dirty, it may be preferable to retype it rather than incur the slower schedule, extra keyboarding costs and less accurate proofs that will inevitably result if the copy is used. Time spent at this stage can save much expense and heartache later in the production schedule: if in doubt, ask the typesetter whether the typescript should be retyped. As well as obtaining the benefit of an expert opinion, this also places a sense of responsibility on the typesetter, the copy is accepted, to ensure that accurate proofs are supplied.

  If the copy is unacceptable in its present form, it may be possible to have it re-keyed by a word-processing bureau, at the same time incorporating a typographic mark-up code system such as ASPIC, to avoid the costs of further keyboarding by the typesetter. Some of the factors involved in this operation are discussed in Chapter Six.

COPY-EDITING

Copy-editing (also called sub-editing in journalism) is a skilled task, and the following brief points are not intended to be comprehensive.

The task of the copy- or sub-editor will include such matters as checking the factual accuracy of the text, clearing any potential libel or copyright problems and clarifying any points of style with the author or journalist. It is, however, the applications of house style and design instructions to the typescript which have most relevance to the typesetting of the work.

House style

Most publishers follow an agreed set of rules to give an overall consistency of style to all their publications; this should cover both the sub-editorial style and typographic specifications and is, ideally, the result of some detailed discussion between editorial, design and production staff.

Sub-editorial style may be modelled on the guidelines given in one of the standard works of reference such as *Hart's Rules for Compositors and Readers at the University Press, Oxford,* Butcher: Copy-editing or Collin's *Author's and Printer's Dictionary,* and may then be covered by a single general instruction to the typesetter to 'follow Hart' or similar.

Alternatively, the house style may take the form of an individual document compiled in detail by the publisher, or it may be covered by an exhaustive mark-up of the individual typescript.

Whichever approach is used, some sort of accompanying overall guidance to the typesetter is essential to cover any individual points accidentally omitted from the detailed textual mark-up; if no instructions of this kind are given, the operator will invariably 'follow copy' as typed.

The house style should provide guidance on at least the following points.

Alternative spellings ise/ize, isation/ization, enquire/inquire, judgement/judgment, etc. The many possible variants are covered by lists in the reference books quoted above.

Punctuation Single or double quotes around speech (single is more usual, with double reserved for quotes within quotes); the use of full points in abbreviations e.g. Mr./Mr, Rev./Rev, H.M.S./HMS (the current trend is to omit these); the use of the en or em rule as a dash; the use and sequence of reference marks or superior figures to indicate footnotes in the text; the use of the ampersand & as a substitute for 'and'.

Quoted matter The use of italic or quotes to highlight titles, foreign names, etc., in the text.

Style for dates and time Whether these should be expressed in figures or spelt out: eg14 April/ 14th April/ April the fourteenth; 6 p.m./ 6 o'clock/ six o'clock.

Numbers When to write numbers and quantities in full and when to use figures (common practice is to spell out the numbers one to ten and to use figures for 11 onward except for weights and measures when figures are generally used throughout); how to use figures in index references, eg 231–9 but 231–42 and 231–307; the use of lining or non-lining figures (this may be limited by the typeface used).

Measurements The style for metric abbreviations, eg 3 mm/3mm, and money, e. £1/£1.00, and percentages, eg %/per cent.

Ellipsis The use of three or four dots, with fixed or variable space between them.

Indents Conventional practice calls for new sections and the first line beneath headings to be set full out, with subsequent paragraphs indented, usually one em of set of the type being used.

Hyphenation Preference over breaks in specific words (lists of optimal break points may be found in reference books such as Collin's Gem *Dictionary of Spelling & Word Division*); the maximum number of successive word breaks allowed at line ends (two is normal for books, three for newspapers and magazines); the prevention of hyphens at the foot of columns and pages; the avoidance of second hyphens in compound words; the prevention of hyphens in dates, times, lists of figures, names and sets of initials.

Closely linked to rules governing word-breaks are the typographic guidelines used to control word-spacing and page make-up. The typesetter should be given guidelines on the following:

Letter-spacing Whether increased letter-spacing is allowed in order to justify problem lines (normally prohibited in bookwork and high-quality composition).; whether automatic kerning is to be used and, if so, whether globally or only between character pairs determined by the typesetting system's program.

Vertical justification Whether interlinear space can be increased throughout the entire page to avoid a page make-up problem; (this is not normally acceptable for quality composition).

Word-spacing parameters The ideal, minimum and maximum spaces allowed between words should be defined, or the typesetter's own default parameters accepted.

Page layout Whether pages must be of equal depth across a spread; how great a variation from the standard page depth is permissible (normally plus or minus one line only); the minimum number of lines which are allowed in various critical positions (the last page of a chapter, before a heading at the top of a page, after a heading at the foot of a page); the treatment of line spaces which fall at the foot or head of a page should also be covered.

Widows, orphans and stumps A widow line is a short line at the top of a page.

An orphan is the first line of a paragraph which falls at the bottom of a page.

A stump describes a broken word at the foot of a column or page.

The circumstances, if any, under which any of these are to be permitted must be defined. Widows are sometimes considered acceptable if the widow line is longer than half the measure but in quality work all three should be avoided if possible.

Display or extract matter The way in which this is to be distinguished from the text should be specified: conventional treatments include a choice of smaller point size; indents at the left or at both edges; and the use of space above and below the extracts.

The publisher must be satisfied that the typesetter understands the particular requirements of the house style before keyboarding commences: a good idea is to dummy up a certain piece of text which includes examples of as many of the above points as possible, and have this set as a check by any prospective new supplier.

The time taken to establish a consistent house style should soon pay for itself; in theory individual typescripts no longer need a laborious and exhaustive mark-up but could be covered by the simple instruction to 'follow house style', leaving both copy-editor and keyboarder free to concentrate on the particular requirements of individual jobs. In practice, however, some instructions still need to be emphasised to the typesetter.

Design analysis

Part of a copy-editor's task is to analyse each job in terms of its structure, to enable the designer to represent accurately the hierarchy of parts, chapters and subdivisions in his typographic treatment of the material.

Conventionally, this is done by identifying the different levels of heading within the text by tags A, B, C, etc., or by names such as *chapter head*, *subhead*, *crosshead*, *running head*, which can be translated easily into the correct degree of typographic emphasis. Text to be treated as extract matter, quotations or verse is similarly marked in the text.

At the same time the copy-editor will mark for the designer's attention any special characters required in the text which might affect the choice of typesetter or typeface, and any peculiarities of the copy needing individual treatment; these might include tabular matter, simulated extracts from newspaper and letters, or any copy which will benefit from special layout.

Details of the number and type of illustrations are also supplied at this stage; if this is a book job being made up straight to page the copy-editor will need to mark cross references in the text for illustrations, with an indication of how many lines of space are to be left at the relevant point to accommodate each one. This instruction must also cater for those instances where references fall too close to the foot of a page to allow the illustration to be included on the same page; a common way of treating this is to tell the typesetter to 'leave xx lines of space as soon as possible after this point'. If the positioning of illustrations is too critical to allow this kind of specification, this is a clear indication that the job should be set first to galley and made up into page following individual page layouts.

The designer requires some brief description of the work and its intended readership to ensure that the typography is sympathetic to content in choice of face, size and page layout; it should not be assumed that the designer or typographer will have either the time or the inclination to read every typescript that comes to him! A brief synopsis from the copy-editor can save a great deal of time as well as the danger of embarrassing misjudgements.

It may also be helpful if a list of the proper names and foreign words used in the work can be compiled as a guide for the typesetter to the consistently correct spelling of such terms.

Much of the above information can be usefully summarised in a form which is handed over from the copy-editor with the typescript; the information can be helpful to both designer and keyboarder alike, and should help ensure sympathetic typographic treatment of the copy and improve the chances of accurate proofs.

Before the typescript is finally released by the copy-editor, a final quick check should be made to ensure that all instructions are clearly legible and that any potentially confusing comments or queries on the copy have been rubbed out or struck through. The typescript is then ready for casting off by the designer.

CASTING OFF AND COPYFITTING

These operations involve the calculation of typescript characters into typeset pages: casting off determines the number of pages copy will make when set in a given typeface and size to specified type area, while copyfitting acts in reverse, calculating the point size, interlinear space and measure needed in a given typeface to fit the copy into a predetermined area. In practice both processes are often used in combination to arrive at a satisfactory typographic specification for a job. If in-house production methods are used, casting off and copyfitting is rendered largely unnecessary, as the act of formatting the type will give the absolute line lengths anyway.

Casting off

There are two separate parts to the cast-off process:

- ☐ Calculating the number of characters and spaces in the copy.
- ☐ Calculating the number of characters and spaces per page in the required type specification.

In all cast-off or copyfitting calculations the term 'number of characters' is understood to include both characters and spaces.

The typescript or a printout from copy supplied on disk is the basis for finding the total character count of the copy. The character count from a microcomputer used to produce an electronic manuscript cannot serve this purpose as it will include in the total any non-alphanumeric keystrokes used for coding or function commands.

Printouts or typescripts produced on word processors should not be printed in justified mode, or the following method will not produce accurate figures.

Typewriter widths in the typescript are normally pica, elite or microelite (10, 12 and 15 characters to the inch) and special rulers calibrated in these measurements can be used to make the counting process easier.

Clean copy which has been prepared in accordance with the above guidelines on copy presentation and which has not subsequently been heavily revised, can be quickly and easily assessed, as follows:

1. Draw a pencil line vertically down the sheet of copy at the end of an average line length.
2. Given the typewriter character widths identified above, calculate the number of characters on the sheet to the left of this line as the number of characters in average line multiplied by the number of lines of copy on sheet.
3. To this total add the number of characters appearing to the right of the pencil line minus the number of spaces at the end of short lines which do not reach the pencil line, but *not* including spaces following the short lines at the end of paragraphs; these will be averaged out by the short lines at paragraphs ends in the typeset version.
4. The resulting total is the number of characters and spaces in the average typescript page. Repeat the process several times on different sheets of copy and average out the results. With clean copy

it is not necessary to repeat the calculation for every single typescript page.

Bad copy which has been produced on different typewriters or different sizes of paper, with varying line lengths, line spaces or with heavy handwritten corrections, presents a more serious problem.

One accurate way to arrive at a total character figure is to laboriously count the number of words page by page throughout the entire typescript. This figure is then multiplied by a factor of six to give the number of characters. An allowance for short lines which will occur at the end of paragraphs when the copy is typeset must also be made, but this will vary according to the nature of the copy: solid text may require an allowance of as little as 5%, while fiction with a lot of dialogue or broken text will result in a greater percentage of short lines.

An alternative approach is to have the copy keyed by the typesetter and formatted in a neutral typeface, size and measure, for example 12pt Times to 24pica ems; after hyphenation and justification but without outputting the text, the typesetter will be able to give the number of lines that the copy makes in this specification, which can then be multiplied out to give the total number of characters in the typescript.

The second stage of casting off is to convert the total character count into a corresponding number of characters in typeset form.

Tables are available from each of the major manufacturers of typesetting equipment which give the number of typeset characters per pica em for each typeface in every size. These figures have been calculated taking into account both the relative occurrence of individual characters in the use of a particular language – for example, the high incidence of vowels and the low incidence of certain consonants – and the proportional set widths of different characters. These tables are based on typefaces set with standard character fitting as supplied by the equipment manufacturer; the situation can be complicated by the ability of modern systems to adjust letterfit in infinitesimal amounts, and by the use of automatic kerning options.

The copyfitting tables supplied by system manufacturers may give information either as a figure of characters per pica em, or as a 'factor figure' which must then be subject to an additional calculation. It is important that only the figures supplied by the relevant manufacturer of a particular system should be used for copyfitting, as variations in typeface design between different typesetting systems produce different results in cast-off calculations.

Where the manufacturer's own tables are not available for some reason, a calculation is still possible, based on the alphabet length of the particular typeface chosen. Although in theory a lower case alphabet is considered to be 13 ems of its own body size in length, the permutations now possible on typesetting systems with regard to letterfitting mean that the safest method of measuring the alphabet length is from a sample setting. This is also necessary when electronically expanded, condensed or sloped variants of the typeface are to be used.

The alphabet length in points is converted into the number of characters per pica by the calculation:

$$342 \div \text{alphabet length in points} = \text{characters per pica}$$

The magical figure 342 is a constant derived from the relative incidence of individual characters in the English language.

Once both the number of characters per pica and the total number of characters in the typescript copy are known, the job can be cast off using one of the following equations:

$$\text{Characters per line} = \text{characters per pica} \times \text{picas in line measure}$$

$$\begin{matrix}\text{Characters per page} \\ \text{or type area}\end{matrix} = \text{characters per line} \times \begin{matrix}\text{lines per page} \\ \text{or type area}\end{matrix}$$

To calculate the type area (or number of pages) a piece of copy will make in a particular type specification

$$\frac{\text{Total number of characters in copy}}{\text{Characters per page or type area}}$$

To the total number of pages made by the main text should be added any extra individual pages required for prelims and end matter, as well as space for illustrations as relevant. If the job is to be divided into chapters or sections which begin a new page, an allowance of half a page per section should be included to cater for pages falling short at these points; for maximum accuracy, each chapter or section can be cast off separately.

Copyfitting

The first stage in fitting copy into a predetermined area is the same as for casting off: the total number of characters in the copy must be calculated.

The depth and width of the required type area are converted into picas and points, and a preferred combination of typeface and point size is looked up in the relevant cast-off tables to give the number of characters per line of the type area. The number of solid lines of type which the job will make is then calculated as:

$$\frac{\text{Total number of characters in copy}}{\text{Characters per line in type area}}$$

To this figure must be added any interlinear space necessary to give an acceptable visual result. The total depth of the job in the particular combination of face, point size and interlinear space can then be expressed in picas and points. Any one of these three variables can then be changed and the calculation reworked until a solution is found that is both mathematically correct (the copy fits the given area) and aesthetically acceptable in terms of the combination of face, size and interlinear space. More than one answer will always be mathematically possible and it is therefore important to start the process, which relies a good deal on trial and error, with a combination of typeface and size which would be chosen in the absence of any copyfitting constraints.

A simple copyfitting exercise is involved in most bookwork, where for maximum economy extents must be an even multiple of 16 or 32 pages; the original typographic specification for a job may often need amendment after it has been hyphenated and justified by the typesetter in order to fit the relevant number of pages. If a solution can be found through changes to the interlinear space or number of lines per page without altering the typeface, size or measure, the job will not require a second h&j pass and proofreading cycle.

Accuracy in casting off and copyfitting depends on two main factors:

- ☐ The accuracy of the initial calculation of characters in the typescript.
- ☐ An awareness of the particular recommendations for the typesetting system to be used to set the job.

The above calculations refer to straightforward setting; allowances must always be made for particular design features – display headings, space, footnotes or illustrations – which would affect these workings.

It is advisable always to check with the typesetter that the manufacturer's tables apply to this use of the equipment and to back up any theoretical calculations with the measurable features of sample setting.

This is particularly important if the specification calls for the set widths or letterfitting values of a typeface to be adjusted from standard.

Sample calculations showing how the different cast-off tables provided by manufacturers of the various typesetting systems are used are given in Appendix Two.

TYPOGRAPHIC MARK-UP

This is not a book on typographic design. There are many excellent studies of the subject by extremely experienced designers, some of which are listed in the bibliography. The basics of typography cannot in any case be learned solely from books, and skilled typographers rely heavily on a practical knowledge and acceptance of the conventions of design as evolved over the centuries. The temptation to break the basic rules in search of fresh effects should be resisted until these well-founded principles have been fully absorbed. A few of the more common conventions of book and magazine composition relate to the following points.

Preliminary Pages

Prelims may contain any or all of the following material, usually in the order given here with preferred positions for left-handed (verso) or right-hand (recto) pages. The majority of these categories only refer to book work:

Half-title page Carries title of book only, and is used to protect the title page; in the binding either the endpaper or the limp cover of a book will be glued on to the left edge of the first page of the book, pulling it out of position, and this can disfigure the title page if a half-title is not used. (Recto).

Half-title verso List of books by the same author, or blank. (Verso.)

Title page Details of author, title and publisher, set in display sizes. (Recto.)

Title verso or copyright page Bibliographic details of publication, copyright notice and printer's imprint. Usually set two sizes smaller than text size. (Verso.)

Dedication (Recto.)

Contents list (Recto.)

List of illustrations (Recto.)

Acknowledgements List of sources and references. (Verso or recto.)

List of abbreviations (Recto.)

Forword Written by a person other than the author. (Recto.)

Preface Written by the author, containing personal remarks about the book. (Recto.)

Introduction Written by the author about the subject matter. (Recto.)

In books, all preliminary pages should be folioed separately from the main text, and with roman figures so that they may be compressed or extended at a late production stage as dictated by the need to fit the book to an even working; arabic figure 1 therefore appears on the first page of the main text. Pages appearing before the contents page do not need folios.

The openings to prelim pages should be treated as chapter openings, although display titling in a smaller size but reflecting the layout of chapter openings is often equally suitable.

In magazines, newspapers and other periodicals, the modern practice is normally to assign a number to every consecutive page, starting with the cover as page 1, and including all advertisements. The cover and advertisement pages rarely carry a printed number, but are still counted when making up the contents list. The practice of numbering all pages consecutively throughout a year's volume of a periodical (so for example the March issue might be numbered from pages 1-96, and April from 97-192 etc) is gradually becoming less common, and so periodicals now tend to start from page 1 in each issue.

Main text

The choice of typeface will be governed by the designer's taste, and limited by the faces available for the typesetter or page description language used. Rigid rules which provide typographic specifications suitable for all purposes and tastes are not possible, but considerations of type design, appearing size and the suitability of different types for specific uses should be carefully evaluated.

The relationship of typesize to measure will have a critical effect on the number of lines which have to either end with a hyphen or have very loose word-spacing; a piece of advance specimen setting will normally indicate whether this is likely to create a problem. This is especially relevant to newspapers and magazines, which often have particularly narrow column widths, hence the popularity of Times Roman, Bembo and Plantin for this type of work – they work well in sizes around 9 and 10 point across narrow set widths.

Subsidiary text

Extracts and tables can be set in a smaller size than the main text, or with the left edge or both edges indented from the main measure to distinguish them from the main text; half-line spaces above and below the extracted matter are also useful. These must be increased to full line spaces in those instances where the opening and closing of the extract do not appear on the same page, to avoid uneven alignment at the foot of facing pages.

Verse extracts can be handled in the same way, and may be centred on the type measure if the verse form allows.

Footnotes are usually set at least two sizes smaller than the main text. They may be numbered by page, chapter or consecutively throughout the book, and may range at the foot of the page, with or without a rule to divide them from the text, or be collected at the ends of chapters or in a separate section in the endmatter.

Type area

The basic page style should be the first element to be decided in book or magazine design. The size and position of the type area relative to the printed page will be affected by the content, style and size of the book, and is usually specified as line measure in picas and points × lines of text in a certain point size and interlinear spacing. For multi-column work, the column width and the gutter between columns should also be specified.

Conventional margins for straightforward non-illustrated text work position the type area so that it sits comfortably on the page, with the two pages of a spread forming a coherent opening; in effect this means that the head must be smaller than the foot margins, and the back margins smaller than the fore-edge, or else the text will appear to be falling outwards and downwards off the page. A useful ratio for the relative proportions of back/head/fore-edge/foot margins calculates these as 1/ 1½ 2/ 2½ respectively.

In practice it is normal to position type on the page by specifying head and back margins only, leaving the fore-edge and foot margins to fall automatically; it must be clear whether the head margin is specified including or excluding the running headline and folio. Periodicals work to pre-printed grids or master pages, so no specification to the typesetter is normally required.

Display matter

Chapter openings, part titles and the title page require very careful treatment to achieve the right visual balance between type and white space on the page, and it is normal practice for the book designer to create rough layouts both to help with the positioning of the various elements on the page, and to serve as a guide to the typesetter. If a pre-printed grid sheet exists, this can be used, together with photocopies of galley proofs (if available), or alternatively a mark-up of the exact type area required. Headlines can be photocopied from type style manuals if available, and assembled by cutting and pasting the required characters together. The typeface, point size and alignment of these headings should be marked on the sheet. The position of any photographs should be marked, together with an identifying number (e.g. page 3, pic B) which should also be attached to the picture itself when sent to the typesetter or repro house. Caption positions should also be marked.

To accompany layouts for a particular page or series of pages, it is a good idea to complete a type specification sheet to cover items which are not in the main text. This includes all headings and captions, and introductory passages if necessary. The headings should correspond to those on the layout sheet, and the captions should be labelled to correspond with the picture labels (e.g. *caption for page 3, pic B).*

Note that mathematically even space above and below a heading causes it to appear closer to the text above than to the text below to which it properly belongs; a good visual effect is usually achieved by allocating space in the ratios of 2:1 or 3:1 above and below the heading respectively.

Running heads and folios

Running headlines repeat for reference the title of the book and chapter, or the subject heading in a periodical. The folio includes the page number, and in periodicals often includes the publication date as well.

Periodicals have no set styles for running heads, and many dispense with them altogether or use them as a graphical element. In bookwork, however, there are recognised styles for the use of running headlines:

Fiction and general non-fiction Verso – book title; recto – chapter or section title. Fiction is often printed without any running heads.

Academic non-fiction Verso – chapter or section title; recto – subsection title.

Preliminary and endmatter pages Normally repeat the section title (Introduction, Appendix, Index) on both recto and verso.

Many variations on the typographic treatment of running headlines are possible; conventional styles call for them to be positioned either a half-line or full line space above the text, centred or ranged on the fore-edge of the measure, in the text size italic or small capitals.

Folios may be positioned at the foot of a page, a half-line or full line space below the last line of text, centred or ranged on the fore-edge of the type area; text-sized figures of the text face are a frequent choice.

If the folio and running head are set in one line at the top of the page, page make-up, if manual, will of course be cheaper than if they have to be positioned as separate items.

Care is needed to ensure that the style of the figures and running head type harmonise: lining figures look better with capitals, while non-lining figures are more suitable with heads set in small caps or upper and lower case.

Endmatter

As the name suggests, endmatter appears after the main text matter. Its use is normally confined to technical or historical books and documentation. The usual sequence for endmatter is:

Appendix or appendices Tables, plans and copy relating to the text but not part of it.

Notes Explanatory notes.

Glossary Explanation of terms used in the text.

Vocabulary Terms in foreign languages, if not covered by the glossary.

Bibliography Lists of sources and recommended reading.

Index Alphabetical reference to subjects in text.

Wherever possible, endmatter should start on a recto page, with opening pages to the various sections echoing the style of the chapter-opening pages of the main text.

Appendices and notes are usually set one size smaller than the text, with glossary, vocabulary, bibliography and index smaller still; frequently the need to force endmatter into a limited number of pages to produce an even working over the entire book will dictate how small a size is considered legible!

A well-designed book always integrates prelims, main text and endmatter into a coherent whole by the use of related or harmoniously contrasting typefaces and a certain consistency of style. Whatever the layout style of the book – centred or ranged left, symmetrical or asymmetrical – all elements of the typography should reflect this.

Composition order

Details of the typesetting specification should be summarised in an official composition order or specification sheet to accompany the typescript to the typesetter. Individual instructions which cannot adequately be specified on the order should be marked in place on the copy and ringed to distinguish them from setting copy.

For work with a high design content, layouts for every page should be sent. In bookwork, layouts for at least the title page, a sample chapter-opening page and a double spread of full text pages should be supplied to the typesetter for reference. Copies of all this material should be kept by the publisher in case of query during the composition of the job. If the first proofs seen are to be in page form, it is important that all instructions are precisely and clearly understood, especially if the page make-up is to be performed manually since any corrections to the specification after page proofs will incur the costs not only of reformatting but also of a second make-up operation.

The following illustrations show a typical composition order form and a rough layout.

Tibi gramen in usus Praebet, et hinc titulos adiuvat ipsa tuos. Polsse placere suis, Floribus effusos et erat redimita capillos, Taenario tuos temeraria quaerit placuit diva Sicana Deo. Nec sine dote tuos temeraria scopuli recubans in vertice pastor, Roscida cum primo sole rubescit humus, "Hac," ait, "hac certe caruisti nocte puella, Phoebe, tua, celeres quae retineret equos." Laeta suas repetit silvas, pharetramque resumit Cynthia, Luciferas ut videt alta rotas, Et tenues ponens, radios gaudere videtur Officium fieri tam penetralia vatum breve fratris ope

Forte aliquies scopuli recubans in vertice pastor, Roscida cum primo sole rubescit humus, "Hac," ait, "hac certe caruisti nocte puella, Phoebe, tua, celeres quae retineret equos." Laeta suas repetit silvas, pharetramque resumit Cynthia, Luciferas ut videt alta rotas, Et tenues ponens, radios gaudere videturr

Tibi gramen in usus Praebet, et hinc titulos adiuvat ipsa tuos. Polsse placere suis, Floribus effusos et erat redimita capillos, Taenario tuos temeraria quaerit placuit diva Sicana Deo. Nec sine dote tuos temeraria scopuli recubans in vertice pastor, Roscida cum primo sole rubescit humus, "Hac," ait, "hac certe caruisti nocte puella, Phoebe, tua, celeres quae retineret equos." Laeta suas repetit silvas, pharetramque resumit Cynthia, Luciferas ut videt alta rotas, Et tenues ponens, radios gaudere videtur Officium fieri tam penetralia vatum breve fratris ope

Forte aliquies scopuli recubans in vertice pastor, Roscida cum primo sole rubescit humus, "Hac," ait, "hac certe caruisti nocte puella, Phoebe, tua, celeres quae retineret equos." Laeta suas repetit silvas, pharetramque resumit Cynthia, Luciferas ut videt alta rotas, Et tenues ponens, radios gaudere videturr

scopuli recubans in vertice pastor, Roscida cum primo sole rubescit humus, "Hac," ait, "hac certe caruisti nocte puella, Phoebe, tua, celeres quae retineret equos." Laeta suas repetit silvas, pharetramque resumit Cynthia, Luciferas ut videt alta rotas, Et tenues ponens, radios gaudere videtur Officium fieri tam penetralia vatum breve fratris opeans in vertice pastor, Roscida cum primo sole rubescit humus, "Hac," ait, "hac

A rough layout of a chapter opening to this book, showing the dummy type used for both the body text and the display titling.

PROVISIONAL SPECIFICATION

Author and Title Barlow | Eccles: TYPESETTING AND COMPOSITION

Date 4 February 1992

Printer Heronwood Press

Copy Prelims + text enclosed

to follow glossary + index (see notes below)

System Apple Mac

Extent to make 288pp

Size: trimmed 216 x 138mm (demy)

Margins: trimmed head 5 picas to top of first line of text

Across back 7 picas

Measure 25 picas

Space between columns

Caption measure max line length indent 1 pica left and right on text measure

Page depth 40 lines

~~Inc~~ex. headline/folio

specimen from m/s page no. 17/18

COMPOSITION Face TIMES

Text 10½ | 12½pt Times justified

Extracts

Verse ———

Indicated as

Tables Only one set as marked in MS

footnotes

Headings

Ⓐ 14 | 12½pt Times caps, ranged left, 2 lines # above, 1 line # below

Ⓑ 12 | 12½pt Times Bold, u/l case, ranged left, 2 lines # above, 1 line # below

Ⓒ 12 | 12½pt Times Italic, u/l case, ranged left, 1½ lines # above ½ line # below

Ⓓ Text size Times Bold, u/l case, start full out, text runs on after fixed em #. ½ line # above can be expanded to 1 line # to fit.

PRELIMS in this order, folios roman/~~arabic~~

Half-title (i) List of books/blank (ii) title (iii) verso (iv) ~~dedication~~ ( ) contents (v), vi + vii

~~PART TITLES~~ ~~pp. text opens following recto/verso~~

CHAPTER OPENINGS begin new page ~~new recto/run on with~~ drop 8 lines

Number 24/25 Times range left, fixed en# to → Title Runs on after No. Position top of No/Title 3 picos from trim ie. top of title aligns top of r/head

~~Subtitle~~ ~~Quotation~~

Text opens on 9th line ~~initial, to align with~~ ~~text line, followed by~~

HEADLINES text size small caps with ~~lead~~/space under 1 line

Text: verso Typesetting and Composition (book title) recto Chapter title

FOLIOS 10½/12½ Times range left (verso) and right (recto) with headline, fixed en# between

---

TEXT ILLUSTRATIONS

Line 54 Allow pp. for figures in cast-off.

Half-tone 14 Captions 9½/10½pt Times Italic, range left, indent 1 pica left + right on text measure

---

TABLES

Total number Horizontal/Vertical ~~Rules~~

Type Captions

ENDMATTER

Appendix(es) 1 (start recto), Bibliography ~~List of sources~~ Glossary,

~~Notes~~ Index

PROOFS 1 ~~Galley~~ Page 4 sets

NOTES Follow house style sheet attached
Allow 15 pages for glossary and 8pp for index in Cast Off.

The composition order for this book.

PROOFREADING

The type of proofs supplied by a typesetter can vary widely and it is important to understand how these have been produced, and how corrections will be made, before proofreading commences.

Depending on whether the typesetter is working with film or paper output, proofs are usually supplied as diazo (ozalid) proofs or photocopies of positive film or bromide paper (see Chapter Seven, *Manual Make-up*). Neither method gives a very good quality of image, and many apparent marks or scratches may be symptomatic of the proofing process rather than indicative of faults in the master image. Most photocopiers also distort the image by a small percentage, and although this may not be critical for straightforward text work, galleys of type which have been stretched or shrunk in this way are not easy to fit to an accurate layout: an enlargement of 2–3% distorts a galley of 60 lines of type in 10/11pt size by a depth of more than a line, which can cause confusion in the make-up of integrated text and illustration work.

Proofing by laser printer, which produces a dimensionally stable and accurate image, is becoming increasingly popular, but note that typesetters may choose to produce only a master proof by this method, and subsequently photocopy this to provide bulk proofs.

Some laser proofers can also be run in a pseudo mode in which they accurately reproduce the set widths of the characters in the specified typeface while not holding the font information to allow them to reproduce the correct design of typeface. The result is that, while the hyphenation and justification of lines on the laser proof represents exactly what will be output by the typesetting machine, the letter-spacing looks very uneven and ragged; in effect the laser printer is outputting, say, Ehrhardt set widths but in Times characters. The publisher must be forewarned to avoid unnecessary anxiety and marking of proofs.

If charges for author's corrections are to be imposed, proofs should be marked with different colours of ink to denote the provenance of errors or changes. Traditionally the following colour scheme has been used:

Green indicates corrections to the keyboarding picked up by the typesetter's reader and marked on the proofs before they leave the typesetter. These are marked on a single master proof and after photocopying they appear in black on all except this master, so it is important that the 'marked proof' is retained by the publisher's editor for the collation of all corrections.

Red indicates errors introduced by the typesetter during keyboarding, and not chargeable to the publisher.
Blue or **Black** is used for both author's and editor's amendments (AAs), which are chargeable by the typesetter to the publisher.

Proof corrections should be made using the marks specified by British Standard BS5261: Part 2, 1976; the most common marks from this are shown in Appendix One.

Typesetter's readers often mark not only keyboarding errors but also queries against possible inconsistencies or errors of fact in the text. Reading departments often harbour specialists in the most arcane fields of knowledge and any queries raised are worth careful checking; even if incorrect, the question itself and a courteous answer on the proofs can only help create a sense of co-operative involvement between typesetter and editor.

Disagreements over correction charges are probably the commonest source of dispute between publishers and typesetters. To minimise these, the publisher should find out in advance how the typesetter proposes to both make and charge corrections, and if possible have these figures presented in a form which can be easily monitored. Depending on how corrections are made, more than one charging rate may be applicable, relating to amendments at the galley, page proof, or final CRC or film stage. The publisher should also keep a record of the changes made to a job by holding all returned proofs until the job has been fully invoiced; accurately colour-coded proofs are the evidence on which an analysis and settlement of fair invoice charges will depend.

On magazines and other work produced to frantic schedules it may prove difficult to keep a record of all the changes rushed through in the face of urgent deadlines. Although some of the more sophisticated typesetting systems provide 'housekeeping' software packages to compile statistics of time spent on the system for each particular job, such records can be difficult for a publisher to monitor on a regular basis. For this reason, a page rate is often agreed in advance, which covers all typesetting, page make-up and normal levels of corrections.

Some allowance for author's amendments should be included in all publisher's estimates. For bookwork this figure is often placed at between 10 and 15% of the total typesetting estimate, after which AAs can, at the publisher's discretion, be charged against the author's royalties; once a typesetter's invoice has been accepted as correct, the production controller will need to advise the editor of this correction percentage. Note that if very low price rates have been agreed with the typesetter for the basic setting of a job, corrections may be proportionally expensive, and the percentage allowed in the estimate to cover corrections may need to be set at a higher level.

ILLUSTRATIONS

To ensure good-quality reproduction, illustrations should be chosen and prepared with care. If any doubts exist over the suitability of an original for reproduction, the typesetter or repro house which will be handling the origination should be consulted before camerawork begins; do not assume that all repro departments are capable of working to the same quality standards.

The following comments apply to monochrome illustrations which are to be combined with typeset matter, and which may often as a result be sent to the typesetter for reproduction.

Line illustrations

Where possible, try to insist on the following:

1. Artwork to be drawn in black Indian ink, on a smooth white board or paper.
2. Detail, stippling or cross-hatching not to be too fine, especially if a significant reduction from drawn size to appearance size is involved.
3. Artwork to be drawn no more than half-up – in other words 150 reduces to 100. A slight reduction on camera helps neaten up any slight irregularities in the drawing of the artwork, but excessively large originals mean extra camera costs and the danger that fine lines may be lost in reduction.
4. Avoid the use of mechanical dry-transfer tints to denote shading or tone; it is difficult to lay these tints evenly, and the camera will pick up irregular blotches in the tint which are invisible to the human eye. In addition, as these tints are manufactured by printing onto backing sheets the dots which make up the pattern are rarely uniformly and densely black; these may burn out to white when photographed.

Tone or tint work should be prepared using overlays registered to the base artwork by corner marks to show the area on which the tint is required. This can then be incorporated photographically and combined at negative stage with the illustrations.

5 Mark all sizing instructions on the face of the artwork in non-reproducible blue pencil.

Halftone illustrations

These are usually photographic prints or airbrushed originals; often no choice is possible as the original photograph is the only one available, but if possible, specify the following:

1 Originals to be glossy black-and-white bromide prints. Avoid originals with a sepia, matt or embossed finish.
2 Originals should be free from marks, tears or dog-eared corners.
3 Focus should be sharp, and detail clearly resolved. Modern electronic scanners can work wonders with poor originals, but they cannot put in detail that is not there in the first place. Avoid the enlargement of photographic prints, which degrades the image – it is always best to start with a larger or same-size print and to reduce it if necessary. Transparencies can be enlarged to a considerable degree, as they carry far more image resolution than prints.

Even where the quality of illustrations cannot be influenced, either because unique originals are involved or because the artwork has already been drawn, there is no excuse for compounding the problems through careless handling. Make sure that the following rules are rigorously applied by all staff in the publisher's office and by the typesetter or repro house.

1 Keep illustrations in protective envelopes whenever they are not being processed.
2 Keep records of which illustrations have been sent where, ideally through the use of self-carbonating delivery notes.
3 Never use paper clips or staples on originals as these will leave marks which, even if invisible to the human eye, may well be faithfully reproduced by the camera or scanner.
4 Write all instructions on sizing or reproduction onto a tracing paper overlay and not on the back of the illustration; always lift

this overlay away from the original before writing. Use a soft pencil or felt-tip pen, never a ballpoint pen, even for writing on overlays: it is easy to forget to fold back the overlay, and a hard-pointed pen or pencil will damage the illustration surface.

5 Draw attention to any illustration which may require particular treatment, either due to a poor original or the need for a special effect.

6 Supply illustrations separately from the text, but keyed into position by markers in the typescript, or alternatively send them in the same package as the layout sheets which refer to them. Captions should be keyed as a separate batch of copy, or with the headlines, cross-referenced to the illustrations.

Illustration scaling

Explanations of picture scaling always make the process sound extremely complicated, especially to those not at ease with the mathematics of proportions. The best way learn is to ask for a demonstration from someone with considerable experience of sizing illustrations, as in practice the process soon becomes familiar.

The following steps cover the basic operation.

1 Determine the general shape of illustration required in the printed result (square, rectangle, etc.). Decide which dimension (depth or width) of the printed result is fixed by the grid or layout of the page and will therefore regulate the area of the original which can be used; this might be a consequence of the type measure, column width or any other dimension from the page grid.

2 Compare the area of the illustration which should appear in this fixed dimension with the space the illustration must fill on the page, and calculate the proportions of these two by dividing the illustration dimension into the page dimension. The resulting figure is the percentage enlargement or reduction factor.

3 Apply this factor to the second dimension of the original, choosing which particular area of the illustration is to appear. This area multiplied by the percentage factor gives the area which will appear in the second dimension of the printed illustration on the page.

If both dimensions of the area of the printed image are fixed – as for example in a full-page illustration – the percentage factor derived from step two will regulate the area of the original which can be included in the second dimension as well: multiply the second dimension of the printed area by 100 ÷ percentage factor to arrive at the area of the original which can appear, and check on the original that this includes a suitable part of the illustration.

4 Mark all dimensions on a tracing-paper overlay, masking out unwanted areas of the original, and note the enlargement/reduction factor and the finished size of the printed result on the overlay: e.g. reduce area marked to 80% to 100mm × 64mm.

5 Never allow the often frustrating mechanics of the illustration scaling process to overshadow the importance of producing a result which is visually attractive and relevant. Check that no important detail has been masked off by the scaling process and that no superfluous detail has been included. Refer to the caption or relevant text to verify this. Try to keep important parts of an illustration at a sensible size in the printed result, and avoid the juxtaposition of illustrations with wildly different proportions.

TOOLS OF THE TRADE

The most important aid for anyone involved in specifying type is a good specimen book showing samples of different typefaces used in various combinations of size, interlinear space and measure. All the major typesetting system manufacturers and many supplier of typesetting services produce specimen books of some kind or other, but these may vary enormously in relevance; a specimen book which shows only an alphabet set in one size may be useful for identifying the individual features of typeface design, but provides no clue to how the type will look when used in a block of continuous text. The most useful type books are those which contain pages of specimen settings with variations of interlinear space for each typesize, set to a depth and measure which can be masked down as appropriate to different type areas. This provides a true visual impression of the final printed result. Unfortunately rising costs have forced many manufacturers to abandon the production of these references.

Many typesetters will provide a collection of specimen settings produced on their own equipment and showing the default spacing parameters. Failing this, one alternative for the buyer is to keep tearsheets from printed books to form an individual specimen collection.

Typescales and rulers come in various shapes and sizes; the most versatile rulers are calibrated in picas, inches and millimetres to enable easy conversion between the various measuring systems.

For checking measurements on films, plastic rulers only should be used to avoid the risk of damaging the emulsion.

Plastic or transparent film depth scales, marked off in $^1/_2$pt units for sizes from 6pt to 14pt, are extremely useful for counting off lines from typeset galleys.

Perspex or film rulers calibrated with grids of parallel lines are helpful when checking that make-up is accurate, and that all elements of type and correction lines are stripped up exactly parallel.

Magnifying glasses used in the printing trade are known as linen testers, after their original use for checking the weave of cloth. They can be bought in various powers of magnification but for general use a factor of × 8 or × 10 is adequate; this allows close examination of any defects or imprecise definition in the typeset image. Metal framed linen testers of the folding type are more convenient to carry around, but should not be used on film; plastic-based lupes are more suitable for this purpose.

All the above items can be purchased at any graphic arts supply shop; they are not expensive, and for anyone seriously involved with typesetting the outlay is well justified.

CHOOSING A TYPESETTER

Contemporary typesetting is a highly specialised and rapidly changing business. The wide variety of technologies available makes it more important today than ever before that the buyer of typesetting services is conversant not only with the basic principles of composition, but also with the specific applications and limitations of individual systems. This does not demand an exhaustive knowledge of technical details but rather a practical understanding of how effectively different equipment configurations will handle particular kinds of work. There are several ways of keeping abreast of the capabilities and uses of the current technology. All manufacturers of equipment publish extensive literature promoting their products, and should be only too happy to pass on this information on request to those who are the eventual end-users of their products, even if the claims made in such sales brochures may occasionally require treating with a degree of practical scepticism!

The trade press is also a good source of up-to-date information on new products.

By far the most useful approach, however, is to learn from the typesetters themselves: they are the people with practical experience of their equipment's strengths and weaknesses, and will invariably be prepared to answer even the most critical queries. Although a supplier's main objective is to market the company's services, publishing is a small world and there is ultimately little mileage for a supplier in selling promises that cannot be delivered. Never be afraid that asking questions weakens your position as a buyer: the technology is changing so rapidly that there are very few people in the industry with nothing new to learn.

The area in which publishers should be totally and confidently knowledgeable, however, is in their own plans and requirements. The choice of the most suitable supplier for any typesetting project will depend on the degree to which a publisher can identify, before the job is put into production, his own overall objectives. The form in which work will be presented, the nature of the end product, the typographic quality, the restrictions of schedule and the available budget are all factors which will need consideration.

Text capture

The publisher must decide how the initial data capture is to be performed; if word processors are to be used, these must be compatible with the subsequent page assembly or output systems. Check the effectiveness of the links and/or conversion processes needed to transfer files into the composition system; are these directly under the control of the typesetter, or does the success of the interface depend on a third party? If input by the typesetter is required, then the type of work may dictate the choice of typesetting company or equipment.

Data processing

The publisher needs to plan in advance exactly what future use is to be made of the data.

Is the job ephemeral, so that no record need be stored in any form, or will revised versions of the data be required for reissue at a later date? What degree of data sorting and manipulation may be necessary? Will the job be re-run in a different typographic format? Has the information the potential for publication in non-print media? Any of these particular requirements will necessitate front-end systems of varying sophistication, with different applications of computing power, and unless the future objectives are planned in advance, the potential value of the information may be seriously restricted by the limitations of the system on which it is held. Conversely, the use of a system with excessive computing power and data-manipulation facilities for straightforward work will probably attract charges which cannot be justified.

Editing, correction and make-up

The levels of correction anticipated in a conventionally typeset project will have a great influence on the choice of supplier. Cut-and-paste techniques work well for small amounts of corrections or changes late in the production cycle, but are not capable of handling extensive alterations or re-sequencing of data. If updates and late revisions play a major part in a job, then it is worth considering bringing the whole keying and layout process in-house.

If illustrations are to be integrated with the typesetting, decide what quality of halftone reproduction will be acceptable and look for a supplier with the relevant facilities to produce either screened PMTs or conventional film negatives. Check the quality of existing work of this kind originated by the supplier.

Typographic quality

Modern imagesetters generate excellent image quality, and the major manufacturers have built extensive type-font libraries. Even so there may be occasional jobs for which only the very highest resolution or certain preferred standards of type design are considered acceptable. The need to integrate digitised graphics and special symbols, lay tints or draw geometric shapes may restrict the choice of potential suppliers and typesetting systems, while demands from designers for specific typefaces can also be a limiting factor. Tension can arise between designers concerned primarily with the visual appearance of printed work and production staff involved in the mechanics of completing a job within the restrictions of budget and schedule. These contradictory influences are probably necessary to enable each side to bring out the best in the other in a spirit of creative co-operation, but a careful balance needs to be maintained. In the final analysis, the suitability of a typesetter for a job should probably be judged on the grounds of overall effectiveness rather than on the wealth of his typeface catalogue; it is ultimately of little relevance to most publishers how good a finished job looks if it arrives too late and over budget!

These guidelines may help to distinguish the kind of typesetting system most suitable for particular projects but to evaluate the merits of different suppliers with similar systems many other aspects of a typesetter's operation need to be considered.

COSTS

Conventional typesetting

The best reason for a competitive price from any supplier is that he has the combination of skills and equipment most appropriate for the job being estimated. This need not mean the most modern and sophisticated plant available on the market, and for certain kinds of work may imply exactly the opposite; equipment which is obsolescent and therefore attracting only low overheads may still be capable of producing perfectly adequate results on straightforward setting. The key point is rather that the plant should be appropriate to the requirements of the job.

Comparative costs should be sought only from suppliers who fit the above criteria: there is little point in swamping every typesetter with demands for estimates on every job. In general, three or four quotes from suitable sources should be enough to give a good idea of the rough price appropriate for the job.

When comparing estimates, always check that the specification is exactly the same, and that your requirements have been correctly interpreted: avoid the temptation to look straight at the 'bottom-line' figure. Different companies couch their estimates in different terms, and for a meaningful analysis of comparative costs it is essential that they are produced to the same set of identical specifications, and provide for the same production stages and final result. If one individual estimate is radically higher or lower than the average range of figures, check it very carefully: excessively high figures may mean that you have misjudged the suitability of the project for that particular supplier, or that some element of the specification has been misunderstood and is distorting the price quoted. Extremely competitive prices are even more worrying: it may be that you have stumbled upon the exact job for which the typesetter designed and installed his system, but it is unfortunately more likely that some part of the specification has been misinterpreted or omitted entirely.

Ensure that you understand the implications of the terminology used in the quotation. Conventional typesetting can be priced in a variety of different ways: as a price for total number of ens keyed, with page make-up and proofing costed separately, or as an inclusive price per page composed. Prices for the first method are normally quoted per thousand ens, but 'ens' in this context can mean either typeset characters or – more probably – keystrokes, including command codes and typographic formats; this will add considerably to the real price per thousand appearing characters.

For conventionally set work, try to give the typesetter an accurate idea of the complexity of the keyboarding and page make-up: a photocopy of the designer's dummy layouts, or pages from previous similar jobs can be useful in this respect. Make sure that the same pages are shown to all prospective suppliers.

Tabular work, endmatter and indexes in particular are usually much more expensive than main text pages, due to the complexity of keyboarding and the greater ennage per page. If a job includes a significant proportion of such copy, include specimen pages or at least a note of the amount of material with the specification for the main text.

The way in which author's amendments are to be charged deserves particular attention. Try to get some firm indication from the typesetter of the method proposed, and in a form which can be translated into a cost per correction: terms on estimates such as 'ad valorem' or 'at an hourly rate of £x' are unsatisfactory. A figure detailing the cost of keyboarding, typesetting and stripping in a simple change at a charge per correction line is of far more use to a publisher trying to control and analyse correction costs; the figure will probably vary for corrections made at different production stages of the job according to the method used to incorporate the changes. Typesetters are sometimes unwilling to be so specific because of the possible implications of so-called simple corrections, which may involve considerable repagination or page make-up; be prepared to show a reasonable understanding of the problems author's amendments may cause when analysing typesetting correction costs.

Payment terms should be agreed before any order is placed. Average credit terms are considered to be thirty days from date of invoice, but this may vary according to the size of the publisher and typesetter. Large customers providing a regular flow of work can fairly demand longer credit and keener prices than those with irregular work and less certain financial stability. Customers who need extended credit to ease cash-flow patterns can similarly expect the cost of this to the typesetter to be reflected in the estimates for their work.

For jobs with an extended production cycle part-invoices are usual, but again the amounts, the dates and schedule stages at which these are to be raised should be mutually agreed before the start of the work.

Direct input

As direct input takes many of the typesetter's former tasks into the client's office, then typesetting charges should be reduced commensurately. There are basically three levels of direct input: the supply of raw or partially formatted text copy in electronic form; the supply of fully made up pages excluding graphical elements such as photographs and illustrations; and the supply of made up pages with all graphical elements integrated.

Each category still has scope for variables in costing. For instance, if text copy is to be supplied, will it need a data conversion process to be acceptable to the typesetter's equipment? Costing for direct input of text only will be worked out along similar lines to that for conventional setting (see above), less the charge for keying-in, but probably including a service charge to cover activities such as data conversion or modem operation.

Charges for the supply of ready made-up pages generally relates to the area of film or bromide/RC paper consumed. With some page sizes, a particular size of imagesetter may be able to fit several pages across the width of the film. Thus a 108 pica (445 mm) imagesetter may be able to expose an A4 page plus bleed in landscape format, and will use an area of film 22 cm deep, and 45 cm wide, or 990 square cm. If two A4 pages were to be exposed side by side in portrait format, then the film area used would be 31 cm deep, but still only 45 cm wide, making 1395 square cm, or 697.5 square cm per page. The rate per page for the two-up exposure would therefore be only 70 per cent of the single page. It is worth doing the mathematics to find the most economical combination of imagesetter and page width.

Note that charges for paper output can be between half and two thirds that of film, but will at some point require a further camera stage to turn pages into film form suitable for platemaking. If colour separations are required from the imagesetter, film should always be used, as paper does not have enough dimensional stability to maintain register between separations.

Each extra separation will cost the same as the main page: the imagesetter will output the same page area whether the colour used is only on one small drop cap in the top left hand corner, or whether it is a full-page of solid colour.

Where graphics are to be supplied on the page, an extra charge may be imposed. Graphics (which will invariably use the PostScript language) impose extra processing loads on the imagesetter's RIP, and can slow it down considerably. The larger the graphic area, the longer it takes to process. Halftones impose an extra processing requirement, and fine screen rulings take longer than coarse screens. Four-colour halftones naturally take even longer. Fine halftones will require the imagesetter to be switched to high resolution of 2000 dpi or more – text is generally exposed at 1000 or 1200 dpi – which halves the output speed. Exposing an A4 page full of colour halftones can literally take hours where a text page only takes a few minutes. If a page takes longer than a pre-arranged time to output, then typesetters will impose an additional charge based on the total extra time taken. This is reasonable, given that an imagesetter tied up in processing could otherwise be making money on other jobs.

High costs currently provide a powerful argument against the adoption of 'desktop colour repro', even if the user is convinced that the quality questions have been solved. Not only does the user have to invest in more powerful front end, storage and data transmission equipment, but the output costs will rise enormously compared with non-graphics pages. By contrast, repro companies have more powerful scanning and data processing equipment, and the work throughput allows them to charge very reasonable prices for scanning.

The introduction of *bridge* systems between desktop and professional colour repro systems provides a useful compromise: the client makes up pages electronically, and passes them to the repro house, which can convert the PostScript page files into their system's internal coding, merge the results on-screen with the high resolution scans, and output the result as a single set of separations. Many of these bridge systems, such as the Crosfield PAT or Scitex Visionary, can produce low resolution view files (with small storage requirements) of the scanned images, which can be passed back to the client, who places them electronically in the desired position on the page. On output, the repro system's computer automatically substitutes the full-quality scans in the specified positions. The data processing computers of repro page assembly systems are very powerful, and can output colour pages much faster than most imagesetters – partly because they do not use the relatively inefficient PostScript language.

Using a bridge system means that the client gets all the benefits of control and cost reduction of in-house electronic page assembly, without the expensive and difficult business of handling colour repro. As the typesetting stage is cut out completely, and only final film is output, the cost is liable to be less than using conventional repro after output by a typesetter. The attractiveness of this route, particularly for colour-heavy magazine, brochure and catalogue work, explains why many typesetters are considering a move into colour – otherwise they may lose trade to established repro houses.

Compensation for errors

The typesetter has no responsibility for errors discovered after proofs have been checked by the publisher except for new errors introduced in the later stages of typesetting. Publishers should therefore be careful not to skip through revised proofs without due care; any pages not marked for attention will be deemed by the typesetter to be approved.

The question of compensation – usually understood in this context as a reduction in the amount invoiced – for poor-quality work is occasionally raised by unscrupulous publishers who are in difficulty with costings or merely as a pretext for delaying payment of an invoice. A responsible print buyer will resist attempts to pressure suppliers in this way: a supplier who misses the occasional schedule date or delivers a below-average set of proofs should be warned that this has not gone unnoticed, but as long as overall performance is satisfactory this is all part of a working relationship.

A typesetter who regularly fails to keep schedules or produce acceptable proofs must be discarded: to demand financial compensation while continuing to accept unsatisfactory work is hypocritical and in no way a solution.

Extra charges

Complex projects, however well planned, may still produce unforeseen complications and, therefore, extra costs somewhere during their production. Suppliers have a responsibility to warn the publisher immediately if work additional to the agreed estimate is necessary, and in all events before any such work is performed: the publisher must have the opportunity to decide whether these costs are to be incurred. If they are unavoidable and reasonable, there is no alternative but to accept them; experienced publishers often include in their project costings a contingency figure to cover such an eventuality.

SCHEDULE

An agreement on an outline time-scale for the job should form part of the estimating process: most work is produced to some kind of deadline which will have implications for a typesetter's costs. If there are no stringent schedule requirements, expect and demand a more competitive price since the typesetting company will be able to use the job as filler work to keep its systems busy at slack periods. It is more likely, however, that discussions on schedule will revolve around provisions for keeping urgent deadlines.

Make sure you communicate to the typesetter the importance of the main schedule stages, including the dates for proofing as well as for the delivery of final film or camera-ready copy. Evaluate the size of the proposed job relative to the supplier's total capacity: most jobs have an unerring tendency to hit problems at some production stage, and a project that stretches a supplier to the limit even on the planned schedule may get into serious difficulties if the supplier has neither the equipment nor manpower to cope with delays and problems. Check that the supplier has experience of working on the kind of project and to the type of schedule being discussed, that back-up equipment is available in the case of mechanical breakdown, and that overtime can be laid on if necessary to meet critical dates.

Communications are also of vital importance. Try to determine how the typesetter's geographical location may effect the schedule if and when problems arise; will the method of sending material then be a critical factor in keeping dates? Is there adequate provision for quick communications – a regular courier service and a fax? If necessary, are there facilities for the publisher's staff to work on the supplier's premises?

Another aspect of communications of increasing importance is modem compatibility. Although in theory practically any modem will talk to any other, in practice it's not that simple. A lot of trial and error is often required to establish the various settings that give satisfactory transmission and reception. It can simplify things if the client and typesetter use the same make and model of modem and communications software.

The schedule should not be constructed on the basis of everything running smoothly and to time, but should include contingencies to cater for late copy, heavily corrected proofs and missed deadlines; these escape routes may in the event not be used, but the time to plan them is before they become vitally necessary.

Any delays, from either side, must be advised as far in advance as possible and the rest of the schedule then renegotiated. If a publisher supplies all material and returns all proofs exactly as agreed in the schedule, it is reasonable to expect the typesetter to meet its side of the bargain (and normally they do – delays are often of the client's making). But it is unrealistic to expect a supplier to abandon other customers' work to retrieve a late schedule of the publisher's own making, and wrong to expect a delay from the publisher's side to mean a delay of only the same amount from the typesetter; once a date has been missed it may be a matter of fitting the work around other jobs which have been delivered on schedule. For this reason, be realistic when agreeing dates: a well-planned schedule about which all parties can feel confident will in the long term probably produce the same result – with less mental and financial strain – as a series of frantic scrambles against impossible deadlines. If a supplier admits that a date is genuinely impossible for him to meet, bear in mind that he is probably not refusing work for the sake of it; the options are either to accept the best dates the typesetter can offer or find another typesetter who can handle the required schedule.

When a typesetter asks if it is possible to miss a date and deliver late, try to be understanding: there may be genuine reasons for this delay, and the reason may be in order to help solve the schedule problems of another customer. Next week that customer may be you! Storing up credits is a rather mercenary term, but it is a fact that a little helpful understanding can often reap its own rewards!

PROFESSIONAL STYLE

Even if the typesetter has the relevant equipment, capacity and experience to produce a project to the required budget and schedule, one important factor still remains, and this is the degree to which the publisher and the supplier can form an effective and harmonious working relationship.

The first point of contact is normally the typesetter's sales executive, and while it is essential that there is a good rapport between the publisher and the person who presents the public image of the supplier, it may be that the personal qualities and capabilities of the account executive – the man in the factory – will at the end of the day be just as important in determining the smoothness and efficiency with which the jobs are produced. As it is the production staff on both sides that will have to work together, it's a good idea to involve them in planning the way that a job will work. Arrange a visit to any prospective supplier as early as possible, and insist on meeting the contact person assigned to your account. Try to establish not only how accessible he or she is on a day-to-day basis but also what level of control and responsibility they exercise over the production process. Will you be able to maintain an effective dialogue, anticipating potential problems and working together to find solutions to them without communications becoming strained? If this seems difficult even at the planning stage of a job, it bodes ill for the future working relationship in times of stress, when only sympathetic co-operation can rescue the situation.

During the visit to the typesetter, try to form an overall impression of how well-organised the company seems to be and how smoothly things are running. Is the operation different from what you were led to expect by the sales representative – and if so, what are the possible implications of this? Look at the kind of work which the typesetter is producing for other customers and consider how this differs from the work which you are considering: evaluate the possible implications for quality and service arising from this. If in doubt, ask a few searching questions and assess the directness of the supplier's replies.

CUSTOMS OF THE TRADE

Estimates from suppliers usually include, somewhere in the small print, a statement of the general trading conditions of the company, and in the event of any disagreement between supplier and publisher this is the official document which may ultimately be invoked. It is in the publisher's interests, therefore, to study these conditions and make sure he understands them.

The Publisher's Association and the British Printing Industry Federation jointly issue a booklet entitled *Customs of the Trade for the Manufacture of Books* which outlines the accepted conventions of the trade, and which provides a useful reference against which to compare any typesetter's specific conditions. A similar booklet covering periodicals is published by the Periodical Publishers Association and the BPIF. Among the subjects covered are the positions of publisher and typesetter in respect of the ownership, insurance and storage of typeset work and intermediary material.

Ownership of material and the typeset image has long been a contentious subject. At one stage a common practice was expressed as 'the publisher owns the image but the typesetter owns the plant material which carries the image' – a transparently absurd distinction, and incorrect if the publisher has been charged for the materials and time spent in the production of the plant material. Publishers should make clear that as soon as full payment has been made to a supplier they consider themselves the owners of all electronic files, tapes, disks, films and other media pertaining to a job, and are free to remove any such material as required. Publishers should not automatically assume, however, that such data will be compatible with another typesetting system, even if the same equipment is being used, unless this requirement has been specified to the typesetter in advance. When disks or tapes are removed, the typesetter has a responsibility to provide information on the type of codes used in the data.

If a typesetter, having agreed to store data, changes his system to a non-compatible system, the onus is on him to translate data into a form which can be used on the new system.

Insurance of work is the typesetter's responsibility up to delivery of, and payment for, the completed work, after which insurance becomes the responsibility of the publisher.

The typesetter is responsible for the safe storage of the work and for the good condition of the disks, tapes, films and other media; the exact nature of any safety procedures or duplication, and the costs that these will incur, should be agreed in advance.

The aim of every working relationship between publisher and typesetter should be to produce a sense of creative partnership. Editor, designer, print buyer and typesetter are all members of the same team trying to translate the author's ideas into published form as effectively as possible, and should strive to reach this goal by working with and not against each other. A good relationship between the involved parties cannot always prevent problems and disagreements from arising, but it does greatly improve the chances of solutions being found that are acceptable to all concerned and that cause minimum disruption to the production of the job in hand. At the end of the day, this is what matters most.

10 The future

Since the first edition of this book, the typesetting industry has undergone a series of revolutionary changes, and the rapid pace of change shows no sign of abating. The predictions in this section of the first edition have proved remarkably accurate, to the point that many of them are now in common use, or at least are on-going trends. As with any look into the future, some things have happened which were not foreseen, notably the ending of any effective trade union resistance to direct input, and the rapid introduction of lower cost colour systems which straddle the gap between the composition and repro industries.

At this point it is possible to speculate on some further trends and developments:

1 The increasing power and falling relative prices of standard platform hardware such as personal computers and workstations will allow the use of ever more sophisticated composition and repro software. Developments in user interfaces will make PC and Unix workstation systems as easy to use as the Apple Macintosh. Proposed new standards will make it easier to run a range of different computers on a network, and to interchange made-up pages between different applications programs.

2 There will be steady progress in the ability to process and store digital graphics, with increased use of digitising scanners, graphic display screens, high-volume storage and associated software.

3 PostScript will become further entrenched as the dominant prepress output language and will extend its grip into high end colour reproduction, aided by higher performance RIPs and increased facilities in PostScript Level 2.

4 The choice of typefaces will widen as low-cost, easy to use type creation software encourages the foundation of small type design houses.

5 There will be no clear cut-distinctions between desktop publishing, composition and repro systems; instead, there will be a large choice of system software ranging from advanced word-processors with page formatting abilities, to fully integrated colour page assembly systems with retouching and press control software. Users (or systems suppliers) will be able to build systems tailored to their individual requirements from off-the-shelf components.

6 As publishers and other clients bring more and more origination facilities in-house, typesetters and to a lesser extent repro houses will be treated as output bureaux, with reduced requirements for their traditional skills.

7 High speed telecommunications and improved data compression will make it possible for publishers to decentralise, and employ more outworkers. At the same time, they can choose to use output bureaux regardless of geographical location. This includes using bureaux in other countries, which may be advantageous on grounds of price, quality, or access to local markets or printers.

8 There will be an increasing market for colour printing as the cost of origination falls. Unless typesetters put in their own colour handling equipment, they may start to lose magazine, brochure and catalogue business to repro houses that can offer a 'one-stop shopping' service. Reflecting this, the margins between typesetting and repro will disappear, and companies will increasingly offer a complete pre-press service.

9 Large publishing concerns may choose to bring the output facilities such as film recorders in-house. This will be a particularly attractive option if laser printers are developed that can handle high quality finished work – laser printers require no special darkrooms or chemical processing facilities.

10 Increasingly sophisticated word processing software will mean that small business stationery requirements can be fulfilled in-house by staff with no typographical skills, taking away a lot of ephemeral business from small jobbing printers and typesetters.

11 Smaller typesetters will replace their third-generation systems in favour of PostScript-based front end and output units, and offer any spare capacity as a bureau service. Instant print shops and jobbing printers will use desktop technology and laser printers to produce short-run lithographic plates.

12 The early years of the 1990s will revolutionise the accessibility of electronic images, in the same way as the middle 1980s saw greater access to type through desktop publishing. All-electronic still cameras are at the start of their commercial life, with predictions that they will be able to match 35 mm film quality in a few years. High street photolabs will offer a high-quality scanning service which will put normal 35 mm film images onto Kodak's Photo CD optical disks which can be used with computer imaging systems – these images will be scanned to current repro qualities and resolutions. Home entertainment systems such as CD-I promise to integrate high quality text and graphics with animation and motion video, plus stereo sound, as well as playing Photo CD disks through television sets. They will undoubtedly lead to specialised 'publishing' systems, able to integrate these disparate elements – already programs such as MacroMind Director are showing that such integration can be handled on desktop computers with a minimum of training. If successful, the new home multimedia entertainment systems carry radical implications for the future of publishing and the industries which serve it.

Appendix
Proofreading marks

The following marks most frequently used in the correction of proofs are extracted from British Standard BS5261: Part 2, 1976.

Instruction	Textual Mark	Marginal Mark
Delete and close up	/ through character or ⊢—⊣ through character e.g. charaacter charaacter	∂
Substitute character or substitute part of one or more word(s)	/ through character or ⊢—⊣ through word(s)	New character or new word(s)
Wrong fount. Replace by character(s) of correct fount	Encircle character(s) to be changed	⊗
Change damaged character(s)	Encircle character(s) to be changed	×
Set in or change to italic	___ under character(s) to be set or changed	⊔⊔
Set in or change to capital letters	≡ under character(s) to be set or changed	≡
Set in or change to small capital letters	= under character(s) to be set or changed	=
Set in or change to capital letters for initial letters and small capital letters for the rest of the words	≡ under initial letters and = under rest of word(s)	≡
Set in or change to bold type	∿∿∿ under character(s) to be set or changed	∿
Take over character(s), word(s) or line to next line, column or page	⊏	⊏

Instruction	Textual Mark	Marginal Mark
Take back character(s), word(s) or line to previous line, column or page		
Raise matter	over matter to be raised under matter to be raised	
Lower matter	over matter to be lowered under matter to be lowered	
Correct horizontal alignment	Single line above and below misaligned matter e.g. misaligned	
Close up. Delete space between characters or words	linking characters	
Insert space between characters	between characters affected	
Insert space between words	between words affected	
Reduce space between characters	between characters affected	
Invert type	Encircle character to be inverted	
Substitute or insert full stop or decimal point	/ through character or where required	

Instruction	Textual Mark	Marginal Mark
Push down risen spacing material	Encircle blemish	⊥
Insert in text the matter indicated in the margin	⅄	New matter followed by ⅄
Move matter specified distance to the right	enclosing matter to be moved to the right	
Delete	/ through character(s) or ├──┤ through word(s) to be deleted	
Change capital letters to lower case letters	Encircle character(s) to be changed	
Change italic to upright type	Encircle character(s) to be changed	
Reduce space between words	between words affected	
Make space appear equal between characters or words	between characters or words affected	
Substitute or insert comma	/ through character or ⅄ where required	
Start new paragraph		
Run on (no new paragraph)		
Centre	[enclosing matter to be centred]	[ ]

Bibliography

BOOKS AND REPORTS

AAPA, *Printing Reproduction Pocket Pal*, fourth edition, Advertising Agency Production Association, 1979.
Baker, J., *Copy Prep (Publisher's Guide Series)*, Blueprint Publishing, 1987.
Bann, D., *The Print Production Handbook*, Macdonald, 1985.
Barnard, M., *Magazine and Journal Production*, Blueprint Publishing, 1991.
Benn, *Printing Trades Directory*, Benn Information Services, 1992.
Berg, N., *Electronic Composition*, Graphic Arts Technical Foundation, 1975.
——, *Encyclopedia of Contemporary Typesetting*, Graphic Arts Technical Foundation, 1977.
——, *The New Era of Electronic Composition*, Graphic Arts Technical Foundation, 1981.
BPIF, *The ASPIC Handbook*, British Printing Industries Federation, 1984.
——, *Printers' Yearbook*, annually in July, British Printing Industries Federation, 1986.
Brown, B., *Brown's Index to Photocomposition Typography*, Greenwood Publishing, 1983.
BSI, *Copy Preparation and Proof Correction*, BS5261, Part 1, 1975, Part 2, 1976.
—, *Specification for Metric Typographic Measurement*, BS 4786, 1972.
—, *Typeface Nomenclature and Classification*, BS 2961, 1967.
Campbell, A., *The Designer's Handbook*, Macdonald, 1983.
Card, M., *Wordprocessor to Printed Page,* Blueprint , 1991.
Collins, F., *Authors' and Printers' Dictionary*, Oxford University Press, 1980.
Craig, J., *Phototypesetting: a design manual*, Phaidon, 1979.
Dowding, G., *Finer Points in the Spacing and Arrangement of Type*, Wace & Co, 1966.
Faux, I., *Litho Printing (Publisher's Guide Series)*, Blueprint Publishing, 1987.
Hart, *Hart's Rules for Compositors and Readers at the Oxford University Press*, thirty-ninth edition, Oxford University Press, 1983.
Heath, L & Faux, I., *Phototypesetting*, second edition, Sita, 1983.
Holmes, A., *Electronic Composition*, Practical Printing handbooks/Emblem Books, 1984.
Jaspert, W.P., Berry, W.T., & Johnson, A.F., *The Encyclopedia of Type Faces*, Blandford Press, 1983.
Johnson, A.F., *Type Designs: Their History and Development*, Gower, 1986.

Kleper, M., *How to Build a Basic Typesetting System*, Graphic Dimensions/ Rochester Institute of Technology, 1979.
——, *The Illustrated Dictionary of Typographic Communication*, Graphic Dimensions/Rochester Institute of Technology, 1976.
——, *Understanding Phototypesetting*, North American Publishing Company, 1976.
Labuz, R., & Altimonte, P., *The Interface Data Book for Word Processing/ Typesetting*, R.R. Bowker, 1985.
Luna, P., *Understanding Type for Desktop Publishing*, Blueprint, 1992.
Martin, D., *Outline of Book Design*, Blueprint, 1989.
McLean, R., *Typography*, Thames and Hudson, 1980.
Morison, S., *A Tally of Types*, CUP, 1973.
——, *On Type Designs Past and Present*, Benn, 1962.
New Western Type Book, The, Hamish Hamilton, 1980.
Peacock, J., *Book Production*, Blueprint, 1989.
Peacock, J., *The Print and Production Manual*, Blueprint, 1992.
Perfect, C., *& Rookledge, G.,* Rookledge's International Typefinder, *Sarema Press, 1983.*
Phillips, A., *Computer Peripherals and Typesetting*, HMSO, 1968.
——, *Handbook of Computer-Aided Composition*, Marcel Dekker, 1980.
PIRA, *Electronic Merging of Text and Tone*, PIRA, 1981.
——, *Linking word processing to phototypesetting*, PIRA, 1982.
——, *Printing Technology Forecast: a ten-year forecast*, PIRA, 1992.
Plumb, D., *Design and Print Production Workbook*, Workbook Publications, 1978.
Raspberry, L., *Computer Age Copyfitting*, Art Direction Book Company, 1977.
Rices, S., *CRT Typesetting Handbook*, Van Nostrand Reinhold, 1981.
——, *Typecaster; Universal Copyfitting*, Van Nostrand Reinhold, 1980.
Romano, F., *The TypEncyclopedia*, R.R. Bowker, 1984.
Ryder, J., *The Case of Legibility*, Bodley Head, 1979.
Seybold, J., *The World of Digital Typesetting*, plus annual suplement, Seybold Publications, 1984.
Simon, O., *Introduction to Typography*, Faber & Faber, 1963.
Steinberg, SH., *Five Hundred Years of Printing*, Penguin, 1974.
Type for the Book Page at the Piman Press, Hamish Hamilton, 1984.
Updike, D.D., *Printing Types – their History, Forms and Use* (2 vols), Dover Publications Inc., 1980.
Wallis, L., *Electronic Typesetting*, Paradigm Press/Institute of Printing, 1983.
Walker, R., *Magazine Design*, Blueprint, 1992.
Williamson, H., *Methods of Book Design*, Yale University Press, 1983.
Wilson-Davies, K., St John Bate, J., Barnard, M., and Strutt, R., *Desktop Publishing (Publisher's Guide Series)*, Blueprint Publishing, 1991.
Xyvision, *Critical Factors in Choosing a Computerized Publishing System*, Xyvision.

JOURNALS AND MAGAZINES

ATPAS Printing Education & Training Journal, 21 Ashley Way, Western Favell, Northants NN3 3PZ. 0604 714326.

British Printer, Maclean Hunter Ltd, Maclean Hunter House, Chalk Lane, Cockfosters Road, Barnet, Herts EN4 0BU. 081-975 9753.

Computers & Graphics, Pergamon Press Ltd, Headington Hill Hall, Oxford OX3 0BW. 0865 64881.

Communications Technology Impact, Elsevier Science Publishers B.V. (Information & Business Division), Amsterdam.

Desktop Publishing Today, Industrial Media Ltd, Blair House, 184-186 High Street, Tonbridge, Kent TN9 1BQ. 0732 359990.

Graphic Repro, Eaglehead Publishing Ltd, 98 Maybury Road, Woking, Surrey GU21 5HX. 0483 740271.

Litho Week, Haymarket Trade & Leisure Publications, 38-42 Hampton Road, Teddington, Middx TW11 0JE. 081-943 5000.

Newspaper Focus, Haymarket Trade & Leisure Publications, 38-42 Hampton Road, Teddington, Middx TW11 0JE. 081-943 5000.

Offset Printing & Reproduction, Maclean Hunter Ltd, Maclean Hunter House, Chalk Lane, Cockfosters Road, Barnet, Herts EN4 0BU. 081-975 9759.

Printing World, Benn Publications Ltd, Sovereign Way, Tonbridge, Kent TN9 1RW. 0732 364422.

Production Journal, Newspaper Society, Bloomsbury House, 74-77 Great Russell Street, London WC1B 3DA. 071-636 7014.

The Seybold Report on Publishing Systems, Seybold Publications Inc., PO Box 644, Media, PA19063, USA.

Typographic, Society of Typographic Designers, 17 Rochester Square, Camden Road, London NW1 9SA.

XYZ, Haymarket Trade & Leisure Publications, 38-42 Hampton Road, Teddington, Middx TW11 0JE. 081-943 5000.

Glossary

AA Author's Alteration See **author's corrections.**
accents Marks added to letters in some languages to indicate stress, e.g. é (acute e) in French.
access The ability to retrieve data from a computer storage medium or peripheral device.
acetate Transparent sheet of film fixed over camera-ready artwork used for positioning repro or for marking instructions.
acoustic coupler A device to which a telephone can be attached and which transmits data over phone lines from one computer to another.
addendum Late addition to book after printing, often as a pasted-in slip.
address The character or string of characters identifying a unique storage location in computer memory or backing store.
advance feed Sprocket holes in paper tape which align with code hole positions to indicate start of tape.
agate Obsolete term for 5½pt type. Also called **ruby.** Standard measurement of advertising columns: 14 agate lines=1 column inch.
algorithm An arithmetical computer routine in the form of programmed instructions which performs a recurring task.
align To line-up type, horizontally or vertically, e.g. **base alignment.**
allotter Computer device which directs files to specific peripherals.
alphabet 1. An ordered set of letters or symbols and associated marks used in a **language.** 2. A set of types of one particular kind, e.g. roman lower case or italic capitals of a specific design and size.
alphabet length Length of a lower-case type font.
alphanumeric Relating to the full alphabetic and numeric character set of a machine.
ampersand Symbol & for the word 'and'.
analog computer A computer which represents numerical data by analogous physical variables such as speed, length or voltage rather than by digital representation. Contrast **digital computer.**
appearing size The physical size of a type, as opposed to its nominal point size. Two typefaces of the same point size can have very different appearing sizes.
appendix Addition to a book or document following the main text.
applications software Programs which are applied to solve specific problems, such as business systems.
arabic figures The numerals 1, 2, 3, 4, etc., as distinguished from the Roman I, II, III, IV. Evolved from Arabic symbols.
archive To store data economically off-line for future use in a computer system.
area make-up Bringing together text and graphics into a page or area layout.
area storage A buffer of storage reserved for 'live' data en route between a peripheral and its storage destination in a computer.
arithmetic unit Computer unit which performs calculations.
art See **artwork.**
art paper Paper coated with china clay and polished to a high finish.
artwork Original illustrative copy or typesetting ready for reproduction at pre-film stage.
Artype Proprietary name for a make of **transfer type.**
ascender The part of a lower-case character which extends above the **x-height.** As in 'b', 'd', 'f', etc. See also **descender.**
ASCII American Standard Code for Information Interchange. The most widely used data transmission code for computers. It comprises 7 or 8 information bits and one parity bit for error checking. Used by most word processors and the IBM PC and compatibles but not by IBM mainframes, which transmit in **EBCDIC**.
ASPIC Author's Standard Pre-press Interfacing Code. System of typographic text coding developed by the Electronic Village typesetting company and adopted by the British Printing Industries Federation as an industry standard of electronic mark-up. See also **SETM, SGML** and **generic coding**.
ASR Answer Send and Receive. Machine which can send to and receive from a computer by paper tape.
assembler A computer program which translates a symbolic language into **machine code.** See also **assembly language.**
assembler box Part of a Linotype composing machine in which the line is assembled.

assembly To bring together pieces of film or paper to make up lines or pages.
assembly language A computer language close to **machine code** which needs an **assembler** to translate.
asterisk Star-shaped symbol (*) often used as a footnote reference mark.
asynchronous transmission Method of data transmission in which each unit of data is delimited by a start and stop bit.
author's corrections Corrections made by the author on proofs to the original copy, as distinct from **literals** made by the typesetter.
author's proof Corrected proof sent to the author for approval.
auto-kerning See **kern, kerning**.
automatic heading The positioning of a heading on consecutive pages by means of an instruction on the pagination set-up program.
auto-reversal film Type of film used for duplication which does not require a second stage of contacting. Used to reverse image on film.
auxiliary storage See **backing store.**
a/w See **artwork**.
azerty Alternative to the standard **QWERTY** keyboard arrangement of characters, in use in Europe and accommodating **accents.**

background Computer-processing mode which can occur concurrently with the main use of the machine, e.g. hyphenation and justification of a text file while other material is being input.
backing store Mass storage medium on a computer, e.g. floppy disk, magnetic tape, etc.
back margin The margin of a book nearest the spine.
back number Copy of a previous issue of a periodical.
backslant Backward sloping typeface, i.e. opposite to italic.
back up Extra standby equipment, personnel or copies of data.
bad break Undesirable end-of-line hyphenation of a word.
bar code Symbol representing a unique product code, presented in standardised machine-readable form and appearing on the outside of a publication for stock control purposes.
baryta Special type of coated paper sometimes used for reproduction proofs.
base alignment Method of aligning characters, e.g. of different sizes, so that they appear to stand on the same base line.
base line Horizontal line on which characters in a line of type appear to stand.
BASIC Beginners All-purpose Symbolic Instruction Code. A widely used high-level computer-programming language.
batch Method of computer processing where input data is collected into batches before processing, as distinct from **real time,** or **interactive**.
batter Broken or damaged type, blocks or plates.
baud Number of computer bits transmitted per second over a data-communications channel.
beard Distance from the bottom of the **x-height** of a piece of metal type to the bottom edge of the body.
bed The flat metal part of a printing machine which holds the type forme during printing.
bell code Code permitting more phototypesetting commands than is normal in a six-channel coding structure.
bf **bold face.**
bi-directional printing Movement both from left to right and right to left in a line-printer machine (e.g. daisy-wheel printer) thus increasing output (conventional printers move only left to right).
binary Numbering system using the base 2 as opposed to decimal which uses the base 10. The only digits used are 0 and 1. See also **bit.**
bit 'Binary information transfer' or 'binary digit' is the basic information unit in computer systems. Each bit is either 0 or 1. A group of 8 bits is known as a **byte**, and defines one character.
bitmap An assembly of **pixels** which describe an image, either as display on screen or as output to an **imagesetter.**
black and white Single-colour black only originals or reproductions as distinguished from multicolour. Sometimes called **mono** or **monochrome.**
black box Colloquial term for an electronic device which converts one type of input into another form of output. See also **code converter, media converter, multi-disk reader**.
black letter Also called **gothic**. A type style based upon a formal manuscript hand of the fifteenth century.
blad Sample pages of a book produced in the form of a booklet and used for promotional purposes.
blind keyboard Typesetting keyboard with no visual display (e.g. screen or marching display) or hard copy of keying.
block 1. Letterpress printing surface (made from etched metal) for printing illustrations. 2. Computer term for a group of **bytes** of information.
blueprints Contact dyeline proofs made on paper from film. Used for general checking purposes especially positioning. Also called **blues** (USA), **diazo** prints and **ozalid** prints.
body 1. Metal composing term for the solid metal of a piece of type carrying the printing surface. 2. Phototypesetting term for the size of the body of type, e.g. 12pt=a 12pt body.
body matter Text pages as distinct from prelims, index, display, etc.
body size Same as typesetting term **body.**
bold Heavier version of a typeface, as distinct from light or medium. Sometimes abbreviated to **bf** (bold face).
book proof Page proofs paperback-bound in the form of the finished book.
borders Decorative designs usually edging the page or type.
BOT Beginning of tape. Mark showing start point of computer tape.
bourgeois Obsolete term for 9pt type.
bowl Typographical descriptive term for enclosed part of a letter as in a 'p' or 'o'.
boxhead ruling Space at head of a ruled column where headings are to be inserted.
BPIF British Printing Industries Federation.
brace Form of bracket, mainly used in tables.
brackets Pair of marks [], used for editorial notes in text. See **parentheses**. 2. In typographic

design, refers to the small curve or cup where a serif joins the letter stem.
BRAD Acronym for British Rate and Data. Publication listing all UK publications and their advertising specifications and requirements.
branch A point in a computer program where one of a set of alternatives is chosen by the computer according to its instructions.
brevier Obsolete type size, approximately 8pt.
brilliant Obsolete term for 4pt type.
British Standards Institution British national co-ordinating body for technical standards in industry.
bromide Photographic light-sensitive paper used in photographic reproduction or phototypesetting, producing a positive image.
brownprint Also known as Van Dyke or brownline. Term (mainly used in America) for a photographic print from a negative used to check positioning before making printing plates. Similar to **blueprint.**
BSI British Standards Institution.
bubble memory Form of backing storage which uses magnetically charged crystal chips to hold data. Not widely used.
buffer Computer storage used when information needs to be held temporarily en route from one device to another.
bug Computer term for a defect interfering with a computer operation.
bullet Phototypesetting term for a large dot used for ornamentation.
byte The smallest addressable unit of computer storage, usually comprising 8 bits. Equivalent to one character.

c&sc Capitals and small capitals, i.e. words which begin with capitals and have the other characters in small caps the height of the lowercase body size.
calligraphy Art of handwriting or script drawing.
camera-ready artwork or **camera-ready copy (CRC)** or **camera-ready paste-up (CRPU)** Typematter or type and line artwork pasted up into position ready for photographing.
canon Obsolete term for 48pt type.
cap height The height of the capital letters of a font.
caps Capitals. Upper-case letters, e.g. A, B, C, etc. See also **lower-case.**
caption Text accompanying and describing an illustration.
card punch Keyboard machine which perforates cards for data storage or input. A **card reader** reads the data.
carding Thin spacing of lines of type using strips of card instead of lead. See **leading**.
caret Proofreader's mark indicating an insertion.
carriage return Keyboard command key which terminates a line of setting and may enter text from a computer screen into memory.
cartridge disk Computer storage disk enclosed in a plastic case.
case Partitioned tray containing type for hand composition. See also **lower case** and **upper case.**
cassette Small reel-to-reel tape holder for audio or data recording.
casting 1. The process of forcing molten metal into a mould to create a character or slug of type. 2. Producing **stereotypes** from **mats** in newspaper printing. A **casting box** is used for this purpose.
casting off Calculating the number of pages a given amount of copy will make when set in a given typeface and size to a given area.
catch line A temporary heading on a manuscript or proof for identification.
cathode ray tube See **CRT.**
CCD Charge Coupled Device. A semiconductor that contains a row of image sensing elements or 'photosites'. The light energy which falls on these phorosites generates a charge proportional to the light energy and the resulting signals can then be controlled and monitored.
CD-ROM Compact Disk Read Only Memory. Pre-recorded non-erasable digital data disk, used successfully for the storage of large amounts of standard information. See **optical disk, optical digital disk.**
central processing unit See **CPU.**
centre To position type centrally in a given measure.
centre-feed Paper-tape sprocket holes that line up with the middle of code holes. See also **advance feed.**
centre notes Notes placed between columns of a page.
chad The waste punched out of paper tape or cards.
channel 1. Electrical path of a data stream. 2. Row of holes in punched tape.
chapel Smallest unit of a print union's departmental or company grouping. **Father of chapel** or **Mother of chapel** is the elected chairperson.
chapter head Chapter title and/or number.
character Letter, figure or symbol of type.
character count Total number of characters and spaces in a piece of copy.
character printer A printer which prints individual characters as distinct from complete lines. Often capable of reproducing specific typefaces.
character recognition Reading characters by machine, often for digital storage.
character set The full range of characters in memory on a keyboard, or available for output from a machine.
chase Rectangular steel frame in which type and blocks are locked up for letterpress printing.
check digit An extra digit calculated automatically from other digits in a data item and used to check its accuracy.
chip A small electronic component containing extensive logic circuits.
cicero European 12pt unit of type measure. Equal to 4.511mm.
circulating matrix The Linotype matrix from which type is cast.
classified Advertisements for job vacancies, articles for sale, etc., set in columns and sorted by classification.
clean line An electrical power line dedicated to one machine and therefore not subject to **spiking.**
clean proof A printer's proof in which there are no errors.
clean tape Computer tape with no data on it or with all unnecessary codes removed.

clear To empty memory (on a screen, a file, etc.).
close up Reduce spacing between characters of type or other elements on a proof.
cluster A group of items of equipment located together.
COBOL Common Business-Oriented Language. High-level computer programming language widely used in commercial data processing.
code A character-string or line of symbolic instructions to a computer.
code converter A device which converts one set of symbolic codes into another.
code structure The structure scheme of a symbolic code.
cold composition Any typesetting method which does not use hot metal typecasting.
colophon A printer's or publisher's identifying symbol, printed on spines and title pages.
'colour' The lighter or darker appearance of a piece of typeset text, created by the combination of typeface, size and interlinear space specified.
colour split Facility of a composition system to output on separate pages of bromide or film, copy which has been flagged for printing in different colours.
column inch A newspaper measure of text space, one column wide and one inch deep.
command A computer instruction specifying an operation.
communications The electronic transfer of data between different hardware.
comp 1. To **compose.** 2. A **compositor.** 3. A **comprehensive:** a layout showing everything in position.
compact disk See **CD-ROM.**
compatibility The ability of two pieces of electronic hardware to emulate each other and to communicate with each other.
compiler A computer program which converts programs from a 'high-level' language to a language understandable by the machine such as BASIC, COBOL, FORTRAN.
compose To make up type into lines and/or pages. The operator is called a **compositor.**
composing stick A hand-held, adjustable tray in which a compositor sets type by hand.
composition sizes Types under 14pt in size, i.e. originally those sizes in hot metal which could be set by a mechanical composition caster. As distinct from **display sizes.**
computer typesetting The use of a computer to store and display typesetting and to perform many other functions such as hyphenation and justification.
concurrent processing The execution of two programs simultaneously.
condensed type A typeface with characters narrower in set than the standard face of the typeface family.
configuration The arrangement of peripherals into a computer system.
console The keyboard which controls the operations of a mainframe computer.
contact print A photographic print of a negative or positive made in contact with, and therefore the same size as, the original.
contact screen Halftone screen used in direct contact with the photographic film for creating halftones.
contents page Page of a book or magazine explaining the contents and where they appear.
continuous tone Coloured or photographic originals containing shades between the darkest and lightest tones, 'continuous' before being **screened** (broken into dots) for reproduction.
contrast The range of tonal gradations in an illustration.
control tape Computer tape containing control information rather than data.
control unit Part of a computer CPU which sequences operations.
converter A computer peripheral which transfers data from one medium to another.
copy Material for publication, especially manuscript for typesetting.
copy block A phototypesetting command treating a block of text as one unit for editing purposes.
copyfitting Determining the typographical specification to which a manuscript needs to be set in order to fill a given amount of space.
copy prep Copy preparation. Putting instructions on manuscript to ensure understanding of requirement by the compositor.
core memory Main storage capacity in the central processing unit of a computer.
corrigenda List of corrections in a book.
counter Part of a letter enclosed by strokes, such as the eye of an 'e', or space within strokes of an 'h', for example.
counting keyboard Keyboard which has logic for hyphenation and justification purposes.
CPI Characters per inch. Unit of measurement of type in a line or information on a linear storage medium.
CPP Characters per pica. Copyfitting method using average number of characters per **pica.**
CPS Characters per second. A measurement of the output speed of a phototypesetter.
CPU Central processing unit. The computing unit in an electronic system.
CRC See **camera ready copy.**
cross-head A sub-heading ranged centrally over a column.
CRPU See **camera ready paste-up.**
CRT Cathode ray tube. Images of type are exposed on a CRT in third-generation phototypesetters.
cumulative index An index which combines several other indices.
cursives Typefaces which simulate handwriting without joined characters.
cursor Moveable indicator on a screen to show a location as instructed by the operator.
cut-and-paste Traditional paste-up methods using scalpel and adhesive.
cut-in notes Notes in an outside margin of a page but which the text runs round in some degree.
cut-out Illustration with the background painted out or removed by process work.
cyrillic alphabet The Russian alphabet.

dagger Dagger-shaped symbol used as a footnote reference mark. Usually follows the asterisk in order of use.
daisy wheel Flat disk with characters on stalks used as the removable printing element of a letter-quality printer. Hence **daisy-wheel printer.**

data Information in a computer store. **Database** or **databank** is a collection of organised information from which categories may be selectively retrieved. **Data processing**, sometimes referred to as **DP**, is the generic term for the use of a computer to carry out business applications. **Data transmission** is the use of telecommunications to transfer information from one machine to another.
data communications The transmission of data between electronic devices, either in **synchronous** or **asynchronous** form.
data compression A processing technique used to save space, especially in the storage of graphics information, by eliminating redundant data and recognising communication signals on a sample basis.
dead matter Type which is finished with, or which will not be used, and may be 'killed'.
debugging The detection and correction of errors in a computer program before it goes into use.
decoding The computer process of interpreting instruction codes.
dedicated An item of equipment or electronics used for only one type of application and maybe only running one program.
dedication Inscription by the author dedicating a book to an individual. Carried among the **prelims.**
definition The degree of detail and sharpness in a reproduction.
delimiter Character used to denote the limit of a computer field.
density Measurement of the tonal value of a printed or photographic area. A **densitometer** is an instrument which measures this on an agreed scale.
depth scale Typographical ruler for measuring interlinear space.
descender The part of a character which descends below the base line, as in g, y and p.
desk top publishing Marketing term describing the concept of technically untrained office personnel producing fully page-made-up documents using a custom-made, graphics-orientated micro linked to a laser printer (a **desk top publishing system**).
diacriticals Marks attached to letters, such as the cedilla.
diamond Obsolete term for 4½pt type.
diaresis Two dots over a vowel to indicate stress.
diazo A chemical coating in photography or platemaking and the term given to a copying process which uses light-sensitive compounds (diazonium). See also **blueprint.**
Didone Group of typefaces more commonly known as **modern**, e.g. Bodoni.
didot The European measuring system for type. Based on the point of 0.376mm and named after Firmin Didot the French typefounder.
die-case Monotype matrix case.
digital computer Computer which uses binary numbers to represent and manipulate data.
digital font A typeface font converted to digital form for storage on magnetic medium.
digitisation The conversion of an image into binary form for storage and manipulation.
digitise To scan a subject and place the digitised information into computer memory for subsequent regeneration.
diphthong Letters joined together, as in æ, œ, etc.
direct access Use of a storage medium which can access information without the need for sequential searching, e.g. a disk as compared with a cassette.
direct-entry phototypesetter Self-contained phototypesetter with its own keyboard, CPU and output device.
direct impression Typewriter-style setting in which the image is created by direct impression from a type character. Also called **strike-on** composition.
dirty 1. Typesetting with many errors introduced at the keyboard. 2. Copy with many handwritten amendments.
disk 1. Computer storage device giving direct access to the information it contains. Available in various sizes and formats. 2. Circular character store used in some second generation photosetters.
disk drive The unit which rotates the disk in use.
discretionary hyphen Hyphen inserted by keyboard and which overrides the hyphenation program in use.
display ads Advertisements 'displayed' to occupy part or all of a page rather than set in columns.
display face A typeface designed for **display sizes** rather than for **composition sizes.**
display matter Typography set and displayed so as to be distinguished from the text, e.g. headings. Hence **display sizes** are sizes of type from 14pt upwards and **display advertisements** are those using display type.
diss Distribute. Return letterpress type to the case after printing.
distribution See **diss.**
ditto Typographic symbol for 'repeat the above matter'. Set as ״.
dot for dot Reproduction of an already screened halftone by photographing it as if it were fine line.
dot-matrix printer A computer printer which forms its printed characters from a pattern of dots.
dotless i An 'ı' available in some photocomposition fonts for the purpose of accommodating ligatures or accents.
double case A hot-metal type case combining upper and lower case.
double-density disk A **floppy disk** which can store twice as much information as its 'single-density' counterpart.
draft-quality output Low-quality high-speed wp printer output from dot-matrix printer. See also **NLQ, letter-quality output.**
dressing The loading of type fonts onto a phototypesetter.
driver Computer routine or device which handles communication between CPU and peripherals.
drop caps Drop capitals. Letters at the beginning of a paragraph which extend beyond the depth of the rest of the text line. Also called **drop initials.**
dropped heads Chapter headings positioned a few lines below the top of full text pages.
dry-transfer lettering Sheets of typographic

characters which can be transferred onto paper by rubbing.
dump Transfer a computer file into or out of storage.
duplex 1. A linecasting matrix with two characters. 2. Modems capable of sending and receiving information simultaneously.
Dvorak Keyboard layout in which the keys are positioned so as to be most readily accessible to the fingers which most often use them.
dyeline prints See **blueprints.**

E13B Magnetic ink font used on cheques.
EBCDIC Extended Binary Coded Decimal Information Code. The IBM code.
edit Check, correct and rearrange data or copy before final presentation.
editing terminal Visual display unit capable of retrieving a file and editing the contents prior to processing.
Egyptian Type style with a squared serif.
electro Electrotype. Duplicate of block or forme made by coating a mould with copper and nickel.
electronic composition Computer-assisted typesetting or page make-up.
electronic erosion Technique of creating an image by vaporising an aluminium surface coating and exposing the underlying layer of black ink.
electronic mail Transfer of documents or messages between computers or word processors using direct links, telecommunications or satellites.
electrostatic printer A device for printing an image on paper in which dark or light image areas are converted to electrostatically charged or uncharged areas on paper. Particles of fine dry powered ink adhere to the charged areas only, and are permanently fused to the paper by the application of heat. See also **xerography**.
electrotype Duplicate of block or forme made by coating a mould with metal.
elite Small size of typewriter type: 12 characters per inch.
ellipsis Three dots (. . .) indicating an omission in the copy or a pause.
em 1. Width of the body of the upper-case 'm' in any typeface. 2. Standard unit of measurement (more accurately called **pica**). One em equals 0.166044 inches.
emerald Obsolete type size of about 6½pt.
emulsion Photosensitive coating on film or plate. Hence, **emulsion side.**
en 1. Half the width of an **em.** Is assumed to be the width of the average type character, and so is used as the basic unit of measurement for casting off copy. 2. Fixed space of one half an em in width.
encode To code groups of characters.
end leaf See **endpaper.**
endmatter The final parts of a book after the main text: appendices, notes, index, etc.
end-of-line decisions Decisions on hyphenation or justification made either by the operator or automatically by the typesetting system.
English Obsolete type size, approximately 14pt.
enlarging/reducing system Typesetting system which creates different type sizes from a limited number of image masters.
epigraph Quotation in book prelims.
epilogue Closing section at the end of a novel or play.
EPROM Erasable Programmable Read Only Memory. Memory which can be programmed and erased by the user. Compare with **PROM.**
errata slip Slip of paper pasted into a book and containing list of author's post-press corrections.
escape code Code which signals a change of mode from, say, text to function symbols.
even pages Left-hand, or verso, pages, with even numbers.
even small caps Small capitals without full capitals.
executive program Program which organises the logistics of a computer system rather than its applications, e.g. allocates priorities of tasks.
exclusive type area Type area exclusive of headline and folio.
expanded type A typeface with characters wider in set than the standard face of the typeface family.
extended type See **expanded.**
extent Length of a book in pages.
extract Quoted matter within a text, often set indented and in a smaller type size.

fax Abbreviation for **facsimile transmission.**
face 1. The printing surface of a piece of metal type. 2. A style of type, i.e. typeface.
facing pages Pages which face each other in an open book or magazine.
facsimile 1. Exact reproduction of a document or part of it. 2. Machine which copies and transmits documents by telecommunications. Hence **facsimile transmission (fax).**
fair copy A correction-free copy of a document.
family A collection of all fonts and sizes based on one basic typeface design.
feed holes Holes in paper tape used by the sprocket on the mechanical reader to feed the tape in.
feet The base of a piece of metal type.
fibre-optic cable A protective glass or plastic cable containing a pure fibre of the same material, used to transmit light from **LEDs** or **lasers** in the communication of signals.
fibre optics The technique of communicating data by the transmission of light through plastic or glass fibres.
field A predefined area of a computer record.
file A collection of related computer records.
filler advertisement Advertisement used to occupy redundant space rather than booked for insertion.
film advance The distance by which film in a photosetter advances between lines of type to create interlinear space or 'leading'. Also called **film feed** or **line feed.**
film feed See **film advance.**
film make-up Positioning pieces of film ready for platemaking. **Page make-up** is used as the term for pages or **assembly** for full imposition.
film mechanical Camera-ready material composed in film rather than paper.
filmsetting Loose term for phototypesetting.
FIPP International Federation of the Periodical Press.
firmware Software which is necessary for the

general routines of a computer and which cannot be changed by the user. Usually held in **ROM.**
first generation Early photosetters modelled after hot-metal machines and largely mechanical in operation.
first proof The earliest proof used for checking by proof readers.
first revise The corrected proof made after errors noted on the first proof have been re-set.
fit The relative closeness of typeset characters to each other; fit can be expanded or reduced by most modern typesetting systems.
fixed-head A disk drive in which the read-write heads do not move.
fixed space An amount of space between letters and words which is not varied for justification needs.
flag An indicator in a program which marks the position of data or signals a condition to the program. In a typeset file a mark which denotes an item for a specific application e.g. index extraction, colour splitting.
flat artwork Artwork which is drawn on a solid base and which cannot therefore be directly scanned on a drum scanner.
flatbed scanner A scanner with a flat platen, rather like a photocopier, as opposed to one with a scanning drum.
flat plan Diagrammatic scheme of the pagination of a magazine.
fleuron A typographical flower ornament used for decorative purposes.
floating accents Accents which are not tied to a given character in a type font and can therefore be positioned over any letter.
floppy disk Small flexible plastic disk widely used for magnetic storage of information on microcomputers.
flush left/right Type aligned with either the left- or right-hand margins.
FOC Father of Chapel. Print union equivalent of shop steward.
foliation The numbering of manuscript pages.
folio Page number at the head or foot of text.
font A complete set of characters all of the same typeface design and point size. Also known as **fount,** especially in hot metal.
foot Bottom of a book or page.
footnotes Notes explanatory to the main text, set in smaller type at the bottom of the page.
foreword Introduction to a book, not written by the author.
format 1. The physical specification for a page or a book. 2. Frequently occurring set of typographical commands stored as a code on a phototypesetter.
forme Metal type and other matter locked up in a chase ready for printing.
foundry chase Chase used in stereo making.
foundry lockup A forme locked up for making moulds of electrotypes, stereotypes etc.
foundry type Hard-wearing metal type characters used in hand composition.
fount See **font.**
fourth generation Output device using lasers for exposure of the image.
front end General term for the parts of a typesetting system used to prepare data for the output device, e.g. keyboards, editing terminals, computers, etc.
full out Set flush with no indentations.
full point Full stop.
function codes Codes which control the function of a phototypesetter rather than generating characters.
furniture Letterpress spacing material.

galley 1. Shallow tray used to hold a column of metal type. 2. Proof pulled from a galley of type. 3. Film or bromide output in unpaged form.
galley stepover Reversal of film or paper transport in a typesetting machine to allow galleys of text to be set side-by-side, as for multi-column work.
Garalde Generic term for the group of typefaces also known as **Old Face.**
generic coding Methods of mark-up, such as **ASPIC** or **SGML,** defining a document typographically or structurally. The codes are programmed to convert into typesetting functions.
gigabyte See **byte.** The prefix giga- denotes one thousand million (10^9).
global search and replace The facility of a computer program to find all examples of a word or group of words in a file and replace them with an alternative.
glossary Alphabetically arranged list of terms and their meanings.
glyphic Typeface based on a chiselled rather than a calligraphic form.
golfball A removable typeface carrier shaped like a golfball such as is found on early IBM **strike-on** composition equipment.
gothic Typeface or script of black letter design.
graphic Typeface whose design suggests it has been drawn rather than written.
graphic display terminal VDU capable of displaying pictures in line or tone.
graphics Pictures and illustrations either in line or tone in printed work.
graphics tablet Calibrated tablet on which, using a **light-pen** or **mouse,** an operator brings together components of a design and fixes them electronically in their correct positions according to the required layout.
gray scale Strip of grey tones from white to black, used to measure tonal range against a standard.
great primer Obsolete term for 18pt type.
grid Sheet with ruled lines used to ensure square make-up of photocomposed or displayed material.

h&j Hyphenation and justification.
hairline Very fine line or stroke in a letter.
hair spaces In metal composition, a very thin space $\frac{1}{6}$ of an em of set or less. Often used for letterspacing characters in a word and still employed in phototypesetting to describe a very fine space of indeterminate width.
half title Title of book, sometimes shortened, printed on right-hand page before title page. Sometimes called **bastard title.**
halftone Process by which continuous tone is simulated by a pattern or screen of dots of varying size.
hand setting The composition of lines of metal type by hand, usually in a 'stick'.
hanging indent Typesetting style in which the first line of a paragraph is set full out and the remainder are indented.

hard copy Copy written, typed or printed as distinct from stored in electronic form.
hard hyphen Hyphen grammatically essential to a word. See **soft hyphen.**
hardware Computer term for equipment as distinct from programs.
hard-wired Circuit or program as constructed by the manufacturer of a piece of hardware and which cannot be changed.
head Top – or top margin – of a page.
headline A displayed line or lines at the top of a page or a piece of text. See also **running head.**
headliner Phototypesetting machine designed to produce lines of display-sized type.
head margin The white space between the top edge of the page and the first line of type.
heading See **headline.**
height to paper Standard height of metal type and blocks. Varies from country to country.
highlights Lightest tonal values in a halftone.
holding lines Design lines which indicate the area of a piece of artwork on a page.
host 1. Main central processing unit in a multi-computer system. 2. Holder of an on-line database.
hot metal Type cast in metal by linecasting or single-letter composition machines.
house advertisement **Filler advertisement** for a periodical's own company.
house copies Copies of a magazine for use within the publishing house rather than for sale.
house corrections Proofs altered by the publisher or printer, as distinct from author's corrections.
house style See **style of the house.**
Humanist Generic term for 'Venetian' style typefaces.
hybrid Twentieth-century typeface designs adapted for phototypesetting from a combination of earlier designs.
hyphenation exception dictionary A collection of words which cannot be broken grammatically by normal rules of **hyphenation logic** and is stored in memory with fixed hyphenation points for access during the **h&j** process.
hyphenation logic Program by which words are broken at line ends according to rules of derivation, constructed from syllable, prefix, suffix and root-word analysis. See also **hyphenation exception dictionary.**
hyphenless justification Justification without breaking words. In general, this creates more widely varying spacing characteristics than hyphenation and justification.

icon A graphic symbol used in screen displays to represent a function, e.g. wastepaper basket, filing cabinet, folder.
idiot copy Unformatted copy with no line ending commands.
image master Photographic original for photosetting fonts. Also, **film master.**
imagesetter An output recorder which can set type and graphics. This normally requires a laser imaging system.
impact printer Printer where the printing element strikes the paper through a ribbon, e.g. daisy wheel or golfball.
imprint Publisher's and/or printer's identifying text printed in a book or other work.
inclusive type area Type area inclusive of headline and folio.
indent Type set further in from the left-hand margin than the standard measure of surrounding text.
index Alphabetical list of subjects contained in the text of a work, together with their page references.
indexing The jagged edges occasionally visible in digitised type, resulting from insufficient resolution in the output device.
inferior Small character set below the base line at the foot of another character.
information retrieval The accessing by computer of text held in an electronic file.
initial First letter in text set in such a way that it stands out, e.g. bigger than its normal cap text size.
initialise Run a program which sets up a storage medium such as a floppy disk to be compatible with the system in use.
ink-jet printer A **non-impact printing** (qv) mechanism which forms the image at high speed by deflecting ink droplets electromagnetically.
input keyboard Keyboard used primarily to enter text into a typesetting system.
instruction Order in a program telling a computer to carry out an operation.
integrated book Book with text and pictures together throughout (as opposed to pictures in a plate section).
interactive Computer system used in real time so that the operator can issue commands which affect the processing.
interactive terminal Workstation at which changes are effected and displayed as they are made.
interface The link between parts of a computer system, varying from a simple cable to an 'intelligent' device which translates protocol.
interlinear space Space between lines in photocomposition of text. See **film advance, film feed.**
intermediates Films used in the intermediate stages of reproduction between the original and final printing films.
Intertype Proprietary name of a linecasting machine similar to a **Linotype.**
I/O **Input/Output** Relating to systems which can input and output to and from a computer.
ion deposition Printing process based on the adherence of a conductive toner to an electrically charged image area.
italic Originally cursive handwriting as found in Italian manuscripts of the 14th and 15th centuries, now understood to mean almost any inclined character; often used in text matter for emphasis. Distinguished from electronically slanted roman type by differences of serif structure and cursive 'feel'.

jobbing General printing.
justification The adjustment of spacing between words to give 'straight' left and right margins.

K kilobyte; ameasure of computer storage. 1Kb=1024 bytes (or Kb) (often used loosely as 1000).
keep standing Instruction to keep metal type made up for possible reprinting.
kern That part of a character which overhangs a neighbouring character.

kerning In phototypesetting, the reduction, by computer controlled operation, of space between characters.
keyboard The array of keys used to input into a system.
keystroke One key depression, often used as a measure of productivity of an operator.
kicker Short line above a headline, set in smaller type.
kill Delete unwanted matter.

LAN Local Area Network. A network of interfaced peripherals linked by cable over a limited area (e.g. an office environment), allowing two-way communication between users.
language In computing and communications, a set of characters, representations and rules for communicating information, e.g. ALGOL, FORTRAN, BASIC.
laser Acronym for Light Amplification By Stimulated Emission of Radiation. Concentrated light beam used to create images, engraving, etc.
laser printer A printer in which digitised characters and images are exposed by laser beam onto a charged drum, and transferred to plain paper by **xerography** (qv).
latent image The latent electrostatic image generated by a photocopier and which powder turns into a visible image.
lateral reversal Change of image from left- to right-reading or vice versa.
Latin alphabet Western European alphabet.
layout Plan of page or area to be composed, showing relative position of all type and graphic elements.
layout terminal See **page make-up terminal.**
leader Row of dots used to lead the eye across a page.
lead-in The introduction in a piece of setting, often in a bold or different face.
leading The spacing between lines of type (strips of lead in metal composition).
LEDs Light Emitting Diodes. Semiconducting light sources used in imaging systems as an alternative to laser technology.
legend Caption.
legibility The ease with which the individual characters of a particular typeface can be identified. See **readability.**
Letraset Proprietary name of sheets of transfer lettering.
letterfit The degree to which characters in any typeface appear closely or loosely fitted together.
letterpress Printing from images with a raised surface which impress on the paper.
letter-quality output Slow-speed, good quality wp printer output, typical of daisywheel printers.
letter space Space inserted between characters.
ligature Two or more letters joined together on one body (ff, fi, fl, ffi, ffl).
light gate array An array of cells which can be programmed to allow or prevent light passing through to expose photographic material in the creation of an image.
lineale Typeface without serifs, otherwise known as **sans-serif.**
linecaster Machine which casts complete lines of metal type, e.g. a Linotype.
line feed See **film advance.**
line gauge Measuring ruler used for copyfitting and measuring type. Also called **type gauge** and **depth gauge** or **depth scale.**
line printer Output device which prints one line at a time usually with non-letter-quality resolution.
linespacing Space between lines of photoset type.
lining figures Arabic numerals the same height as capitals. As distinct from **non-lining** or **old-style figures.**
Linotype 1. Manufacturer of digital typesetting equipment. 2. Linecasting machine formerly manufactured by Linotype, now L&M, a separate company.
listing Computer print-out of data or a file.
literal Mistake introduced in keyboarding, often affecting only one or two characters.
lith film A high contrast film.
lithography Planographic process in which ink is applied selectively to the plate by chemically treating image areas to accept ink and non-image areas to accept water. Shortened to **litho.**
litho prep American terminology for repro, film make-up and other pre-press camerawork.
lock up To secure metal type in a forme ready for the next stage of production.
logo scanner A device which converts a logo, or other special symbol, into digital signals for computer input and display on a VDU. The image may then be manipulated or changed in some way before output.
logotype 1. Company name or product device used in a special design as a trademark. Shortened to **logo.** 2. In metal composition, a whole name or word cast and used as one piece of type.
long primer Obsolete type size, approximately 10pt.
lower case Small letters as distinct from capitals. Abbreviated as **lc.** See **upper case.**
Ludlow Proprietary name of a display-size type-casting machine which uses hand-assembled matrices.

machine code Primary code used by the computer's processor.
machine composition General term for composition of metal type using typecasting equipment.
macro Single keystroke programmed to activate the commands necessary to access special characters, symbols, etc.
magazine The container for storing matrices on linecasting machines.
magnetic inks Inks with magnetic content that can be read by electronic sensing. Used on cheques.
magnetic tape Narrow tape magnetically coated for the storage in serial form of computer data.
magnetography Printing process based on the magnetisation of tiny recording heads by digital data, creating an image area to which magnetic toner adheres.
mainframe Large computer.
make-up Making up typeset material into pages.
manuscript Abbreviated to **MS**. Typed or handwritten copy for setting.
marching display Visual display of one line of

type displayed sequentially as keyboarded.
margins Areas of white space left around printed matter on a page.
mark up Instructions on a layout or copy for the compositor to follow when typesetting or making up pages.
marked proof The proof on which the printer's reader has marked corrections.
master proof Printer's proof or reader's proof. See also **marked proof.**
masthead Graphic device which displays a newspaper's name on the front page.
mat See **matrix.**
match (or merge) and drop Process of eliminating repetition of the same term in computerised data sorting. See **match (or merge) and replace.**
match (or merge) and replace Process of merging, by computer, duplicate appearances of the same term in data sorting, or replacing it with predefined characters. See **match (or merge) and drop.**
matrix 1. In metal typecasting, the recessed die which imparts the design of the letter onto the face of the type being cast. 2. The photographic image master of a character.
Mb Abbreviation for **megabyte** (qv).
mean-line Imaginary line level with the tops of lower case letters. Also called **x-line.**
measure Length of a line of type.
mechanical Camera-ready paste-up.
mechanical composition See **machine composition.**
media converter Hardware device which converts computer coded data into intelligible information.
megabyte Unit of computer storage; 1Mb=1,000Kb, or 1 million bytes.
memory Internal storage of a computer.
menu The display of a list of functions available for selection by an operator.
menu-driven Software program laid out in the initial form of a number of questions to which the operator replies in order to action the program.
merge Combine two or more files into one.
metric system The decimal system of measurement.
microcomputer Small computer, usually without multi-user capabilities.
microfiche Sheet film, in size typically 105×150mm, containing on it a large number of pages of information photographically reduced to very small size and readable only with a **microfiche reader.**
microform Generic term for **microfiche.**
microprocessor See **microcomputer.**
microsecond One-millionth part of a second. Measurement used in computing.
middle space or **mid space** Fixed space equal to one-quarter of a 'mutton' or em space.
middle tones Tonal range between highlights and shadows.
'milking machine' Colloquial term for portable text retrieval device which records data on to a cassette tape or disk, to be downloaded to a typesetting system through its RS232C port.
millisecond One-thousandth part of a second. Measurement used in computing.
minicomputer Powerful computer, between mainframe and micro in size, usually dedicated to one job rather than general data processing.
minion Obsolete term for 7pt type.
mixing Usually applied to typefaces of different fonts in one line of text.
mock-up A layout or rough of artwork. Also called **visual.**
modem or **Mo**dulator/**Dem**odulator. Device which converts analog communication (e.g. telephone transmission) into digital form and vice versa.
Modern Late 18th-century type style, also called **Didone.**
modern figures See **lining figures.**
modular Hardware system capable of being expanded by adding on compatible devices.
mono See **black and white.**
monoline Typeface with all strokes appearing to have the same thickness, e.g. Univers.
Monophoto Proprietary name of a British photosetting system.
monospaced Typesetting system in which all characters have identical set widths.
Monotype Proprietary name of a 'hot-metal' typecasting machine which assembles characters individually rather than line by line.
mould In metal typecasting, the shape through which hot metal is forced, creating the rectangular metal body on which the character is cast.
mouse A palm-sized unit with buttons, attached to the display terminal, and used in preference to the keyboard to manipulate the screen display. The mouse is moved by the operator over a tablet, and its movement is monitored by the computer. Different control functions are accessed by the use of buttons on the mouse, or by moving the mouse to defined 'menu' areas on the tablet. Used to position elements of a job in electronic page make-up systems.
MS See **manuscript.**
multi-disk reader Device capable of reading many kinds of disks, varying in size, storage capacity and recording density. The information can be written onto new disks, with the existing codings converted as relevant.
multiplexor Device enabling communication between central storage and peripherals.
multiprocessing Concurrent computer processing of several tasks.
multitasking See **multiprocessing.**
mutton An em quad.

nanosecond One-thousand-millionth part of a second. Measurement of computer processing speed.
narrow band Data transmission at speeds lower than 200 bits per second.
negative Photographic image on film in which dark and light areas appear exactly transposed from the original.
newspaper lines per minute Standard measure of photosetter speeds. Specifically, output measured in 8pt lines to an 11em measure.
NGA National Graphical Association, the UK print union.
nick Groove in metal type which appears uppermost during assembly.
NLQ Near Letter Quality. Used to describe higher-density dot-matrix printer output. Between **draft quality** and **letter quality** output.
noise Disturbance on an electrical circuit.

non-counting keyboards Keyboards which cannot access justification logic and whose output therefore must be h&j'd either by the front-end system or the typesetting machine itself.
non-impact printing Electronic methods of image transfer without striking paper. See **ink-jet printer, laser printer.**
non-lining figures Also called **old-style figures.** Numerals which do not align on the base line but have ascenders and descenders. As distinct from **modern** or **lining figures.**
nonpareil Obsolete term for 6pt type.
nut An en quad.

object program Machine intelligible program.
OCR The interpretation of typewritten characters by a machine which scans the text and stores it in memory, often for subsequent typesetting.
OCR paper High-quality bond suitable for optical character recognition equipment.
OEM Original Equipment Manufacturer. Acronym (and misnomer) for manufacturer who buys original equipment, adds features (and therefore value) before re-selling as a new package.
off-line Mode of computer peripheral operation in which equipment is not physically linked to a CPU and must be operated through an intermediate medium, by disk or tape.
offset Printing which uses an intermediate medium to transfer the image on to paper, e.g. a rubber blanket wrapped around a cylinder as in offset litho.
Old Face Early 17th-century type style. Also called **Garalde.**
old-style figures See **non-lining figures.**
on-demand publishing The concept of printing books one at a time from computer store 'on demand', rather than tying up capital by printing for stock.
on-line Mode of computer peripheral operation in which equipment is connected direct to, and communicating with, a central processing unit.
'on the fly' Colloquialism for process which occurs as output is being performed, such as the screening of halftones as they are output to an imagesetter.
opacity The quality of opaqueness in a paper.
operation Result of a computer command.
optical centre The 'visual' centre of a page, about 10% higher than the mathematical centre.
optical character recognition See **OCR.**
optical digital disk A **video disk** which stores information as bits of data, rather than as visual images, allowing large amounts of data to be written on to a small surface. See **optical disk, CD-ROM.**
optical disk A disk which holds data in a series of indentations etched onto its surface, and read by laser beam. See **optical digital disk, video disk, CD-ROM.**
optical letterspacing Space between letters which accommodates their varying shapes and gives the appearance of even space.
original Photograph or drawing to be reproduced.
origination All the processes involved in the reproduction of original material, including make-up, up to platemaking stages, and also including typesetting.
ornamented Typeface embellished with decorative flourishes.
orphan First line of a paragraph at foot of page. Considered undesirable.
orthochromatic Photographic materials sensitive to yellow, blue and green rays but not red.
outline Typeface comprising only an outline with no 'solid' area.
output Data or any form of communication coming out of a computer after processing.
output recorder Loose description of any machine capable of outputting type and graphics by non-photographic means, and therefore distinguishable from a **phototypesetter.** See **imagesetter.**
overmatter Typeset matter which was not used in the final printing.
ozalid Form of copying process often used for proofing film. See also **blueprint.**

package Set of software bought 'off the shelf' rather than specifically written for a purpose.
packing density Amount of information which can be stored on a magnetic medium.
page description language Software necessary for the composition of combined text and graphics, encompassing factors such as scaling, font rotation, graphics and angles. Some examples, such as Adobe's Postscript, are device-independent. Other contenders in the market are Interpress from Xerox, DDL from Imagen Corporation and Interleaf's RIPprint.
page make-up Assembly of the elements in a page into their final design.
page-make-up terminal Specialised workstation used to electronically assemble type and graphics into finished page form.
page proof Proof of a page before printing.
page-view terminal VDU which can display a page in its made-up form.
pagination 1. The batch processing of volume data into a sequence of composed pages. Compare with **page make-up.** 2. The numbering of a set of pages in sequence.
paper tape Strip of paper which records data as a series of punched holes arranged in 'channels' or 'tracks' across the width.
paragraph opener Typographic device marking the start of a paragraph which needs emphasising, e.g. □.
parameter A variable set to a constant value for a specific operation.
parenthesis Pair of marks, (), used for interpolation in text.
parity bit A check bit added to a series of binary digits to make the total odd or even according to the logic of the system.
paste-up Dummy or artwork comprising all the elements pasted into position.
patch Corrections pasted or stripped over or into original setting.
patching Pasting corrections into film or artwork.
pc personal computer Microcomputer for home or office use.
PE printer's error Normally a literal in typesetting.
peculiars Special characters outside a normal font range.
perforated tape See **paper tape.**

perforating Punching a series of holes in paper, as a coding process.
perforator Keyboard which produces punched paper tape.
peripheral Computer input or output device which is not part of the main CPU, e.g. a printer.
photocomposition Typesetting performed by a phototypesetter.
photocopy 1. Duplicate of a photograph. 2. Duplicate of a document, etc., produced on a copying machine.
photogravure Printing process in which the image is held in a screen of tiny cells on the surface of a cylinder. These cells are filled with ink which is transferred by contact to the paper. Used for long-run magazines and catalogues.
photolettering Method of setting display-sized type from photographic fonts.
photolithography Lithographic process with photographically produced plate image.
photomechanical transfer Abbreviated to **PMT.** Paper negative which produces a positive print by a process of chemical transfer.
photosetting See **phototypesetting.**
phototypesetting Typesetting using photographic principles, i.e. film masters, lens systems and light sources. Hence **phototypesetter.** See **imagesetter, output recorder.**
pi characters Special characters outside the normal alphabetic range and not normally contained in a standard font, e.g. special maths symbols. Some typesetting manufactuers now hold a huge variety of special symbols.
pica 1. Unit of typographic measurement equal to 12 points or 4.21mm. 2. Size of typewriter face with 10 characters to the inch.
pie Jumbled metal type. Sometimes spelt **pi.**
pitch Measurement of the number of characters per horizontal inch in typewriter faces.
pixel The minute individual image/non-image areas created by the digitisation of type or graphics. A pixel is the smallest element of a digital image that can be addressed.
planning All the processes involved in imposition, laying pages down onto foils in imposition sequence, etc., ready for platemaking.
PMT See **photomechanical transfer.**
point size Description of a size of type. Not usually directly equivalent to the size of the printed image of this type.
point system The main system of typographic measurement. 1pt=.013837″ or 0.351mm. See also **didot, em, pica.**
port An input and/or output connection to or from a computer.
portrait The shape of an image or page with the shorter dimensions at the head and foot.
positive An image on film or paper in which the dark and light values are the same as the original, as distinct from **negative.**
PPA Periodical Publishers Association.
preface Formal statement before the text of a book by the author. As distinct from **foreword.**
prelims Abbreviation of **preliminary matter.** The matter in a book which precedes the text.
pre-press costs All the costs associated with bringing a job ready for press up to but not including printing the first copy. As distinct from **press costs.**
pre-screened illustration Illustration original which is already screened in halftone form. Subsequent reproduction handles such an originals 'dot for dot', with each existing screen dot recognized by the camera as a line image.
press costs The costs associated with printing and manufacturing a job from plates onwards. As distinct from **pre-press costs.**
preview screen. A VDU which allows a piece of composed work to be viewed exactly as it will appear in print. See **soft typesetter.**
printer's error See **PE.**
print-out The text printed out by a computer printer.
program The complete set of instructions which control a computer in the performance of a task.
PROM **Programmable Read Only Memory.** Memory which can be programmed but not subsequently altered by the user. See **ROM, EPROM.**
proof A trial printed sheet or copy, made before the production run, for the purpose of checking.
proofreader's marks Symbols used by a proofreader in marking corrections on proofs.
proofreading Checking typeset proofs.
protocol Set of conventions controlling the exchange of data between communicating devices.
pseudo font Typeface used to represent text with character widths (and therefore line endings) from a different typeface. This allows text to be proofed via laser printers in typefaces for which the relevant low-resolution font information is not available.
puck See **mouse.**
pull 1. A proof (metal composition). 2. A single print for subsequent photo-litho reproduction, often called a **repro pull.**
punch In hot-metal typefounding, the relief image of a character used to create a matrix.
punched tape See **paper tape.**

quad Letterpress spacing material used to fill out lines of type.
quad left, right or centre To set lines flush left, right or centre.
quoin An expanding wedge used to lock up letterpress chases.
quotes Inverted commas.
QWERTY Standard typewriter-keyboard layout, QWERTY being the arrangement of keys on the top left-hand row of the board.

RAGA Reproduction and Graphics Association.
ragged right Text with an even left margin but an uneven right margin.
random access Method of directly accessing a specific address on a computer file without the need for a sequential process. **Random access memory** is often abbreviated to **RAM.**
range Align (type, etc.).
rapid-access processing Method of quick film and paper processing using heated chemicals.
raster image processor (RIP) Device which organises the symbolic description of a page made up of individual **pixels** and pre-defines this description into the scan lines needed for output to a laser device. See **bitmap.**
raster scan The technique of recording an image line by line in sweeps across the whole image area.

raw data Data before processing or preparation.
readability The ease with which printed matter composed in a given typeface can be assimilated. See **legibility.**
reader 1. Person who checks proofs for accuracy. 2. Device which can 'read' from magnetic media or in the case of OCR, from typescript.
reader's proof First proof used by the printer's reader.
reading head See **read/write head.**
read/write head The component which reads from and writes to a magnetic disk or tape.
real time Method of computing in which operations are performed on data simultaneously with input and output.
recall To call a computer file from backing store into memory.
record A block of computer data.
recto A right-hand page.
reflection copy Copy viewed by its reflected light, e.g. a photograph, as distinct from **transmission copy.**
reformatting Setting new typographical parameters for a previously set piece of copy.
refresh rate Rate at which an image is flashed on a VDU, e.g. 60 times a second, etc.
repro Pre-press camerawork, scanning and film make-up.
repro paper Coated paper suitable for use in camera-ready artwork. Also called **baryta paper.**
repro pull See **reproduction proof.**
reproduction proof A proof taken from metal type for subsequent reproduction.
resin-coated paper Abbreviated to **RC paper.** Photographic paper with good longevity of image used in phototypesetting.
resolution The definition or sharpness of characters produced by digital imagesetters, usually measured in terms of 'lpi', the number of output strokes per inch used to create the image. The resolution of an imagesetter usually varies in inverse proportion to output speed.
response time The time taken to display the result of a command on a VDU.
retouching Correcting a photographic print or transparency before reproduction.
reverse leading Ability of a phototypesetter to move film or paper 'backwards', used in column or tabular work.
reverse out Type printing white out of another colour.
reverse reading See **wrong reading.**
revise A revised proof for subsequent reading.
right reading Film which reads 'correctly', i.e. from left to right, as distinct from **wrong reading.**
rigid disk Aluminium-based disk with magnetic coating, of greater storage capacity and less corruptible than a **floppy disk.** Needs a carefully controlled environment to avoid corruption.
RIP See **raster image processor.**
river Undesirable formation of word spaces into a vertical 'river' of white in the text.
ROM or **Read Only Memory** Computer memory which cannot be altered by the user.
roman figures Roman numerals such as iii, xviii, xxv, etc.
roman type 1. 'Upright' letters as distinct from **italic.** 2. Type of normal weight as distinct from bold or light. Usually clear from context which sense is.
rough proof Proof for identification rather than reading.
routine A computer program with a selective task.
ruby See **agate.**
rule A line (of specified thickness).
run The activation of a computer program.
run-around Type set around a picture or other element of design.
run on Continue copy on same line.
running head A title repeated at the top of each page. Also known as **running headline.**

same-size system Typesetting system which holds unique image master for each type size.
sans serif A typeface with no **serifs.**
scaling Calculating the enlargement or reduction of an original for reproduction.
scanner Electronic device which reads the relative densities of an image and records the information, usually in digital form.
screen The dot formation in **halftones.**
screen ruling The number of lines or dots per inch on a screen.
screened negative See **halftone.**
screened positive See **halftone.**
script A typeface which simulates handwriting.
scrolling Moving text vertically or horizontally into and out of the display area of a VDU.
second generation Photosetters using electro-mechanical means of exposing type.
sequential access Reading items in computer memory in sequence rather than by **random access** (qv).
series A set of fonts of the same design, but graded in size.
serif Short terminal stroke at end of main stroke of a typographic character.
set 1. To typeset. 2. The width of a character.
SETM Specifying Electronic Typographic Markup. New language for typographic markup of text, proposed by BSI in April 1987.
set width See **set.**
SGML Standard Generalized Mark-up Language. A system of text coding for electronic manuscripts, devised in the USA and now a Draft International Standard. It defines a document by its structure. See **generic coding.**
shank In hot-metal, the stem of a piece of type.
shift A key which, when depressed, gives a different designation to all the other keys, e.g. turns a lower-case letter into upper case.
shoulder notes See **side notes.**
shoulder head A heading in text, ranged left in a line on its own.
show-through Lack of opacity in a sheet of paper to the point where the printed image on one side of a page is excessively visible from the reverse side.
side-head Heading ranged left with the text.
side-notes Short lines of text set in the margins.
single tasking Computer system capable of performing only one operation at a time.
slab serif Typeface with heavy, square-ended serifs. Also known as **Egyptian.**

slave or **slave unit** A remote device which is driven by logic from a central processing unit.
sloped roman A synthetic (as distinct from 'true') italic form created by third-generation typesetting machines and their successors by electronic slanting of the roman form.
slug Line of metal type cast in one piece.
small caps An alphabet of capitals designed to the same size as the x-height of the normal lower case.
small pica Obsolete term for 11pt type.
soft copy Non-paper version of text, e.g. on a VDU.
soft hyphen Hyphen introduced in a word by the h&j program. See **hard hyphen.**
soft typesetter A VDU, such as a **preview screen,** usually non-interactive, showing an exact replica of a piece of work as it will appear in print. See **WYSIWYG.**
software Computer programs.
SOGAT Society of Graphical and Allied Trades, one of the UK unions for trades closely associated with printing.
solid Type set with no extra interlinear space.
sort 1. A single character of metal type. 2. To order data into a given sequence, e.g. alphabetical.
spacebands Spacing wedges used by linecasting machines.
spaces Pieces of metal type used to space out letters or words.
spec Specification.
special sort Unusual character necessary in a job.
specimen Sample setting used as a check on the typographic specification.
spelling-check program A computer program which checks the accuracy of each word of input against the spellings of a dictionary held in memory.
spiking Inconstant surges in power on an electrical power line causing interference with sensitive electronic equipment.
spot colour Single additional colour used in the printing of a job.
spread Pair of facing pages.
sprocket holes Feed holes in paper tape.
s/s Abbreviation for 'same size' in reproduction specifications.
stabilisation paper Photographic paper used for phototypesetting output. Has short image-retention span once processed and will discolour.
stand-alone A self-contained hardware system which needs no other machine assistance to function.
standing type Metal type stored after printing or proofing pending subsequent re-use.
stem Main stroke of a letter or figure.
stereotype Duplicate printing plate cast in a mould taken from the original. Abbreviated to **stereo.**
stet Proofreader's instruction meaning 'ignore marked correction', i.e. let it stand as it was.
stick See **composing stick.**
stone The surface (now metal) on which pages of metal type are assembled and planed down (levelled).
storage Computer memory or a magnetic medium which can store information, e.g. a floppy disk.
straight matter Straightforward text setting.
stress Angle of shading in typeface character design. May be oblique or vertical.
strike-on composition Typesetting created by direct impression of image-carrying surface, e.g. typewriter composition.
string A sequence of alphabetic or numeric characters in a computer program.
stripper film Very thin film used for hand corrections.
stripping Film handling, correction and assembly (American).
stump Term coined by the typesetting systems manufacturer Miles 33 to describe a hyphenated word at foot of column or page. Considered undesirable.
style of the house Typographic and linguistic rules of a publishing house. Also **house style.**
sub 1. Sub editor: journalist who edits copy. 2. Subscription to a magazine or journal.
subscript Inferior character. Small character printed below the base line as part of mathematical equation.
superior Small character set above the line, especially used in mathematical statements (e.g. 10^2) or to indicate footnotes; also called **superscript.**
swash letter An ornamental italic character, usually a cap.
swelled rules Rules which are wider at the centre than at the ends.
synchronous transmission Method of data transmission in which streams of data are transmitted at a given rate between a perfectly synchronised transmitter and receiver.
systems functions Functions relating to the movement of data within a system and controlled from the keyboard, e.g. writing to memory, or transmission between peripherals.

tabular material Typeset tables or columns of figures.
tail Downward stroke of a letter.
take An amount of copy for typesetting allocated to one operator.
tape merging The combination of data from a master tape and a correction tape to produce a third, error-free tape.
tape transport The device which moves tape past the reading heads.
telecommunications Communication over the telephone wire.
teletypesetter Abbreviated to **TTS.** Linecasting system driven by six-channel paper tape generated on separate keyboards.
terminal Keyboard and/or screen for computer communication or text generation.
text The body typesetting in a book as distinct from headings and display type.
text pages The principal matter in a book as distinct from the prelims, index, etc.
text type Body type of a printed work. Loosely, type smaller than about 12pt.
thick space Fixed space equal to one-third of an em.
thin space Fixed space equal to one-fifth of an em.
third generation Typesetting machines using cathode ray tubes to generate images.
time-sharing Concurrent processing of several jobs or programs on a computer.
title page Page of a book carrying the title,

author's name and publisher's name. Always recto.

torn-tape system Paper-tape typesetting system involving manual removal and feeding of tape from one machine to another.

track A path on which information is carried on a sequential storage medium such as tape or disk.

transfer type Pressure-sensitive type on carrier sheets. Can be 'rubbed-off' to create type in position. Also known as **transfer lettering.**

Transitional Type style such as Baskerville which evolved between **Old Style** and **Modern.**

transmission copy Copy which is viewed by transmitted light, e.g. a transparency.

transpose Abbreviated **trs.** Exchange the position of words, letters or lines, especially on a proof. Hence **transposition.**

TS Abbreviation for typescript.

TTS See **teletypesetter.**

'turnkey' systems Systems based on standard hardware, developed for specific applications.

type area Area occupied by text on a page.

typecasting Casting type in metal by a machine such as a Linotype or Monotype.

typeface A specifically designated style of type, e.g. Times or Helvetica.

type gauge A rule calibrated in picas for measuring type.

type metal The alloy for cast type, comprising lead, tin and antimony.

type scale See **type gauge.**

typewriter composition See **strike-on composition.**

typographer Designer of printed material.

typographic errors Abbreviated to **typos.** See **literals.**

u and lc also **u/lc** Abbreviation for upper and lower case. Instruction to follow copy for caps and lower case.

UDF An instruction assigned to an input key to access a particular command or string of commands over and above any normal function; keys programmable by the user in this way are also known as UDKs (User Defined Keys), user programmable keys, or macros.

unit Division of the em measurement into smaller units of width used to allocate different widths to different characters.

unit value The number of units in a character. See **unit.**

unjustified Text set with an even right or left edge with even spacing and therefore a ragged left or right edge. Setting ranged left (unjustified) is also known as **ragged right,** setting ranged right (unjustified) as **ragged left.**

un-shift Keyboard designation for lower case.

update Edit a file by adding current data.

upper case Capital letters. See **lower case.**

variable space Space between words used to justify a line.

VDU/VDT See **visual display unit/terminal.**

vector scanning A method of storing a digital typographic image by vectors or outlines.

verso Left-hand page with even number.

vertical justification Spacing a column of type to fit a set depth. Automatic process on some typesetting systems.

video disk An optical disk which stores information as visual images rather than digital data. See **optical disk, optical digital disk, CD-ROM.**

visual A layout or rough of artwork.

visual display unit/terminal Cathode-ray tube screen and keyboard for input and editing of copy.

weight In typography, the degree of boldness of a typeface style (e.g. light, medium, etc).

wf Wrong font. Proofreader's mark indicating a character from an incorrect font has been used in setting.

white line Line of space in phototypesetting.

widow Short last line of a paragraph at the top of a page. Considered undesirable.

WIMPS Acronym for the set of features—Windows, Icons, Mouse and Puck—often provided as aids for the manipulation of data by a workstation operator. See **icon, mouse, puck, windows.**

Winchester disk Hard disk with extensive backing store capacity.

Winchester disk drive Sealed unit of multiple **rigid disks.**

window 1. Clear panel left in litho film for halftones to be stripped in. 2. A description of the contents of different computer files on screen for easy viewing by the operator.

word break Division of a word at a line ending.

word processor Machine using computer logic to accept, store and retrieve documents for subsequent editing and output.

word space The variable space between words which may be increased or decreased to justify a line.

WORM Acronym for Write Once Read Many, an optical digital disk on which data can be recorded but not erased by the user.

workstation Part of a computer typesetting system manned by an operator, e.g. an editing terminal.

wp See **word processor.**

write To record or output electronic data.

wrong font See **wf.**

wrong-reading Film which reads 'incorrectly', i.e. reversed from left to right.

WYSIWYG **What You See Is What You Get.** Acronym used to describe a visual display showing an exact replica of typeface, size and relative position of all elements of the final output image.

xerography A process which places an electrostatic charge on a plate. When an image is projected onto the plate it causes the charge to dissipate in the illuminated areas. Resinous powder is applied, and adheres only to the dark, (image) areas. The powder is transferred to the paper and fused by heat.

x-height Height of body of lower-case letters, exclusive of ascenders and descenders, i.e. height of the letter x.

x-line See **mean line.**

Index